JIM CROW'S LEGACY

Perspectives on a
Multiracial America Series
Joe R. Feagin, Texas A&M University,
Series Editor

JIM CROW'S LEGACY

The Lasting Impact of Segregation

Ruth Thompson-Miller, Joe R. Feagin, and Leslie H. Picca

ROWMAN & LITTLEFIELD
Lanham • Boulder • New York • London

Published by Rowman & Littlefield
A wholly owned subsidiary of The Rowman & Littlefield Publishing Group,
Inc.
4501 Forbes Boulevard, Suite 200, Lanham, Maryland 20706
www.rowman.com

Unit A, Whitacre Mews, 26-34 Stannary Street, London SE11 4AB,
United Kingdom

British Library Cataloguing in Publication Information Available

Library of Congress Cataloging-in-Publication Data

Thompson-Miller, Ruth, 1957–
Jim Crow's legacy : the lasting impact of segregation / Ruth Thompson-Miller, Joe R. Feagin, and
Leslie H. Picca.
pages cm. — (Perspectives on a multiracial america series)
Includes bibliographical references and index.
ISBN 978-1-4422-3027-9 (cloth : alk. paper) — ISBN 978-1-4422-4163-3 (pbk. : alk. paper) —
ISBN 978-1-4422-3028-6 (electronic) 1. African Americans—Segregation—History. 2. United
States—Race relations—History. 3. Whites—United States—Attitudes. 4. African Americans—
Civil rights—History. 5. Racism—United States—History. I. Feagin, Joe R. II. Picca, Leslie
Houts, 1975– III. Title.
E185.61.T465 2015
323.1196'073—dc23
2014029700

♾ ™ The paper used in this publication meets the minimum requirements of
American National Standard for Information Sciences Permanence of Paper
for Printed Library Materials, ANSI/NISO Z39.48-1992.

Printed in the United States of America

Dedicated to
Dorothea Laverne Thompson

CONTENTS

PREFACE

As trained social scientists, our job is to collect appropriate data, analyze it carefully, and draw reasonable conclusions based on our findings. However, in spite of the narrative of social science objectivity that has been asserted by numerous social scientists, the inevitably subjective reality of doing research into people's everyday lives and how that manifests itself in the lived experience of researchers are important issues frequently left out of scholarly research discussions. As longtime researchers of the Jim Crow era, we have learned well the importance of actively and accurately voicing the lived experiences of African Americans who survived the horrors of Jim Crow. The ever-savvy respondents in our extensive Jim Crow research contributed major insights and extraordinary wisdom to this lengthy project, a type of social-depth education that most graduate students are not afforded in all the training they receive in the academy. Let's be clear: The interviews for this project were read numerous times, coded, and analyzed before we could understand and present well what these Americans have experienced across their lives. Our previous training about, and research on, white racism did not prepare us to face the extraordinary, deep-lying, painful, and horrific realities of the Jim Crow experiences recounted by these older African American respondents. If the reader learns half as much as we have learned from these African American elders about U.S. racial matters, we will have achieved our goal in this research and in writing up this book.

Sadly, the realities of white-imposed racial privilege and racialized pain that our respondents endured under Jim Crow are still constantly experienced today by African Americans in what many inaccurately term a "post-racial" America. One of us was recently privy to an intense conversation involving a talented young black girl attending a prestigious private school. Camella (a pseudonym) gave her mother a copy of her writing assignment, for which she needed her mother's signature. The white teacher had written several negative notes on it: "This is careless of you. This is confusing what you wrote here (twice). I don't understand this word." She gave the child a "C" on this assignment. Adults reviewing the paper could quickly see it was by no means a "C" paper. Looking over the paper, her mother calmly said, "Sweetie, we have talked about this before. Didn't I tell you that you will be judged more harshly because you're black? I know that this is not a 'C' paper and you know it. But you have got to do better so that they [whites] can't find anything else that they can use to give you a bad grade. I know it isn't fair, but that is the way things are and you need to understand. And be sure that you don't give them anything to use against you. Do you understand?" The innocent black girl stood with her head hanging down, acknowledging the harsh reality of current white racism.

We understand the supportive actions that most Americans of all backgrounds make to help their children thrive in school. Most parents want what is best for their children and will do whatever they can to ensure that. Yet, such parental support is especially difficult if it must be done, as here, during the too-long struggles to fight racial discrimination and oppression in this country. As our interviews frequently show, the black targets of white racism regularly face two types of oppression—the first being the racist acts themselves, and the second being the pain and effort of trying to deal with the aftermath of such racist acts.

Our elderly African American respondents have lived through Jim Crow, and much contemporary racial discrimination as well. As the reader will see throughout the chapters, their insights about, and interpretations of, white racism in the past and present are regularly revealing, savvy, and awe-inspiring, and oftentimes they left us astounded or in tears. For the most part, they remain resilient, hopeful, and especially concerned about young African Americans. As later chapters reveal, this resilience is very powerful. In spite of the great stress, violence, and degradation they faced daily from whites, they often pushed back by drawing on family and communal support and religious beliefs to help them endure this oppression. Amazingly enough, they even express significant and generous concern for the souls of white folks who have brought such oppression on them. Moreover, as much as these older African Americans clearly deserve it, almost none seek reparations for their decades of suffering mightily from white oppression. All they really want today, as they did in the past, is societal *fairness*, *equal access* to socioeconomic resources, and a *level playing field* for their children and grandchildren. Much of the source of their continuing anguish today, as we will see in their interviews, comes from realizing that their children and grandchildren are still facing some of the same white-imposed racial barriers they faced and experiencing similarly horrific personal and family consequences.

We see much evidence of this reality in recent incidents where children like Camella are still treated unjustly and harshly because they are black and face powerful and hateful whites who do not care about their humanity and life chances. Camella actually deserves, but did not get, routine praise for her intelligence and creative thinking. She is not being placed in advanced classes for her decidedly unique abilities. Sadly, little Camella still faces today the white-imposed barriers similar to those that her great-grandparents, grandparents, and parents have faced, as children and adults, in a system of racial oppression that has been maintained now for four centuries.

African Americans know that most oppressive white actions are grounded in institutionalized racism and are part of a racially structured society. In their everyday worlds children like Camella often learn much about this racist reality from white teachers who force them to question their academic abilities and who crush their self-esteem. Even in this brief account, we can also see the heavy toll that this one event makes on one black child and her loved ones. Some might suggest the apparently easy solution—that is, the parents should just change her school. But such a strategy usually does not work in this society, for white racism follows a black person of any age or status almost anywhere. Indeed, this view posits an individual solution for what is a problem of well-institutionalized racism. Certainly, it is the responsibility of black parents to help their racially abused children, and they routinely do so. But fighting racist educational systems and white teachers' racist framing and trying to get the latter to see the academic talents and abilities of black children is yet another, much more difficult challenge.

We understand well that the necessary societal racial transformation is not just about the attitudes of these individual whites, but centrally about the centuries-old institutional and systemic racism of this society. Yet, we still can't get the words of our elderly black respondents about hundreds of individual white assaults out of our heads or the image of contemporary black children like Camella learning similarly difficult lessons about situated racial barriers. And we know well from both our own experiences and from much research that we have done here and elsewhere that whites have the option to close their eyes and ignore the grave and grievous individual and societal consequences of everyday racism. But African Americans like our respondents and children like Camella, who endure and witness this racism every day, generally do not have that *option*.

ACKNOWLEDGMENTS

We are indebted to all the African American respondents who were willing to share their lived experiences even when it was emotionally painful to recall the memories. All agreed to share their lifetime experiences, for a variety of reasons, including the relief that sharing such memories often brought to them. Unmistakably, this book would not have been possible without their bravery, candor, tears, and even laughter. We three authors feel privileged to share their stories. Both Ruth and Leslie feel it was an honor to work together on this project, and to work with our Ph.D. advisor, Joe Feagin.

Before writing up the analysis for this book, Ruth and Leslie conducted workshops on the legacy of Jim Crow at the annual White Privilege Conference in Seattle, Washington. We are grateful to the conference founder, Dr. Eddie Moore, Jr., along with Dr. Abby Ferber, for taking an interest in our research. The workshop participants of various ages and racial and ethnic backgrounds shared their own stories with Jim Crow, and through their eager questions, urged us to quickly publish the book.

This research was funded in part by Ruth's support by the American Sociological Association's National Institute of Mental Health Minority Fellowship Program (MFP), the McNair Scholars Program, the University of Florida's Scholars Program, and the University of Dayton's Seed Grant Program. We wholeheartedly thank each organization for supporting this work.

Ruth and Joe would like to thank the faculty, staff, undergraduate and graduate students at Texas A & M University, including Jane Sell, the late Howard Kaplan, Alex McIntosh, Holly Foster, Joseph Jewell, Rogelio Saenz, Wendy Moore, Verna Keith, and, most particularly, Christi Ramirez.

Ruth and Leslie would like to thank the faculty and staff of the Department of Sociology, Anthropology, and Social Work at the University of Dayton for their support and assistance, particularly Nancy Terrell, Ashley Seni, Michaela Herrick, Glenna Jennings, Patty Alvarez, Daria Graham, Sr. Laura Leming, and Paul Benson.

Leslie is grateful to the University of Dayton for her sabbatical, allowing her the opportunity to dig deep into Ruth's interviews. Leslie also thanks Mike Picca and their children Katie, Sarah, and Megan; it takes a village to raise the Picca kids, and Leslie couldn't do it without Carol Wethington, Karen Gardner, Krista Lorenz, Miho Sakama, Gail Rice, Julie Frame, Dawn Azennar, and Betty Houts.

Ruth would like to thank Theresa C. Schile for all her support and assistance during a critical phase in the writing of this book. She is deeply thankful to her beloved family, mother Carolyn, sisters Anita and Loretta, brothers Joseph and Jeffrey, and brother-in-law Joseph Royal, who have supported her throughout the process. She extends her deepest thanks to her deceased father Millard and sister Dorothea (I miss you both terribly). Ruth is deeply indebted and thankful to the three loves of her life, who made her laugh when she needed to and kept her moving forward when she was stuck: Nefertiti, Myia, and Yasmeen. Without them, Ruth could not have done this work—thanks for your love and support.

Joe would like to thank Ruth for her long years of devoted gathering of these interviews with the African American respondents who make up the heart of this book and especially to thank these awe-inspiring respondents themselves. He would also like to thank Leslie for agreeing to come into the project and for helping us bring the project to conclusion.

I

INTRODUCTION

We didn't even think about, being ugly to white people. . . .We did have a trouble with the Ku Klux Klan. . . .They put the sheets on and they would ride down Fifth Avenue. We would hide . . . under the house, in the house we would hide from them. They didn't bother us; they just parade down the street . . . lots of them, and just blowing their horns and you know howling and stuff like that. But they didn't shoot at us or they didn't say anything, 'cause we was hiding. But we didn't have any trouble with them robbing us or nothing. I guess they just wanted to show us how big they could be. . . . I'd say about once a year. . . . It would be a big parade, it would last and last hours, and they'd be gone. . . . We keep out of the windows and keep the light off. . . .Our parents didn't allow us to look, at the street. . . . it was throughout my childhood. (*Janice Evans, 70s*)[1]

Janice Evans shares with us the white terrorism that her family experienced while she was growing up in a town in the Southeast. Her mother worked for a police officer, who would warn her that the Ku Klux Klan would be parading through the neighborhood. This event and daily violent experiences of Jim Crow segregation profoundly affected the lives of the older African Americans interviewed for this book, in individual and collective ways. They coped with and survived the experience of Jim Crow, and they shared their often poignant narratives with us. As we will see throughout the chapters, older African Americans frequently still feel the need to pass on their hard-learned survival strategies, which date back 50 or more years, to the next generation living in this town. The intergenerational transmission of racial oppression and its countering strategies are built into the fabric of their everyday lives.

As you drive through this town where Janice Evans lives, you see small signs of a time that signal what the town may have looked like during Jim Crow. In the African American community on the east side, there are still dirt roads, dilapidated houses with tin roofs among modern houses, large forested areas intertwined with signs of development, and poor people in need of employment. In the white community on the west side, there are million-dollar homes, gated communities, mega malls, hospitals, modern industrial sites, and country clubs. Although the racial makeup of the town is largely segregated, with most whites on the west side and the large majority of African Americans living on the east side, there are some exceptions. A small number of whites, mostly students, live in what was historically the black community. At the same time you have a token population of professional African Americans on the west side of town.

The east side is mostly poor, underdeveloped, and struggling with issues of school closings and gentrification. As in other towns and cities, gentrification often involves a government-supported process that results in the uprooting of black renters and moderate-income homeowners and their replacement by higher-income, disproportionately white, residents. Here it has meant the involuntary displacement of low-income people of color in a community plagued by social problems and a history of lack of investment. Meanwhile, the predominately white west side is booming with new schools, new industry, and thriving businesses. This town is growing almost entirely in accordance with the economic and political goals of its white citizens.

The majority of African Americans work at service jobs such as janitors, bus drivers, food service workers, and health or day care providers. The jobs usually pay close to the minimum wage. Many jobs service white families or business or government facilities that most African Americans there rarely get to enjoy. The university in town employs many black workers who live on the east side. On work days, an exodus of groundskeepers, custodians, cooks, and maintenance workers come to the university from their communities on the east side. In contrast, many whites work at the university as professors, administrators, or other staff members. Other whites work throughout the area, a majority in higher-paying jobs such as businesspeople, doctors, lawyers, realtors, or teachers. The majority of students at the university are white and middle class, with a small number of students of color among them. The political climate of this town is shaped by the relative disenfranchisement of the black voter and, thus, a neglect of the major needs of the black community.

The contemporary life in this town resembles in many ways the social, political, and economic descriptions of the legal segregation that once characterized it. Our respondents project the image of little room to maneuver when they recall memories of that extraordinarily difficult era. Although the Jim Crow era officially ended about 1969, painful memories of that totalitarian experience are still shaping their lives and those of the next generation of African Americans. Our respondents often suggest that in certain ways racial patterns have changed little.

We conducted our research in some of the many towns and cities that once had well-developed Jim Crow segregation. The description of the town above and its economic layout helps to put the narratives of our participants into the social context in which they are living. It is important to contextualize the contemporary scene to understand why our participants feel the need to pass on their antiracist strategies and to understand that much has not changed for them since Jim Crow. In this research we analyze how, during legal segregation, white-generated fear through racial violence and terror was used to routinely keep African Americans under social, economic, and political control. We examine how fear of physical harm (including death) motivated their survival strategies. To alleviate the contemporary effects on the minds and health of African Americans, the long history of imposed racialized traumas must first be fully acknowledged by both black communities and the larger society.[2]

Without hearing the voices of African Americans who lived through legal segregation, it is difficult for non-black people generally, and for younger people of all backgrounds, to comprehend the extensive and oppressive experiences of legal segregation. One reason for this is that most U.S. history books, especially those used in primary and secondary schools, are still white-framed and typically downplay or ignore the horrific realities of the brutal Jim Crow era, which ended only a half century ago. One purpose of this book is to provide some counterpoint to this whitewashed history and to voice the historically subjugated and silenced voices of these elderly African Americans. Growing up in the era of legal segregation taught them many harsh and bitter lessons, and it is important for many reasons, including contemporary social justice efforts, to document the ways they used to survive. There is an undeniable power in listening to the voices of older black southerners who share their narratives of daily experiences. Throughout this book we document the voices, perceptions, and experiences of older African Americans in southern towns who survived this country's extreme but legal segregation.

Here we examine how racially traumatic events—for example, lynchings, rape, torture, humiliation, church and house burnings, Klan marches, and the threat of white violence—were routinely utilized to keep black southerners under economic, social, and political control. The correct term for this violent social context is *white terrorism*. The standard definition of terrorism runs something like this: the "calculated use of violence, or its threat, against ordinary people to attain ideological or political goals."[3] In the Jim Crow era, white terrorism, the reality and threat of white violence, was the everyday reality, and it induced a widespread state of fear in the African American community. Fear is a powerful and repressive emotion that was then, and still is to some extent, felt in all African American communities across the country. Indeed, the towns and cities where we conducted this research will remain anonymous to protect the identity of our participants, who often expressed concern for their safety if that identity was exposed. They still fear the consequences of speaking out about racialized oppression during legal segregation.

We will also examine how fear motivated the coping strategies that millions of courageous African Americans used to survive the recurring onslaught of terroristic violence inflicted upon them by whites. This induced state of fear is still, unbeknownst even to them in some cases, affecting their health, minds, and bodies as they continue to heal wounds that keep them in a persisting cycle of white-imposed victimization. The cumulative experiences with racially traumatic events caused long-lasting psychological consequences for African Americans as individuals, families, and communities. We refer to this significant lifelong reality as the *segregation stress syndrome*.

HISTORICAL BACKGROUND: SLAVERY AND JIM CROW

In 1619, the first enslaved Africans arrived in the English North America. These and other Africans were violently separated from their families, cultures, and heritages. The voyage through the middle Atlantic passage was brutal and traumatic; thousands fought back on ships or leaped to their death in the waters of the Atlantic.[4] Once they arrived, they were sold like cattle on an auction block. They endured beatings, rape, torture, lynchings, and decimation of their families. The people, places, and things that Africans knew and revered in Africa were replaced with unfamiliar people, places, and things in North America—leading to an overwhelming fear at what they surely didn't understand initially. Not surprisingly, over subsequent decades many fought to gain their freedom, as individuals and groups.

During slavery there were whites of various social, political, and economic backgrounds who enslaved African Americans, traded goods with slave farms and plantations, or performed other functions connected with the institution of slavery. In this process many whites gained significant wealth. Many descendants of both elite and ordinary whites are thus still reaping the benefits of the unjust wealth that was created as a result of the system of slavery.[5]

No events in the collective memory of African Americans are more profoundly impactful than those involving the capture, enslavement, and kidnapping of millions from the continent of Africa, their ultimate homeland.[6] With the "total institution" of slavery came the simultaneous formation of Africans as a collective group in America.[7] In a total institution, groups of individuals are cut off from the "wider society, for an appreciable period of time" and every major aspect of their lives is controlled and monitored—from the language they use to their ability to protect loved ones.[8] After about 246 years, the total institution of slavery was finally abolished at the end of a bloody Civil War by the 1865 Thirteenth Amendment to the U.S. Constitution. We should note too that the exploitation and oppression of African Americans had been originally enshrined in the foundational U.S. legal, economic, and social institutions. Thus, the U.S. Constitution, and later federal court decisions, created the early forms of numerous racist institutions that are still functioning today.[9]

After the end of slavery, there was a brief time, a little more than a decade, when many freed African Americans gained better economic, social, and political footing and opportunities. During the post-war era of Reconstruction, the newly desegregated state electorates elected the first African American members to U.S. Senate, House, and other legislative positions. However, these black elected officials, in most instances, were soon replaced with whites and/or had modest political influence while they served. After the Reconstruction era, between the 1880s and early 1900s in former slave states, extensive racial segregation ("Jim Crow") laws were set in place with conditions in many ways similar to those of slavery. Segregated agencies of local, state, and federal governments exercised extreme control over major aspects of the lives of African Americans.

In 1896 the white racist judges of the U.S. Supreme Court ruled that this expanding Jim Crow segregation was constitutional. This landmark case involved Homer Plessy, an African American who refused to sit in the "colored" section on a Louisiana train, and in effect it upheld the laws reinforcing local Jim Crow segregation across the United States. The structures of totalitarian racism were extended for many more decades by the Jim Crow system.

Today, when we are taught in schools about Jim Crow, we mostly learn about Rosa Parks, Martin Luther King, Jr., and the separate water fountains, sections of buses, and sections of restaurants. These were important aspects of Jim Crow segregation, but there was much more to this totalitarian system. In most former slave states African Americans could not vote, testify against whites, or serve on juries, and they could only use segregated schools, orphanages, and hospitals. All major aspects of public life such as transportation, hotels, and parks were legally segregated. There were major racial disparities in the treatment of black Americans in financial, employment, educational, political, and other societal institutions. The total institution imposed by Jim Crow laws even included provisions for imprisoning African Americans who whites thought were "vagrants."[10] These laws thereby gave whites permission to force them to work in white fields and factories, or else go to jail.[11] The legal and informal Jim Crow practices meant racial subordination and an imposed badge of racial degradation for all African Americans in southern states and in many other areas of the United States.[12]

Yet more extreme racial oppression also characterized the legal segregation era. Our respondents periodically recall that there were numerous lynchings of black Americans, for a variety of reasons including disrespect for Jim Crow norms or laws. The number of men, women (including those pregnant), and children who were lynched is estimated by historians to be in the range of 6,000–10,000, although the actual number is unknown. Moreover, the lasting, often severe psychological impact that recurring lynchings and other white violence had on black individuals, families, and communities over the long Jim Crow decades has rarely been documented or adequately analyzed. The larger issue for these black individuals and communities was the daily, never-ending fight for survival and dignity, as well as the constant pushing back against second-class citizenship.

In the 1950s and 1960s, pressures from black leaders and protestors in the African American civil rights movement began to press the white elite to end this official segregation. Together with other societal and international factors, these civil rights pressures did eventually end legal segregation. However, long centuries of slavery and Jim Crow greatly shaped the foundation and institutions of this society, and thus many types of white racial oppression continue to flourish today in this country.

OUR CONCEPTUAL APPROACH

In this book we use the term *systemic racism* for the many institutionalized structures of white-created racial oppression that have for centuries greatly shaped the lives of African Americans and other Americans of color. Implemented by European Americans in the seventeenth century, white-on-black oppression has been central to this society ever since, to the present day. As we will demonstrate throughout this book's chapters, this systemic racism involves these key societal features: (1) a complex array of oppressive racial practices implemented by whites, (2) the unjustly gained privileges and power of white Americans that result from this oppression, (3) the substantial, well-institutionalized, and unjust impoverishment inflicted by this oppression on African Americans, and (4) the extensive white racial frame that has been used for centuries to rationalize and maintain white privilege and power over the centuries.

In the Jim Crow era this systemic racism was very similar to what some social scientists have termed a "total institution." We use this term and concept to accent the all-encompassing reality that was legal segregation for about a century of this country's history. Under this form of systemic racism African Americans were often criminalized, treated like animals, and excluded from numerous freedoms and valuable resources available to white Americans. The sociologist Erving Goffman emphasized the concept in the 1960s in research on mental institutions and prisons. A total institution is "a place of residence and work where a large number of like-situated individuals, cut off from the wider society lead an enclosed, formally administrated round of life."[13] Some of the characteristics of such a total institution include controlling a person's language, regularly humiliating a person, and denying acknowledgment of a person's real name. A total institution also usually entails a rigid hierarchy, extensive economic control, a loss of personal safety, forced deference, sexual and other assaults, an inability to protect loved ones, constant surveillance, and suppression of feelings.[14] In some political histories, such as of Nazi Germany, "totalitarianism" is often portrayed as a societal set of such total institutions.

We show in this book that most aspects of the previous total institution of slavery continued during the Jim Crow era. To make up for the end of the extreme physical barriers and mechanisms of slavery, an array of Jim Crow laws and unwritten rules were established as the new means of racialized social control. The concept and practice of this racial social control was utilized to dictate and shape the everyday social interactions between whites and blacks in southern states, border states, and some areas of northern states.[15] We prefer the term "racial social control" instead of the "racial etiquette" phrase most scholars use.[16] The word *etiquette* is too tame and implies that there is an interactive agreement, even some equal status. The continuation of racial social control from slavery days was instrumental in maintaining the extreme racial hierarchy in which blacks were treated as second-class citizens and rarely afforded the protection of most state and local laws. In addition, the practices of racial social control included those of ordinary whites who had the unwritten authority to keep black people in "their place" by any means necessary—which included beatings, torture, rape, murder, humiliation, and other forms of inhumane treatment.

In summary, in this book we address the following important questions:

1. What were the realities experienced by African American during Jim Crow segregation?
2. How did the survivors of Jim Crow cope with the everyday occurrences of white violence and other oppression?
3. What have been the long-term psychological, physical, and economic consequences for these black survivors of Jim Crow?
4. What is the intergenerational impact of the traumas experienced by these survivors of Jim Crow?

To our knowledge, no existing book probes these questions as thoroughly and deeply as we do here, and no one has examined these questions in sociological depth with people who survived the Jim Crow era. Some significant narratives of the events of Jim Crow segregation have been collected by McGovern, Smead, Wexler, Tyson, and Bernstein, among others.[17] They and others have mostly focused on documenting historical events and narratives, including those connected to publicized lynchings. A few other scholars have documented certain important aspects of everyday life for African Americans under Jim Crow.[18] This book builds on this previous work and focuses not only on a more thorough sociological analysis of Jim Crow events but also on the contemporary legacies and impacts of the legal segregation era.

OUR RESEARCH METHODS AND PARTICIPANTS

While several scholars have researched the experiences of African Americans during the Jim Crow era, no previous research probes deeply into the long-term physical, psychological, and social consequences experienced by its survivors and their descendants. No research that we have found examines important intergenerational consequences, including legal segregation's long-term impacts on black young people today. Here we report on 92 in-depth interviews with the black survivors of the Jim Crow era. Their ages range from 52 to 95 years old; they reside in the Southeast and Southwest. The interviews detail accounts about the oppressive legal segregation experience, including incidents of beatings, torture, rape, and lynching, as well as recurring nonviolent acts of white humiliation, acts of everyday resistance, and other individual and group coping strategies. Among other results, our data provide some significant insights into the long-term health consequences of racialized violence and other trauma and provide a complex and revealing picture of the extraordinarily oppressive Jim Crow era that is missing from conventional history books.

We began this project by contacting key local informants, such as ministers and teachers, in two black communities in the South. They provided us with a few names of people who might be willing to participate, and we collected further names by making presentations at organizational meetings and from references of the initial respondents. The first author, who is African American, interviewed 52 respondents in the Southeast (37 women and 15 men). A substantial majority were over 70 years old, with the rest between 52 and 69 years old. In the Southwest, she also interviewed 40 respondents (25 women and 15 men). Again a substantial majority were over 70 years old, with the rest between 58 and 69 years old. In both regions about two-thirds had held relatively low-paying jobs, such as domestic worker or hospital aide, during their primary work lives under legal segregation; most of the rest held modest-paying jobs like schoolteacher in a segregated school. From the interviews, we learned that all were strongly committed to education, and a majority managed to secure at least a high school diploma,[19] with a quarter having some college. Most interviews took place in the respondents' homes and lasted one to two hours. We used a flexible interview schedule with a series of open-ended questions about their lives under the total institution that was Jim Crow.[20]

In their interviews our African American respondents shared events that happened decades in that past, and yet the details of what they recall are often extensive and staggering. Some readers may be tempted to think these older respondents are exaggerating. Unfortunately, this is a strategy used by some whites to deny or deflect the reality of centuries of racist experiences experienced by African Americans, experiences they often prefer to ignore. Commonly, whites will question African Americans' experiences with doubting questions like, "Are you sure you aren't reading too much into it?" Some will also offer rationalizations for the extensive white violence reported by those who lived through Jim Crow segregation, comments such as "that was only an isolated incident" or "alcohol was probably involved." However, the many incidents of racial violence and other racial oppression reported by our respondents are not only often detailed, but also validated by much historical evidence, including the newspaper accounts we also cite in several chapters of this book.

Thus, for this research project we went beyond our interviews to examine the broader historical and societal contexts of our respondents. We utilized the documentation of historical events in important white and black newspapers. Historically black newspapers thoroughly reported the experiences of black Americans during the legal segregation era. Some respondents mentioned that there were rapes by whites in their families and communities, yet were often reluctant to talk about the details. The subject of rape is unquestionably sensitive. Thus, we searched newspaper archives in order to gain more information about these many white rapes during the Jim Crow era. We began our search in newspaper archives to answer the questions: What was the frequency of rapes in the black community, who were the perpetrators and victims, how were they reported in newspapers, what newspapers reported them, what were the details, how did law enforcement respond to the crimes, and what was the frequency and severity of the punishment. We used the ProQuest Historical Newspapers' searchable archive of the *Atlanta Constitution* (1868–1942). This major white-run paper has long had an established reputation and regional influence and is one of the only Southern newspapers that survived the Civil War. We also used the searchable ProQuest archives of three important African American newspapers, the *Baltimore Afro-American* (1893–1988), *Chicago Defender* (1910–1975), and *Philadelphia Tribune* (1912–2001). Using the search function of these archives, we were able to document many cases of rape by whites during the legal segregation era. The newspaper articles we have quoted in this book often provide a more detailed account of the victims, rapists, and circumstances that led to the rapes.

OUTLINE OF CHAPTERS

Let us briefly provide an overview of the chapters to come. In chapter 2, we detail the long-term consequences of racial violence and trauma, and how the consequences are transmitted intergenerationally. We examine how the traumatic experiences of one generation can be passed along, verbally and nonverbally, to subsequent generations. We develop the concept of the "segregation stress syndrome" to explain the collective psychological and physical consequences of Jim Crow. The causes of this segregation stress syndrome are rooted in historical racial traumas, including those generated by violent racial events. These racial traumas were generated by the individual, collective, and institutionalized actions of whites that were physical, written, or spoken. They inflicted or threatened to inflict injury on the black targets, who often resisted. The experiences of racial violence and other racially traumatic events, and the ensuing negative consequences for African Americans, were individually and collectively endured, and they created a cumulative loss of psychological well-being. Similar to the post-traumatic stress disorder (PTSD) experienced by U.S. soldiers and others, the segregation stress syndrome often includes an intergenerational aspect, as the impact of that segregation trauma is passed on from generation to generation.

In chapters 3 and 4 we show that African Americans experienced constant surveillance, forced deference, and coercion in public spaces such as in mass transportation and on public streets. As might be expected, white police officers and security guards enforced the omnipresent racial hierarchy, but so did other whites. During legal segregation white violence was commonplace, and African Americans were under constant surveillance by ordinary whites, who were in turn usually supported by the white representatives of the government agencies, especially police officers. This racial control included spoken and unspoken rules that forced African Americans to live as second-class citizens who daily faced major human rights violations. African Americans weren't even guaranteed personal or collective safety like most whites were. On any given day, without warning, a black presence alone could be enough to set off a white person to act in a racially aggressive or violent way. Here, as in other chapters, we detail numerous accounts from the interview participants who experienced or witnessed racial violence and other discrimination at the hands of whites of all ages, from small children to elderly adults. We continue here to detail the many social, material, and psychological costs of recurring racial violence and other trauma. We also link these recurring Jim Crow experiences with research that has found a higher incidence of cardiovascular diseases, high blood pressure, stroke, and psychological problems among African Americans.

In chapter 5 we detail the seldom-discussed, but everyday, occurrence of rapes and other sexual assaults by white men during the Jim Crow era. We discuss the long-term psychological consequences for the victims of this sexual violence, and for their families. We examine how black men were usually unable to protect their daughters, sisters, wives, and mothers from white male assaults. In the chapter we rely not only on our interviews but also on our content analysis of historical documents, especially the newspapers discussed in the methods section, to discuss the prevalence of sexual assault of black women, including its use as one important tool of white terrorism in the Jim Crow era. As we will see, the women rarely had any recourse and almost never received any justice for the crime. Those who attempted to report an incident to white authorities feared retaliation. In rare instances when a rape case did go to trial, the white rapist typically was set free by the white judge or all-white jury. If the African American girl or woman who was raped got pregnant, she was forced to leave town in shame. Given the pervasiveness of sexual assault, it is important to understand the physical, psychological, social, and economic consequences for these black girls and women, as well as for their families.

In chapter 6 we detail how African Americans coped with the many laws and unspoken norms of Jim Crow. Our respondents frequently described the important role of the black community, especially churches and schools, as relatively safe places of comfort and socialization for younger members of the community on how to prepare for interactions with whites. Although legal segregation was a bloody, extensive, and legitimized system of racial assault and violence, African Americans actively resisted its oppression. In our interviews we learn that, even though the respondents understood that to resist might cost them their lives, they were willing to take chances to change the totalitarian racial system. The respondents described numerous strategies of resistance, such as filing lawsuits, organizing protests, and everyday small-scale acts of resistance.

In the final chapter we will summarize and further analyze our findings by connecting these African American survivors' experiences of Jim Crow segregation with contemporary racist realities. The *official* era of Jim Crow oppression ended less than 50 years ago. Living in southern areas of the United States, these older African Americans do sometimes—though not always—report that racial conditions have gotten better. Yet, they still report instances today where they hear, witness, and experience organized and random acts of serious racial discrimination, including white violence such as police brutality, sexual assaults, modern-day lynchings, and cross burnings. In addition, they report numerous everyday, more subtle and covert racial aggressions at the hands of whites of all ages. These contemporary experiences reignite and legitimate their racialized fears as Jim Crow survivors.

In this book we probe and demonstrate the deep societal reality that *the racially violent experiences of Jim Crow are still profoundly affecting and shaping the lives of older African Americans in individual and collective ways.* Our respondents' accounts periodically demonstrate that the legacies of legal segregation are still very much with us today, not only in the physical and psychological trauma evident in Jim Crow survivors, but in the racialized views and actions of people in all racial groups as well. By no means are we in any type of "post-racial" society, and white racism is certainly not a "thing of the past," given its extensive and persisting individual and systemic forms.

2

THE REALITY AND IMPACT OF JIM CROW

[In this town] my brother was very outspoken. . . . He fought back and stood up for our rights. . . . One day he just disappeared. Weeks went by and we didn't know what happened to him. . . One night, I will never forget it. Mama and I were getting ready for bed and I heard her scream, "They found him." It was on the news. My mama fell apart. [She begins to cry]. That thing hurt me so bad. I will never get over it. [She begins to cry harder.] We found out later that he was lured to the secluded place by a lake where he was killed and where they found his decomposing body in a refrigerator . . . There were signs that he fought back. . . . My mama never got over it. . . . I will never get over what [whites] did to my brother. (*Elaine Pearson, 70s*)

Elaine Pearson, a respondent living in the Southeast, shares the great pain she experienced when the decaying body of her brother was found in a refrigerator in a secluded location where he had been lured and brutally murdered. The pain of remembering is evident in her continuous crying throughout the recollection. Although in tears, she didn't want to stop the interview. She wanted to share the traumatic events that she endured throughout her life under the oppressive system of Jim Crow.

In this chapter we examine the *segregation stress syndrome* as a major type of post-traumatic stress disorder (PTSD). We assess how the causes, symptoms, risk factors, and intergenerational transmission of this stress syndrome can be applied to a collective group, the elderly survivors of Jim Crow oppression.

JIM CROW TRAUMAS AND RACIAL STRESS: THE SEGREGATION STRESS SYNDROME

Jim Crow was defined by millions of recurring traumatic events forced on African Americans. These painful events included verbal and violent attacks on individuals and families, including those involving the loss of material properties. If whites wanted land or houses owned by blacks, they would often engage in legal chicanery, assaults, or killings. One historical example of whites' mass expulsion of black residents involved Rosewood, Florida. In the 1930s an entire African American town was destroyed by a white mob that killed numerous residents. The town was never rebuilt. The alleged cause of the weeklong massacre was a married white woman who claimed to have been sexually assaulted by a black man. However, the limited evidence suggests the woman was blaming a black man instead of the white male lover with whom she was actually having an affair. White mobs doused black homes in kerosene, lit them on fire, and shot at residents who emerged. According to historian Thomas Dye, "The Rosewood riot was not an anomaly, but rather an all too common expression of racism in the 1920s."[1] Historian Maxine Jones reports that the black survivors "exhibited symptoms associated with a post-traumatic stress disorder [which] included fear, avoidance, hyper-vigilance, recurring memories, denial, and emotional numbness."[2]

Many of our respondents shared stories of racially traumatic events. These included witnessing a black person being injured or killed by whites and being unable to protect them, or personally experiencing violence, rape, or other assault. They also included white violence in the form of burning of houses and churches; entire black communities were sometimes forced out of town by whites. In addition, many people reported the loss of family members whom they were unable to protect and loss of self-respect from personal humiliation, such as whites using demeaning nicknames, compelling deference, and making false accusations.

Witnessing, experiencing, or hearing about a racially traumatic event often generated symptoms of the segregation stress syndrome: the loss of trust, discomfort, being fearful, and being nervous around whites, the dominant group that caused the racial trauma. Like other researchers, we see much evidence in our interviews of primary trauma that stems from a person directly experiencing the racist actions of whites, individually or collectively, as well as of the secondary trauma that comes from seeing or hearing about the racist actions endured by others.[3] The racially traumatic events also often generated a feeling of uncertainty about what the whites might do and avoidance of places and things that were reminders of the traumatic events. These latter symbols of Jim Crow included trees, buses, water fountains, stores, and lynching exhibits. Other reactions to racially traumatic events included denial of an event, individual and collective forgetting, being emotionally upset when recalling memories, and feeling anxiety, rage, shame, or sadness. The reactions also included hyper-vigilance in regard to the white perpetrators of the traumatic event, the latter in turn being prone to inaccurate labeling of blacks as paranoid.

In making sense of these racially traumatic events we draw on the research literature on the post-traumatic stress disorder (PTSD). In this literature, war, a disaster, rape, and other terrorism are strong predictors of a person developing PTSD. The segregation stress syndrome is created by similarly stressful events. African Americans living in the Jim Crow era were constantly faced with the threat of racial violence and other discrimination of the types previously mentioned. As with PTSD victims, they too often were unable to protect themselves or their family members in dangerous situations.[4] African Americans who suffered under Jim Crow faced a significant risk of developing symptoms of PTSD, but this varied somewhat depending on their specific experiences. A number of factors affected the severity of their PTSD-type reactions to Jim Crow. These included the time of earliest exposure, the length and frequency of their exposure, and the severity of witnessing the racially traumatic events. In the next section we consider important excerpts from our many interviews that deal with particular types of racially traumatic events.

RACIALLY TRAUMATIC EVENTS: LOSS OF LAND

One important type of racially traumatic event involved the loss of property, an event that usually entailed an inability to protect one's land or other belongings. Historically, there are documented cases of entire black communities being banished from their lands in a short period of time. The white message was, "Get out or die." In his book on "sundown towns," James Loewen[5] documents the disturbing history of many African Americans who were regularly kept out of or chased out of many towns in states such as North Carolina, Michigan, Florida, and Missouri. One dramatic example that we referred to previously involved the mass expulsion of African Americans in Rosewood, Florida. It was a very common occurrence during the Jim Crow epoch for African Americans to lose lives, property, and family members to white treachery and violence. Significantly, most of the likely huge number of such personal and property losses to African Americans throughout the southern and border states over a century of Jim Crow remain unrecognized and undocumented.

The intergenerational transmission of family assets is fundamental to family survival over time. Mary Ingram, a respondent in the Southwest, who was living in the grip of Jim Crow, discussed the importance of land that some African Americans had. She noted the significance of land assets for her family's survival:

> My grandfather owned a lot of land down there. My grandfather was one of the, if we could call it, one of the important blacks down there. He had over 500 acres of land. He had his own farm. He had people who worked for him. I've never known a hungry day in my life. There are other people that might have. We were poor; I don't mean that we had money. But we had, we lived on the farm with my grandfather that had the resources, and he wasn't an educated man. He was just a man that had common sense, good mother wit, and know-how to do things. But I've never known a hungry day in my life. (*Mary Ingram, 70s*)

In her interview, Mary Ingram further describes how her grandfather eventually had to sell his substantial landholdings and go to work for whites. The wealth, or opportunity for wealth-generating resources, was thus lost to the family, apparently under discriminatory pressures from whites.

Historically over many generations, most white families had far more opportunities to build up family assets and wealth than black families, especially given that the latter faced slavery or extreme racial segregation over more than three centuries of this country's development. Over nearly 400 years now, the unjust enrichment of whites and unjust impoverishment of blacks has been fundamental and foundational to this society. Much of this wealth development was assisted by white "affirmative action" programs such as the major homestead acts of the nineteenth century and early twentieth century, and other federal and local government programs that assisted whites in gaining land and other assets.[6] Other assets were directly stolen by contemporary whites' ancestors who used some type of racialized treachery or violence. Hearing the voices of black individuals who lost their land, their assets and inheritance, adds much to our acknowledging and understanding the great price that African American families have paid for racism over centuries of time.

Significantly, the history of land theft in this country dates back to the first years of the colonization of this country, during which Native Americans lost much land to white treachery and violence. African Americans have had similar experiences, especially during the Jim Crow era. Periodically, respondents like Mary Ingram recalled how their family once owned land that is now a source of wealth for the descendants of the whites who stole it. The history of this land theft has not been discussed enough by historians. Jaspin has noted that "whites had driven blacks out, and yet the memory of this expulsion worked at whites like a stone in a shoe."[7] The expulsion of African Americans from their lands, as well as from towns and other areas across the country, was not achieved just through legal chicanery and other nonviolent means. The expulsions often included mob violence and the loss of life.[8] Certainly, one major effect of this white land theft was to deny a great many African American families the ability to pass land resources to their generations—thereby perpetuating such lack of socioeconomic resources over many decades to the present day and thereby reinforcing certain white-racist depictions of impoverished black individuals and families in the age-old white racial frame.

Not surprisingly, such substantial loss of land and related socioeconomic resources is a major source of shame, anger, and rage for many African Americans. The anger and rage felt by many African Americans about such white-racist actions is thus quite reasonable and easily explained. Helen Gaines, a respondent in the Southeast, recalls how her father, on his deathbed, shared how his land had been stolen by whites:

> My father never did tell us about it, the land. But when he was dying he told us how whites stole his land. They forced him to sign papers that gave them control of the land. They threatened him, and he was afraid and didn't know what to do. Before he died he begged me to see if I could get the land back for the family. I'm not sure what to do. (*Helen Gaines, 60s*)

Indeed, many African Americans had good reasons for keeping the theft of their land a secret from family members. These reasons included the impact of the segregation stress syndrome, including feelings of uncertainty and fear of the serious consequences of fighting back, not only consequences for oneself but also for one's relatives. They also included a desire to ensure the safety of their loved ones.

Today, one can reasonably argue that African American communities do have an opportunity to investigate these land theft issues, form a rights movement, and regain their rightful inheritances. However, if this is to be accomplished, time is of the essence as the survivors of Jim Crow age. As U.S. history shows, whites then (and now) in power usually maintain a collective amnesia about these land thefts and their long-term consequences in creating the racial "wealth gap." In the Jim Crow case, the specific victims of this land theft are gradually leaving the scene.

RACIALLY TRAUMATIC EVENTS: LOSS OF LIFE

As we will see throughout this book, during the long legal segregation era, racially traumatic events often involved the loss of acquaintances and family members to major white violence. Frank Wilson, a respondent in the Southeast, recounts an extremely painful event that happened to a person he knew:

> There was a fellow named John. Now we can't prove it, but we know that white folks had something to do with taking him out in the woods and burn[ing] him up in the house. . . . This was right around here . . . somewhere, but it was out in the woods. . . . They burned him up in the house. [*Why?*][9] [He whispers.] White girls. White girls. You didn't cross no lines. That was automatic death. And there was nothing nobody could do about it. (*Frank Wilson, 80s*)

Note the level of *contemporary* pain and fear signaled in Frank Wilson's account, including in the whispering. In these Jim Crow situations the white killers often acted under cover of night or in isolated wooded areas. Black men who were just suspected of sleeping with white women were often murdered by white men. Ironically, in the past and the present, white men have inflicted physical violence on many black men for alleged sexual violations of white women, yet they have not assumed any responsibility for centuries of raping and molesting black women and children. When white perpetrators commit acts of racial violence and don't face criminal charges, they and their crimes are thus officially sanctioned by the larger white society. Moreover, in their accounts our respondents indicate that they often knew *who* tortured, raped, and murdered their neighbors, acquaintances, or loved ones, yet they had nowhere to turn for effective legal assistance and justice in their highly segregated towns.

Another respondent, Margaret Flowers, in the Southwest was asked if any of her family members had warned her about being especially careful around whites, and she recounts the warnings her brother received from their father about white women:

> My father would always warn my brothers never look directly at a white woman or white girl. Or whistle, or make . . . gestures to them because they would go back and say that you were trying to flirt with them. And they would . . . come and kill you or lynch you, you just don't even try those kinds of things and if you are with other boys that's doing this you separate yourself and you get back towards home. Never! . . . They had this thing that if a white girl or white lady was walking on the same sidewalk that you were walking on or road that you were walking on you were supposed to step aside and let the white girl or white boy, white lady pass. My father always says, "If you see one coming just turn and go another direction. So you won't have to meet these ladies or young women.". . . You don't want to get caught up in anything like this. You want to keep yourself always safe from things like this. [*What would whites do?*] . . . If they felt that you were trying to whip the law, haze them or something they would jump on you! Fight you! Do everything they can to kill you, harm you! (*Margaret Flowers, 70s*)

Repeatedly in our interviews, we see African American parents and other relatives warning male family members about possible encounters with white women. The common white racial framing of black men and white women contributed to this respondent's brothers being warned that they could lose their lives for just looking at a white woman. The intergenerational transmission of great white-imposed trauma is evident as the respondent recalls emotionally that her brothers were warned by their father about several actions in regard to white women.

Shaking her head back and forth in disgust, another respondent in the Southeast, Virginia Lane, recalls reading in the newspaper that several African American men were arrested and tried for merely looking at a white woman:

> I remember when [a black man] got six years in prison for looking in the direction of a white woman who was 75 feet away from him. He was charged with reckless eyeballing, and he spent six years in prison. . . . If you look at whites too long, white women, you could be put in jail. That man went to jail for years, and he was standing a long ways from the white woman. (*Virginia Lane, 80s*)

This supposed crime was so frequent that some African Americans referred to it as "reckless eyeballing."[10] It bears repeating that in this long segregation era white men frequently raped black women with impunity. Yet, if a black man merely looked at a white woman too long, he would often face punishment, including lengthy imprisonment or even death.[11]

The huge number of black boys and men who were tortured and lynched for fictional or greatly exaggerated "crimes" during the Jim Crow era has yet to be acknowledged by most white leaders, or whites collectively in any significant fashion. Yet it was a reality that the African American community dealt with on a daily basis. For example, in 1952 in Tallahassee, Florida, whites charged and convicted a 17-year-old black teenager with the rape of an older white woman. His mother, Mrs. Bard, fought to free her son and wrote the state governor and Supreme Court. The governor promised to help if she assisted in his reelection, but later ignored his promise. Black parents like Mrs. Bard and the larger black community had all the evidence they needed to develop a major mistrust of the white police and other government officials, as well as most other whites. In the face of death, her son insisted in a letter to her, "Mama, I didn't do it." According to newspaper reports from Mrs. Bard, "He told me on the day before he died,

'Mama, you pray for me. Hold your head up high, I didn't do it.'" On the day of the execution, the reporter noted that everyone "remembers the heartrending cries with which Mrs. Bard filled the dawn air . . . the day they strapped her teenage son . . . in the electric chair and pulled the switch." Reflecting an element of the segregation stress syndrome, his mother commented poignantly that "his being killed hurt me."[12] There are few media reports of the last words of black boys and men who were illegally or legally lynched as in this case of a teenager accused of raping a white woman. There were doubtless thousands of black parents and sons who during the Jim Crow era hoped that they could get a fair trial in the criminal justice system. Yet, they did not. Despite reports of a grief-stricken mother wailing for the death of her son, we see parallels with contemporary suffering of African Americans that often falls on whites' deaf ears. Civil rights activist Jesse Jackson famously noted in 2005 that America has "an amazing tolerance for black pain."[13] Unfortunately, as we discuss in chapter 7, this is true both for the Jim Crow era and for our contemporary era. Note too that African Americans have always had to live with an awareness that most whites in this racially oppressive society have a high tolerance for African American pain—yet one example of the *cumulatively* oppressive and traumatic effects of systemic racism.

THE SEGREGATION STRESS SYNDROME AS COLLECTIVE EXPERIENCE

Racially traumatic events had an array of negative impacts on their victims, their families, their neighbors and friends, and the larger black community. That is, they had both individual and large-scale collective effects. We have already touched on some of these impacts. In the rest of this chapter we will dig even deeper into the many dimensions of the segregation stress syndrome.

Recall that the traumatic experiences of Jim Crow were quite cumulative and systemic. Throughout our interviews the respondents constantly referred to individuals who lived through the era of Jim Crow as "we," "black people," "our women," "our men," and other terms that indicate they were talking about blacks *as a group*. This accents a shared collective experience with systemic racism. As we have seen previously, segregation stress syndrome is both an individual and collective experience. Sociologist Maurice Halbwachs has underscored the difference between individual and collective memory: Personal memory "refers to shared understandings of the past [but] collective memory is broader and more durable than personal memory."[14] The shared experience of living with everyday discrimination, coupled with knowing that the black body carries the white-constructed stigma of an inferior "race," shapes a person's trauma and reactions to it. A respondent in the Southwest, Delores Fowler, somewhat cautiously talks about the collective experience of living under Jim Crow decades ago:

> Well sometimes if they ask me questions, I will share it with them. . . . It's tough, and it hasn't been easy on a lot of people . . . people will tell you things that happened to them . . . some things that [whites] did you know it was wrong. . . . But you couldn't say anything about it. . . . When you got in trouble when you tried to speak up for something that you thought was right. . . . Your voice is not being heard. (*Delores Fowler, 80s*)

With tears in her eyes, Fowler continues with some savvy comments on the difficulties of raising black youngsters under Jim Crow:

> You raise some kids that is quick tempered . . . they say "I just ain't going to do this, today" and "I ain't going to do that." But you can't say what you ain't going to do, you can't do that. [She begins to cry.] I know that we have, the black-race people, and, you know, they had a hard time. . . . [Cries harder.] I've been around [whites] all my life. . . . I know that they still didn't care for me. . . . You see things you don't like; you know you can't do nothing about it. . . . You can't just tell them, let them know that you, you are a human, too. . . . I would like to have respect too because you are black does not mean you need to be treated like you are not nobody. And you find some [whites], and they just as good as gold, I mean they just as good as a black is towards you. Just like you're another one, just a human being. That's all you want, that's all I would want. I don't care about them. They don't have to hug and kiss me. Just treat me nice, that's all I ask, you know. Some people have a short temper and if things don't go just like they want to well they flies all off the handle and a bunch of cussing and stuff like that. (*Delores Fowler, 80s*)

She shares how the collective "black-race people" have had it hard in this society. In her sharp and revealing responses she exhibits significant symptoms of the segregation stress syndrome, including the emotional response of crying as she recalls the era of Jim Crow. She accents the pain of knowing she is despised just because of the color of her skin.

Numerous researchers such as Sharon Wasco have accented the dimension of oppression that involves the "devaluing of an individual's social status because of a characteristic of their identity (e.g., gender, race/ethnicity, sexual orientation, physical ability)."[15] Additionally, however, during Jim Crow an entire group of people experienced the insidious white-imposed trauma of being racially devalued. Other aspects of the segregation stress syndrome similar to those of PTSD include avoidance, isolation, the inability to forget the trauma, and the inability to reconnect with individuals one was close to before the major trauma. In addition, our respondents and other black Americans have mentioned how hard it was in the Jim Crow era to get adequate health care and assistance in times of great stress. They note too that white health caregivers and counselors usually did not understand their struggles and often dismissed them as just "paranoia."

THE SEGREGATION STRESS SYNDROME: MISTRUST OF WHITES

Similar to the consequences of trauma signaled by the much-discussed post-traumatic stress disorder (PTSD), the consequences of witnessing, experiencing, or hearing about a racially traumatic event can cause numerous symptoms of the segregation stress syndrome. One of these is a loss of trust in, and feeling uncomfortable, fearful, and nervous around whites. Additionally, the mistrust that many African Americans have for the white-created legal system and for various white representatives of government agencies, especially the police, is substantially rooted in a long history of discriminatory events.

An older female respondent, Elizabeth Ware, in the Southwest recalls how she warned her son about even the language he used about whites in one town:

Like my son be down there, and he called back, "Hey, mama, I'm in
this town. Ain't nothing here, but peckerwoods." And I would say,
"Boy, you better shut your mouth because them people will carry
you back down there in those woods and kill you. And we'll never
find your body." There's a lot of black people that have been killed or
hung and their bodies have never been found. And they don't do
nothing to them white people. Now you got, you got a little leeway,
but I *still* don't trust them, I don't trust them folk. That's the way
they are. That's the way it is. (*Elizabeth Ware, 80s*)

She knows what the Jim Crow era and afterward has meant for black
Americans in many areas of the South and Southwest. For racially traumatic events to have an impact, one did not need to witness them.
Hearing about them was enough to have a negative impact on psychological well-being. Like the respondent here, other respondents note
that "black people just disappeared" and they "kill you and we'll never
find your body." Throughout the interviews the respondents mentioned
that they didn't want their children to end up dead somewhere. This
respondent states that individuals would disappear, a common comment that leads one to wonder if we do have an accurate picture of the
actual number of blacks who were killed during this segregation era, as
official records and white newspapers oftentimes ignored or downplayed white violence targeting African Americans.

In addition, black residents of these southeastern and southwestern
areas, long taught to repress their anger in dealing with hostile whites,
usually developed a general mistrust of whites as a daily coping strategy.
Emphasizing Elizabeth Ware's words, an older child-care worker living
in the Southeast, respondent Florence Tyler, who earlier in her interview speaks about being scared for her mother, then adds this comment:

My mama told me to always keep my distance from white folks. . . .
She said, "You can't trust them. They will grin and smile in your face
but they are not your friend." This is what I tell my children. (*Florence Tyler, 80s*)

Once more, the ever-present threat of physical violence generated a
rational distrust of whites across the generations and most sectors of
black communities. In these accounts, we constantly observe the cen-

tral importance of families in enabling their members to survive racial oppression. Parents and grandparents often taught lessons of caution and distancing to their children, grandchildren, and other relatives.[16] Raising youngsters meant a great expenditure of energy and time in teaching them how to deal with oppressive whites, and thereby in protecting them from harm. This brief narrative again speaks to the effects of living in a total institution and experiencing recurring white-imposed traumas. Florence Tyler's segregation experiences occurred 50 years earlier, yet she still instructs her children and other relatives to distance themselves from often-untrustworthy whites. We see again the intergenerational transmission of lessons learned from Jim Crow traumas, and likely of the segregation stress syndrome.

These insightful accounts add to our understanding of how Jim Crow operated as a system of quotidian violence to human bodies and minds. In everyday life, African Americans had to respond to whites and racist practices, not surprisingly, with great caution, significant distrust, and some distancing. Reflecting on working conditions in the fields where she used to work in North Carolina, Anna Reese, an elderly female respondent in the Southeast, develops this view of mistrusting whites in a bit more detail:

> I just don't have any trust. . . . They had like strawberry season to pick strawberries. . . . I can remember . . . when you're going through those working conditions, they kind of treated you like cattle. . . . I can remember that but it was like one of those things that you never let it bother you 'cause you know you had to work, you had to bring the money in, so you did what you had to do to survive. But it never got to a point where we just said, "We hate white people." I can't stand them, but I didn't hate them. And to this day I just don't have any trust, I don't trust them and I really don't like them. . . . As I get older I come to realize how hateful they were and that's when I started to tell my grandkids how things was as far as getting educated and you know, they always consider you second class no matter how educated you are. And you have to work twice as hard as them to get where you want to get. (*Anna Reese, 70s*)

Like most African Americans in other research studies, Anna Reese links her ongoing assessments of whites to her direct experience, in this case to migrant farmwork experiences under Jim Crow.[17] Some public acceptance on their part of this being treated with hostility and like cattle was usually necessary for everyday survival. They often had some agency in dealing with Jim Crow, but that agency was severely limited. Sadly, they often had to distance themselves somewhat from their own real selves—a key feature of the dehumanization that is central to the operation of systemic racism. Remarkably, too, this memorable experience, communicated now to her grandchildren, did not lead her to hatred but rather to caution and distrust.

A respondent in the Southeast, Frank Wilson, mentions, in emotional terms, several important issues associated with his lessons about dealing with whites on an everyday basis:

> They said don't trust them because you don't know whether they would turn on you or not. Don't befriend them too much. It is all right to befriend them, but not too much. Don't put too much confidence in them. Because they will laugh in your face today, and go home and tell their parents something. And then you are subject to wake up with your house on fire. You know what I am saying? No. Because the black man was just, he was just a tool for nothing but working. . . . I could be playing with the white boy. The white boy could say something to me and I would get offended. I better not say nothing too much to him to offend him though. He would go home and tell his daddy, and he would come down [pauses, seems exasperated] and ain't no telling what will happen to you. [*If you had one word to describe how you felt?*] The way the white folks have treated me? Terrible [voice filled with pain]. There is nothing. Like when I was coming up. There is nothing I could say good about the white people. Nothing. (*Frank Wilson, 80s*)

He describes the two-faced character of much interaction with whites, as well as the tenuous character of his relationships growing up, even in play with white boys. We also see the dramatic impact on him due to decades of racial discrimination by whites. In all these quotations from the interviews we observe a well-justified black mistrust for a large racial group, virtually all whites, based on decades of personal and collective racial traumas. Ironically, whites have often embedded in their racist framing of black Americans the view that the latter are paranoid in this mistrust, that is, are only imagining their problems with white racism. This white-racist framing then further burdens blacks with having to defend why they often mistrust and keep their distance from whites. Note, too, that this mistrust is a normal reaction for human beings. Research on the impact of other types of traumatic events accents this mistrust and related emotional reactions. For example, researchers Evans-Campbell, Lincoln, and Takeuchi note that individuals who suffer through traumatic life events can suffer from sadness, worry, fear, hopelessness, humiliation, and shame, which can contribute to survivors having trust issues and feelings of worthlessness.[18]

In most of the previous accounts we clearly see the severe psychological injuries suffered by black citizens. These also include great fear and necessary caution. Respondent Ralph Hill shares this account of the fear and caution that the threat of lynchings regularly generated in the local community:

> They had a fear that if they did something that aggravated the white folks, that that night about midnight, they would come to [find the person]. They would knock on the door. . . . "Is [names person] in there? Well, send him on out here. They would take him to a tree. . . . Then you found the person dead the next day. (*Ralph Hill, 80s*)

Constant caution in regard to one's everyday actions, as well as those of one's children and other relatives, was necessary for survival. Black citizens knew that anything they did that incited significant white anger might result in death. The great stress associated with negotiating the white spaces of the Jim Crow community is a type of well-documented harm that remains uncompensated to the present day.

THE SEGREGATION STRESS SYNDROME: DIFFICULT AND RACIALIZED MEMORIES

One symptom of the segregation stress syndrome is a black person's attempts to avoid the symbols, sounds, and people that can trigger a flashback to the racially traumatic events of the Jim Crow era. A similar reaction has been reported in research on the survivors of the Nazi Holocaust who experienced extreme, violent, and racialized experiences at the hands of German Nazis and their allies. Long after the war they have reported symbols, sounds, and people that generate flashbacks to earlier times of great pain and oppression.[19] This research

reveals that individuals often want to avoid recalling their extraordinarily painful past. Similarly, several decades after World War II, veterans suffering from PTSD reportedly experienced flashbacks of that
war after watching the movie, *Saving Private Ryan*.[20] Exposure to substantial trauma at a relatively early age not only leads to painful remem-
brances but also is a significant predictor of a lifelong struggle with
depression.[21]

In our interviews several elderly African Americans report organizing much of their lives around their Jim Crow traumas and responding
negatively to the symbols and places that remind them of racialized
traumatic events. Coupled with the mistrust of whites previously discussed, avoidance is often involved—avoiding buses, drinking out of
water fountains, and shopping in certain stores. Decades after the official end of Jim Crow laws, older African Americans frequently avoid
symbols and places that trigger memories of the earlier racial violence.

Historians estimate that there have been 6,000–10,000 lynchings of
black Americans since the Reconstruction era after the civil war, most
of them during the Jim Crow era but a few still occurring in our present
era.[22] Not surprisingly, during and after the legal segregation era, the
trees that were utilized to lynch African Americans often became painful symbols for whole communities of black Americans. Sometimes the
treed areas where these tortures and murders took place were permanently called something like the "lynch woods" or the "hanging trees."
Respondent Ruby McKnight recalls the place where African Americans
had been lynched as being called and symbolized as "lynch hammock":

> The Ku Klux Klan. . . . If you had sons, you were just frightened. . . .
> People were hung right here. . . . It was a place called "lynch ham-
> mock." They would take people out and lynch them. They would
> take those kids out and you would find a black body hanging any day.
> Anytime. People were frightened. There was nothing they could do.
> If you talked too much, then the younger black would go and, you
> know, tell on the others. It was terrible. . . . In order to keep a lot of
> confusion down and sleep well at night and try to protect their boys,
> and protect their girls, they just had to accept it and be quiet about it.
> That's the way it was. People were afraid. People were afraid. If you
> had a few who weren't, you had no backup. . . . It was bad, but it was
> something that you grew up with. (*Ruby McKnight, 70s*)

This respondent recalls numerous lynchings in this one community, yet no one could speak much about them for fear of white reprisals. They also avoided these discussions in order to protect their own sanity and to protect their children as well. To the present day, this area is feared and symbolized as the "lynch hammock" area, one that some black residents of the area still avoid. Similarly, Jack Greene, a respondent in the Southwest, remembers a particular tree in the local area that had been used for at least one lynching:

> They had a tree they called it the "hanging tree." A man was hung on there, but that was way before my time, so I don't know. The tree is still there. If you go to [names place] now they'll show you where the "hanging tree" is. They just keep it as a memory I guess. [*What was the reason for the man getting hanged?*] Segregation. At that time I didn't know the reason why, but I guess because they seen, he did something that he wasn't supposed to do, and they hung him. And he got the word; they got the word "hanging tree." (*Jack Greene, 50s*)

These events were frequent. Jack Greene recalls that he was shown this "hanging tree" and mentions it was before his time because older people recalled its use. The segregation stress syndrome often involves an intergenerational transmission of recalled racial traumas. Another respondent, Lloyd Reed, remembers, "You could ride through a black community during any given day and see a black man hanging from a tree." Horrific white violence often took place in numerous states' treed and forested areas. Thus, it is not surprising that, in contemporary research studies on U.S. recreational activities, African American families are found to frequent forested areas, such as national parks and national forests, *much less often* than do white families.[23] This is yet another serious consequence of Jim Crow violence over many decades.

For several of the respondents even riding the bus today is stressful because that triggers memories of traumatic bus events during the Jim Crow era. One respondent in the Southeast, Thelma Pierre, remembers riding segregated buses. In her narrative we observe the long-term consequences of these earlier racial traumas as she notes that she tries not to ride buses:

> I do that because I was never comfortable in the back, I was comfortable in the front. I will sit in the driver's seat if I have to! I just came

back from England in the summer, and baby, I tell you that was a hard trip for me. I am not going to sit on the back of no bus. . . . I hate buses. To this day I hate buses because that was "our place." . . . You can hardly get me on a bus. And the only reason that I rode on the buses in England was because we were not familiar, and driving on the wrong side of the road, and for me to rent a car I would just have been kind of lost. And so we took the tour, we took the buses, instead of trying to rent a car . . . but I don't like bus rides. . . . [Also] when you can't go . . . into a café, and you can't go into the front you have to go in the back. You know about it. You know about it but still, it really bothered me. (*Thelma Pierre, 60s*)

Like several other respondents, Thelma Pierre avoids riding buses because they remind her of the difficult segregation traumas of her youth. Her account reflects much pain that the very degrading events of the Jim Crow era regularly created for her. Not surprisingly, thus, African Americans as individuals and as a group often, knowingly or unknowingly, display many symptoms of the segregation stress syndrome resulting from many years of experience with Jim Crow and contemporary racism.

CONCLUSION

In the psychological research on post-traumatic stress disorder (PTSD) in military and other settings, typically an otherwise healthy individual develops symptoms after traumatic events in the present. However, as we have seen, the segregation stress syndrome is much different in that African American survivors of Jim Crow were usually raised by already traumatized parents and grandparents, who were themselves often raised by enslaved African Americans. They also grew up in a lifelong oppressive environment of the many traumatic events enumerated previously, events that were not onetime occurrences. They were recurring over a long Jim Crow period in all African American communities, and thus African Americans today have a substantial communal legacy. In addition, racially traumatic events were usually sanctioned and legitimized by local and state institutions, including the legal system and its white police and judges. These totalitarian contextual realities predisposed black citizens, as individuals and a group, to develop major elements of the segregation stress syndrome. The segregation stress syndrome was and is a *collective* reality, not just a reality like PTSD that is experienced mostly by individuals.

Throughout this book we argue that the extensive racial violence and other shocking traumas experienced by African Americans during the Jim Crow era was, intentionally and unintentionally, *imposed* trauma. Moreover, it was trauma imposed *on a whole group of people* and thus represents a distinctive and collective form of PTSD. In the revealing interviews of these older African Americans, in their narratives as well as body language (verbal and nonverbal cues), we witness clear parallels with the symptoms and indicators documented in the recent literature on PTSD. As we have seen, some of the similar symptoms include avoidance of certain settings, triggered flashbacks, and being emotionally upset.[24] Let us be clear here. As sociologists, our purpose is not to psychologize their experiences or to diagnose and "treat" the individual respondents. Rather, our goal is to better understand their traumatic life experiences, then and now, within the context of the broader U.S. racial hierarchy and history. It is our goal to understand the experiences of elderly African Americans and to give voice and validity to their harsh everyday experiences with whites in an obviously unjust society.

3

EVERYDAY SURVEILLANCE AND RACIAL FRAMING

We [had] gone overseas to fight for this country. . . . I came home on leave I had to get in the back of the bus in Washington, DC. . . . I couldn't get out for about 10 hours. I am in uniform. I only had about four or five days at home. I'm waiting in Washington. . . . [Even as a soldier for this country], you lower than all the white people, you lower than all of them. I finally squeezed in on the bus and they had a revolution [on the bus] to get me off. . . . I said I wasn't getting off the bus. The bus left the station and after they were about 100 miles from [southern city], a white Irish police officer came up to me and hit me with an object similar to a blackjack of today. The police officer said, "There is that nigger." He hit me on the side of my head and that is all I remember. I was found on the railroad tracks miles outside of [names southern city]. I was severely beaten. I had 500 dollars on me and my leave papers and they were all taken. I was in uniform. My injuries were so severe that four years later I had to have brain surgery because of the injuries sustained in the beating. Several men, who served and fought for the country, were beaten and lynched in their uniforms after they returned from the war. (*Harold Moore, 80s*)

This World War II veteran, now in his 80s, recalls the long-term impact of riding public transportation to get home to his family while on active leave in the military. Great irony is clear here. This soldier's degradation started in the capital of the "world's greatest democracy," which had just fought a war for "freedom." He was not only denied the honor and prestige typically awarded to military personnel, but suffered severely for standing up for his rights—physically, emotionally, economically, and psychologically.

His injuries can be partially measured in economic terms, not only in the $500 stolen (equal to thousands of dollars today) but also in the cost of subsequent medical care and of replacing leave papers. He was beaten by an Irish American police officer, who obviously considered himself to be white and superior in what was then part of the Jim Crow South. Considering the country's immigration history, it is likely that this black veteran had deeper ancestral roots in the United States than did the Irish officer. Indeed, at that point in time the average African American had ancestry going back some eight to fifteen generations, more than for the average Irish American. The many Irish Catholic immigrants in the mid-nineteenth century did face blatant discrimination by white Anglo-Saxon Protestants, but by the late nineteenth century they were being accepted as "white" by Anglo-Saxon-Protestant whites in ways unavailable to African Americans.[1]

Like many black veterans, this brave man had his humanity totally discounted and was reduced to the harshest of racist epithets—the N-word, a white-framed term and concept often used to justify anti-black violence. The efforts of these black soldiers were not usually celebrated with medals and parades by whites, and frequently they paid a terrible price in physical injury or death. They faced significant risks in returning home, including violence at the hands of the white men they had risked their lives abroad to support or protect. Indeed, this respondent was one of the "lucky" ones, for numerous African American soldiers after both world wars were unable to escape death by lynching. Some veterans were even lynched in their uniforms.[2] Although all African Americans in the southern and border state areas had to live with the terrors of lynching, these soldiers were probably targeted for extra reasons: white retaliation for entering the military (considered "white space") or for attempting to secure white social and educational benefits; the white fear that a militarily trained "negro"[3] might threaten the established patterns of white supremacy; and actual resistance to white-imposed segregation by black soldiers like this respondent. Indeed, many black soldiers did challenge white supremacy in various ways, including assisting in civil rights organizations that eventually brought down Jim Crow segregation.

In this set of events one sees evidence of another concept we will periodically draw upon. As noted previously, the racist reality that is systemic in this society is constantly interpreted and rationalized by a white racial framing of U.S. society. This white racial frame is an overarching and racialized worldview from which whites of all class, gender, and age backgrounds operate in implementing and interpreting the discrimination they direct against Americans of color. As with the other features of systemic racism, this white-maintained racial frame has been in operation since the seventeenth century. As laid out by Joe Feagin, this white frame encompasses at least these important dimensions:

1. racial stereotypes;
2. racial narratives and interpretations;
3. racialized images and language accents;
4. racialized emotions; and
5. inclinations to discriminatory action.[4]

In the example just noted, numerous whites on the bus, and especially the white police officer, not only stereotyped this black soldier as undesirable and out of his "place," but also exhibited intense racialized emotions that led them to extreme violence on a man they viewed in dehumanized terms. Clearly, the white racial frame, which is still dominant, includes extensive antiblack stereotypes, images, and emotions that are regularly acted upon by whites. Also in this account, and most others throughout this book, we observe how this white racial frame includes a very positive white orientation to white racial views, virtue, privilege, and societal dominance. From the beginning of this country, whites have rationalized the long-dominant racial hierarchy by accenting a "superior" white group viewed as legitimately dominant over an "inferior" black group.

In this chapter and the next, we consider how the painful everyday experiences of Jim Crow impacted black lives, including the denial of human necessities and of personal respect and integrity, and even the denial of a desired name. We examine the surveillance and forced deference when African Americans encountered designated "white-controlled spaces," such as white homes, stores, streets, and other public spaces. We examine how African Americans were regularly monitored by whites to ensure that they stayed in "their place," especially in interactions with the police and with ordinary whites. We end the chapter with an examination of how these traumatic experiences created and maintained economic and material costs for the targets, including generations of unjust impoverishment.

DENIAL OF ONE'S NAME

During the era of African American enslavement, whites eliminated most enslaved African workers' names and renamed them in English. The reader might recall that in the 1970s television miniseries *Roots* the central character Kunte Kinte was renamed "Toby." Enslaved persons were often renamed with Christian names or demeaning or diminutive names such as "Buck" or "Queenie."[5] The process of whites renaming or partially renaming African Americans continued during legal segregation. Blacks were often denied their full names, but instead referred to as "uncle," "auntie," "boy," "girl," or just "nigger." Some of these slights may seem relatively innocuous. However, one's name is more than an identifying marker. Naming imparts meaning and often represents a distinctive knowledge or family communication.[6] Typically, a person's name indicates to others that she or he is part of a collective group, yet also is a unique individual. Erving Goffman noted the critical significance of one's name: "The most significant of possessions is not physical at all, [it's] one's full name . . . the loss of one's name can be a great curtailment of the self."[7] As such, one's name signifies one's identity and sense of self.

For example, Richard Thomas, a respondent in the Southwest, remembers being called "uncle" as an aural representation of his lack of power:

> You have to look for that because you, you going to hear things. Right or wrong, you going to hear things. It may not be right, but you going to hear it. See, because you know what you up against. . . . From the time you born until you die, you up against. One strike is going to be on you, or with you all your life. Why? Because you're a Negro. And the black is going to stay on you everywhere you go, and they [are] never going to really just get down and do away with it. Before they will call you by your name, a colored person, they'd call you "uncle."

You know damn well they ain't—you ain't they "uncle." They call you "uncle." (*Richard Thomas, 80s*)

Being called something besides your actual name and being referred to as a false family relation were insults that African Americans dealt with on a recurring basis. Thomas makes a powerful point about the stigma of being black. No matter what his accomplishments were or how hard he worked, he still faced over a long lifetime the strikes against him for being black. The everyday racial norms dictated that whites could deny blacks the dignity and acknowledgment of their humanity by referring to them in diminutive and other demeaning ways. Additionally, African Americans were often required to address whites of all ages by titles such as "Mr." and "Mrs." or face racialized punishment.

Numerous respondents noted their hurt at being called the N-word and being targets of other types of hate speech. A domestic worker in the Southeast, Edna Daniels, describes an excruciatingly painful memory from when she was a child:

I remember that I went to town one Saturday, a little white girl was on the street, just start picking, starting picking at me. Me and my Aunt she was teasing: "Hey, nigger, nigger, nigger." Just kept calling us that. I told her, "You better go on home and leave us alone because we are not bothering you." So she just kept on right behind us . . . "Nigger, nigger, nigger, nigger, nigger, nigger, nigger." . . . I told her, "Come on, come on, I'm going to show you what a nigger is!" I was probably about . . . nine or ten, eleven. [*Did your Aunt say anything?*] No. She just didn't. No, no. She said, "Just don't bother, don't say nothing to the others." (*Edna Daniels, 70s*)

The racist epithet here as elsewhere in white hate speech symbolizes power, authority, and a desire to humiliate. As is evident in this account, African Americans repeatedly endured being called the harsh N-word by both white adults and children. Although some scholars have argued that children lack the cognitive ability to understand the racial order and are merely repeating language they hear from other whites, research by Debra Van Ausdale and Joe Feagin found that very young white children do comprehend and can individually manipulate racist terms and meanings.[8] Edna Daniels notes that she first attempted to reason with the white child before defending herself assertively. Yet, her aunt warned her that silence was the appropriate and safest response to such white verbal attacks.

Another respondent in the Southwest, Jean Horton, remembered being forced to endure the humiliation of being called the N-word by whites:

> Well, I had to comply with whatever was going on, and there was nothing I could do about it. I either complied with it or got hurt trying to not comply with it. Because of the ways [mumbles] "Hey, nigger, come here." They talked dirty to you; then asked, "Did you like it?" What could you do about it? Take some sticks and beat them? There was nothing you could do about it. (*Jean Horton, 70s*)

She couldn't bring herself to say the N-word clearly in the interview and instead just quickly mumbled it. For many respondents, this powerful word is loaded with so much hatred and threat of violence that they couldn't bear to utter it. She notes the complete lack of power and access to resources that blacks had in this racially totalitarian era. Traditional avenues of defending oneself against all types of Jim Crow discrimination—for example, calling on the police, seeking justice in a court of law, exposing injustices in the media, or physically striking back—were not viable options because whites dominated every major institution. As is evident in the white mockery and ridicule in numerous interview excerpts, whites were often quite aware of this black helplessness.

White mockery was evident not only in auditory language, but also in visual signs. A respondent in the Southwest, Fred Hall, described the racist signs in some areas of his town:

> Oh, I just know that in, you know, certain parts they had these signs "If you can read, nigger . . . if you can read, nigger, run" . . . or something like that. And it's just down not too far from here. And they still don't have any coloreds that live there because they all prejudiced, you know. . . . People are still prejudiced. (*Fred Hall, 60s*)

Yet again, African Americans are dehumanized and reduced to a racist epithet. Here we see evidence of explicit warnings given to African Americans that their presence was not welcome in a "designated white space." Significantly, although the sign was likely intended for all African Americans, it particularly called out those capable of reading. Social scientists have found that Americans of color with greater access to resources, including literacy and economic capital, sometimes face greater racial hostility and violence than do those with less.[9] Thus, African Americans who were then literate and otherwise better-resourced were regularly seen as threatening the Jim Crow order, such as by taking up resources reserved for whites. Note too the respondent's connecting of the hostile sign when he was growing up to persisting racial hostility and discrimination today. As we discuss later, the racialized experiences of the past do not remain in the past, but are remembered and even re-experienced in the present.

SURVEILLANCE AND CONTROLLING BLACK BODIES: DENIAL OF NECESSITIES

In the 1940s, psychologist Abraham Maslow wrote about a hierarchy of basic human needs. The physiological necessities—food, water, air, shelter, excretion—form the base of this needs pyramid while self-esteem and self-actualization are depicted as at the top of this human pyramid. For black Americans living under legal segregation, even meeting these basic physiological necessities was not guaranteed. For example, the great novelist Richard Wright wrote about hunger in an important 1945 memoir on his life under Jim Crow: "Hunger stole upon me slowly that at first I was not aware of what hunger really meant. Hunger had always been more or less at my elbow when I played, but now I began to wake up at night to find hunger standing at my bedside, staring at me gauntly."[10] Wright's basic necessities were not being met, and he suggests in the novel a great hunger for self-esteem and self-actualization as well.

Many African Americans lived in poverty and lacked adequate access to the physical resources necessary to sustain their survival—food, water, and shelter. Even for those with resources, the opportunity to eat was usually denied to them in white-dominated establishments. This was especially true when they tried to travel from one area of the country to another. Army veteran Roy Turner recalls traveling with his white colleagues and difficulties in just getting food:

I served in the army. There was time when they sent me from Oklahoma to El Paso. Back then, you couldn't go in a place to eat. We started riding about, during that whole trip they stopped about three times to eat, but uh, the driver came up to me and said, "Man I'm sorry, but you can't come in this place to eat, I'll bring you something." I said, "Never mind, if they don't want me to eat I just won't eat." So we made the second stop, he said the same thing. Early in the morning, about 5:00 we got over there into Mexico. He say, when we get over into Mexico, I could stop and get out. Ain't that something? All the white folks is eating, but the Negro can starve to death. And that's when I ate. (*Roy Turner, 70s*)

In his interview Turner recalls how African Americans had to "eat their rage." Additionally, this U.S. veteran notes that he was treated with more dignity in Mexico than in his home country. We see sympathetic whites who offered to assist the respondent, yet this gesture could not undo the indignity, evident in *two* stops, of a discriminatory denial of food. Under legal segregation blacks repeatedly were denied nourishment of their bodies, as well as their self-esteem and self-actualization.

Another veteran respondent, Ernest Bell, recalls going to restaurants when he was on leave from active duty in the military in the early 1960s:

When I finished basic training, AIT jump school and I was in Fort Campbell, Kentucky, and I was authorized to leave. So I took this seven-day leave, me and my friends. And we left from Fort Campbell, Kentucky. . . . We got into Tennessee. . . . So about 6:30–7:00 in the morning, we go into the restaurant to get a cup of coffee. Even though we were in the military, we had to stand separately. However, during this time I was not thinking. So we stopped at this restaurant, so we sit down on these round stools, as we sit there one minute, two minutes, five minutes. Nobody says a thing. But as soon as I say, "Can I have a cup of coffee please?" the lady said, "I'm sorry, we can't serve black people." And I go and I looked, and my wife got up and started using city school language because she was really angry. "Let us get out of this bad, bad place." I said to her, "Take it easy." She was upset. (*Ernest Bell, 70s*)

Bell continues with his detailed account of Jim Crow's daily indignities and assaults:

There was a sign that said, "No blacks allowed." They used the term *black*. It said, "No blacks allowed." We left out of there. It was in the year of 1962. So we came on out of there, and we got in our vehicle, and I say that we have to find some place to eat. But we was thinking that since we were in Tennessee that this place is really racist so we need to get closer to home. We need to get all the way home and forget about eating. But I said, "We need to stop and eat someplace." So we stopped and we were very cautious . . . we stopped in Virginia and we had our breakfast, and so we went on. . . . Well that was one of the most embarrassing situations because, in the military, it was what you called "organized discrimination." Then you go out into the public, then you find people acting that way, and it was really surprising to me. (*Ernest Bell, 70s*)

This took place in the mid-South in the 1960s, an era when John Kennedy was president. Many Americans viewed him as a supporter of the civil rights movement. This insightful respondent notes the institutionalized nature of his experiences by referencing his military training on "organized discrimination." He also notes an array of negative and painful emotions as he recalls this degrading incident from over decades back, including his understandable anger, distress, embarrassment, and self-blame. In a later chapter we will observe that in oppressive southern settings, numerous African Americans defied the rules and intentionally resisted the racial hierarchy, but here the respondent was tired from the long drive and simply forgot "his place." Being black in the Jim Crow era often meant that one could never really relax, especially when in public places.

There were often severe repercussions for forgetting one's place. Many respondents commented on this reality of segregation in public places in a matter-of-fact way. A retired teacher in the Southeast, Patricia Lucas, recalls her experiences in restaurants:

I can remember that we automatically knew to go around to a place that was kind of like . . . it was a sitting area, it wasn't a bar, but it was stools. We could sit there and eat and order. But the white people were sitting at tables. They were sitting at tables and chairs. And we had to go in the side door. (*Patricia Lucas, 60s*)

Even when African Americans were permitted to eat in restaurants—a privilege that whites simply took for granted, that one could *eat* in a *restaurant*—they were reminded by whites of their second-class citizenship. The racialized practice of entering through a side or back door was "automatic" according to this participant. This segregating practice demanded by whites, along with other indignities, served as visual and tangible reminders to blacks that they lived in a system of white supremacy.

The visual indicators of black subordination and white superiority were aggressively depicted in public establishments with signposts and place cards. Ethel Chapman, an interviewee in the Southwest, recalls these "whites only" signs:

> And they would have signs, "for whites" . . . then they have water fountains in public places the same way. As I was growing up, in that one store I told you about, at the counter . . . in that store they had water fountains and one had a sign for whites and one for colored. Back then people were so ignorant that people thought that if you were to drink out of the same fountain it would somehow hurt you, they had it all like that. As I grew up, same for the restrooms. If they had one for us, it was nasty. (*Ethel Chapman, 70s*)

Another respondent in the Southwest, Josephine Floyd, recalls the consequences for not obeying these racist signs:

> You know I never really went to too many of [restaurants] because they had, let me put it this way, when I was coming up the sign said black or colored, and white. You didn't go in the white one, no. You went in the colored door. When you needed water that fountain there said for colored or Negro, and that fountain said for whites. If you went to that white one, you might get beat down or put in jail. (*Josephine Floyd, 80s*)

The consequences for challenging the racial order of Jim Crow were often severe. Defying, even unintentionally, white supremacy could be deadly to oneself, one's family, and one's community. Punishments were doled out regardless of the reason for the infraction: resistance, forgetfulness, ignorance, or illiteracy. Such repercussions were necessary to maintain white power and dominance—and often benefited whites economically, psychologically, socially, or politically.

In order to sustain control, whites created a broad racial frame to justify that African Americans were deserving of their subordinate position and whites of their superordinate position. This white racial frame was created to legitimize slavery and continued to defend Jim Crow. Stereotypes and images of black Americans as "criminal," "dirty," and "subhuman" were developed, and these stuck as whites reiterated them and created the socioeconomic conditions that forced some black Americans into the conditions suggested by the labels. For example, during the slavery and Jim Crow eras those who fought for their freedom and resisted the oppression were often portrayed by whites as inherently criminal. Whites treated African Americans as property or animals and then stereotyped them as animal-like.[11]

Whites viewed black Americans as unworthy not only to eat together but also to use the same public facilities as whites. For example, respondent Louise Vaughn recalls the indignities of not being allowed to use the same facilities as whites:

> You just didn't have to do anything to them for them to not like you. They just didn't like you because you was black. And it's kind of sad that we had went to a restaurant that we couldn't go in the front door. We had to go in the back door, and sat there where they washed the dishes at. . . . So that, and then the bathrooms. You could not go to, you know, get up and go to a bathroom like the other peoples went, other white peoples went. You had to go around and go outside, and go to the bathroom, you could not you know, use their bathroom. (*Louise Vaughn, 60s*)

Vaughn echoes what numerous other interview respondents stated: Whites didn't like you for the simple reason that you were black. She remarks with sadness at the memory of being forced to enter through a back door where the custodial duties took place.

Louise Vaughn also accents the segregation of bathroom facilities. Indeed, when facilities were provided for black Americans, there often was only one bathroom for both genders to make use of: white men, white women, and "colored." White fear of catching "blackness," seen as a type of "disease," was a common rationale for insisting on separate public restrooms. Central in the white racial frame is "black" being synonymous with uncleanliness or a contaminant of whiteness. This issue was highlighted in the 2011 award-winning movie, *The Help*, which focused on experiences of black women domestics under Jim Crow oppression. In that movie only certain Jim Crow experiences were portrayed, often from a white woman's perspective. A key white woman in the movie argues that private toilets in white homes with black women domestic workers should be legally segregated by race. Significantly, this movie trivialized black female experiences with Jim Crow by focusing on this silly proposal and whitewashed much else about the Jim Crow segregation that oppressed black women. More generally, the denial of dignity and denial of significant roles for black actresses persists in the contemporary movie industry and other mass media. [12]

In the cruel logic of racism, African Americans suffered greater health debilitations than whites in this era, but not because of their biological nature. Their everyday problems frequently stemmed from impoverished families and segregated surroundings, including grossly inadequate medical and hospital services and facilities. [13] A respondent, Bernice Gibbs, in the Southwest recalls that going to the doctor's office was one of the worst experiences:

> Now the worst part was the doctor's office. You went until they had no more [whites]. . . . You know, you would go in one side, a little room and . . . the other people would go in the front. And they didn't put your name down. You just came, and when it was no more whites, well then they would take you. But you would be there for a long, long time—no matter how sick you are. You had to wait until they had saw all the [white] patients, then they'd see you. And that was really hard. . . . Well, by not going out a lot. The only thing was like stores and doctor's office. You knew that you had to wait. (*Bernice Gibbs, 70s*)

She notes that part of coping under Jim Crow was to not go out a lot. However, some trips—like a doctor's visit—were inevitable. Whites justified legal segregation by suggesting that African Americans needed to stay in "their place." Although many whites to this day have claimed that there were "separate but equal" facilities during this era, actually there was rarely a black equivalent of white medical care in particular areas. In addition, because African Americans were almost always denied an education in white-constructed medical schools, African American patients usually had no choice but to visit white doctors when they were ill. [14]

Another respondent, Martha McClain, reports a difficult experience in a doctor's office when her son was injured:

> My son got his leg broke, and I had to go to the back of the doctor's office and I went to the back. I cleaned the office, and I couldn't go to the front. I had to take him in there. He was playing right there; I carried him out to the doctor. The secretary told me the doctor, my regular doctor, was out on vacation. [She] said but the doctor here, his name was Dr. Smith, he don't doctor on blacks. So he won't see him. He should, but he won't 'cause he's black. [*And what did you do?*] So I said, "Oh please doctor on him, my child is in pain." So she went and asked him, so he said since I cleaned his office—I cleaned his office every day—Every day! . . . I will take care of him, until her doctor gets back. . . . And he took care of him because I cleaned his office. . . . And I said, "Oh I'm so glad that you saw him 'cause he was in pain, so much last night just hollering in pain." But he said so many black people after they come to visit him, they don't even come back no more. "So I never doctor on them, a black person no more." I said I wasn't one of them. . . . And he's going to have to put his hands on him. The child was hollering and crying. (*Martha McClain, 70s*)

The physical presence of a black child in great pain was not enough for the doctor to treat him. Only because she endures the drudgery of cleaning his office would he reciprocate and treat her son. McClain had to push the doctor to see her as an individual mother and not as a caricature of all black people. In contrast, whites can usually rely on their racial characteristics not working against them as they can assert their individuality and know that their missteps will not be attributed to those characteristics.

Some readers may sympathize with this white doctor, as he justifies not treating black patients because they supposedly don't return for follow-up care. However, he is overgeneralizing to an entire population based on his limited experiences. We can also speculate that the doctor is not merely relying upon individual experiences, but is parroting conventional racist thinking of the Jim Crow era. Although we see evidence of sympathetic white doctors, such as her doctor who is on vacation, taken as a whole African Americans were systematically denied access to adequate medical care.[15]

Note too that treating people badly often creates bad health responses. The legal scholar Vernellia Randall has argued that the negative socioeconomic and other negative societal conditions forced by whites on African Americans in all eras have created many physical infirmities that are not genetically derived.[16] (Poor health conditions created by decades of white racism can affect later generations as well, through negative effects on a person's epigenome.)[17] Given that health reaction to oppression, whites then stereotype what they have caused as an "innate" black condition and add that racist stereotype to their dominant white framing of African Americans.

SURVEILLANCE AND CONTROLLING BLACK BODIES: MORE TRAVEL RESTRICTIONS

As we have seen, a popular image of the legal segregation era involves physical signs stating a separate "white" water fountain from an inferior "colored" fountain. There were also signs in public transportation sites indicating "colored people" must ride in the back of the bus. Indeed, when we ask college students in our classes what image comes to mind when they think of Jim Crow, many will respond with these images of separate water fountains and bathrooms or segregated buses. Riding in the back of a bus might be seen as a mere inconvenience. However, bus boycotts and other protests by civil rights demonstrators were not simply about people of all racial groups being allowed to sit next to each other. They were centrally about protesting for the human dignity of African Americans and for an end to segregation and the terroristic violence lying behind it.

Our elderly African American respondents recalled countless stories of forced deference to whites and surveillance by whites in white-controlled public spaces, including the area of transportation such as buses and trains. Consider the response that Lillian Wilson, who worked as a nurse, and now works as a teacher, gives to a question about her first encounter with a white person:

> I remember going to my grandma's on the bus and my mom having to stand and hold one of us while she's standing because all the seats were taken. We may have started out with a seat, but as we went along the pathway, if the front seats filled up, white people could sit

all the way to the back. I remember my mom telling us about the little brother that we, she lost, because she's pregnant and on one of her trips home she had to stand all the way from Georgia to here and therefore she miscarried the baby. (*Lillian Wilson, 70s*)

Black women were often denied the perks granted to white women in pregnancy such as being offered a chair or having the door held open for them. While numerous scholars have cogently argued that such rituals are embedded in a patriarchal system and are thus problematical offers of "help," black women's experiences with pregnancy were steeped not only in patriarchy but also in this type of trumping white supremacy.[18] As we discuss in the next chapter, historically black women had no autonomy over their bodies, as they could be bought and sold in slavery and usually assaulted with impunity at the hands of white men during the Jim Crow decades.

Note too that in Lillian Wilson's account her mother was far enough along in the pregnancy to know that she was carrying a son, whom she lost. Unfortunately, these miscarriages were then, and are today, exceedingly common for African American women. Contemporary statistics suggest that, controlling for education, black women experience infant mortality at a rate of nearly three times higher than that of white women.[19] Much research suggests that the chronic stress associated with being an African American or other person of color tends to lead to worse health outcomes from cradle to grave. For example, stress can limit fetal growth by constricting blood flow to the placenta and can contribute to inflammation in the uterus, thereby triggering premature labor. Some epidemiologists suggest that the health disparities between white and black women are related in part to the black life-course experience of excessive weathering on the body: The activation of constant and chronic stress wears on the body's organs, systems, and functions. Numerous research studies support the statement that social stress is deadly.[20] While everyone faces life stress, this is the chronic stress of second-class citizenship that is reactivated with every racial insult and assault. Significantly, the chronic daily stress that was connected with merely surviving has not been studied and measured for the elderly African Americans who have survived the Jim Crow era.

In their interviews many respondents used phrases such as "that's the way it was" or "what are you gonna do?" Although they may come across as self-defeating, such statements signal the coping strategies that often were necessary in order not to be abused and assaulted by whites. In the Southwest, respondent Dolores Arnold noted the array of customary and legal practices that whites used to control black bodies, including in public transit. Throughout her interview she states, "That's the way it was," as a way of reminding the listener of her everyday reality:

> I used to have to ride the bus going to New Orleans to visit the charity hospital, I was pregnant, and you sit in the back, had to sit in the back of the back of the bus, you couldn't sit up front. It didn't make no difference if you [were] . . . pregnant . . . you had to sit in the back. And if there was no seats in the back, then you had to stand up. You always had the sign say "colored" and "white." Even when I came to Killeen in 1968 they had a sign . . . that had said, "Killeen" meant "Kill Each and Every Nigger." That's what the sign meant and it stayed up for quite a while. (*Dolores Arnold, 70s*)

She clearly recognizes overt and blatant signs of second-class citizenship. Unlike the account of Harold Moore in our chapter opening where a police officer imposed white supremacy in mistreating a veteran, many of the oppressive practices of Jim Crow were created by ordinary white citizens. Dolores Arnold references the "colored" and "white" signs, as well as the hostile acronym created out of the city's name by whites. Many whites used their "creativity" in coining mocking racist descriptions as a way of maintain racial superiority. Today, whites still do this sort of thing for existing acronyms, such as for the metropolitan transit systems of Atlanta, Dallas, and other cities. (For example, MARTA in Atlanta becomes "Moving Africans Rapidly Through Atlanta.") These racist acronyms are crafted by whites to remind African Americans that they are unwelcome, stereotyped, and to be denied their individuality and dignity.

Dolores Arnold continues with more details about events that took place during the legal segregation decades:

> Jackie Robinson, I know he died, been dead before your time was. The first major league baseball player, he was stationed here at [names town] and they put him in jail for riding on the bus, where he wasn't supposed to ride. But now, they wanted to give a plaque to his daughter, you know, like apologizing. She wouldn't even come and accept it. That's the way it was.

Then she notes some bus events in which she was involved:

And like I said, my first child was, [I was] pregnant. We was in Atlanta, and I had to ride the bus to New Orleans. And they could have fifty dozen seats empty up front, you didn't sit down, you sit in the back. They didn't care if you're pregnant as big as a house, you were black, so you sit in the back. That's why I don't too much trust for white folks. I don't, I don't respect them, 'cause they didn't care nothing about you, you know. Like I said my grandfather was white and black, and you couldn't tell he wasn't white. You know what I'm saying? But that mean nothing to them. They don't care. If you got a little bit of color in you, you black. A "nigger," that's what they call you. Negroes was "niggerous" women. . . . "Nigger, what you want?" You know that's the way it was. That's how it was. I am serious! And when I'm at that nursing home, and I be running my mouth I can see them old white ones in there saying, "She must think she's something." Don't say nothing to me, 'cause you might get hit! Yep. [She laughs]. Yes. (*Dolores Arnold, 70s*)

The laughter in the interview illustrates Arnold's resiliency, yet also the fact that she still harbors resentment for the way whites treated her during the legal segregation era. She references the "one drop rule" as her white-looking grandfather was still treated as black, and with potential to contaminate whiteness. Like the rest of her community, he was denigrated as the N-word. She describes the discrimination on public buses, such as pregnant women forced to stand, and how black celebrities like Jackie Robinson were arrested for violating racial norms. Interestingly, the respondent underscores the fact that Jackie Robinson's daughter, more recently, refused to accept a discriminatory town's award in her father's honor. Many whites today claim that blacks need to "get over" the racism of the past and "move on." However, what this sentiment ignores is that whites expect to be easily or cheaply absolved of past racial transgressions. In 2008, the U.S. Senate finally did apologize briefly for slavery and Jim Crow, but no serious reparative response to this large-scale wrongdoing was offered by the senators. The great and unjust impoverishment of the racialized slavery and Jim Crow past is still manifested in black communities today, a point we will discuss in a later chapter.

Another respondent, Gerald Jenkins, recalled an incident of riding a public bus in the Southwest:

I remember when I was in high school. I think I was a junior, and during the summer I had a summer job. I was washing dishes at a cafeteria . . . I had to be there at 5:30 in the morning, and the buses started running at about 5:00. There was nobody on the bus but the bus driver. . . . They had this thing that you had to go to the back, but wasn't nobody on the bus but the driver. I got on there, paid, and just sat right there in the front. He wanted to raise hell about that, and made me go to the back. Nobody was on the bus! So, I told him, "Man! Ain't nobody else on this bus, and I'm just going . . . just six to eight blocks." He told me if I didn't get to the back of the bus he was going to stop and call the police on me. So, you see what we go through? This wasn't something that needed to even be talked about, you know? He could have just went on and drove the bus and let me off. But, no. (*Gerald Jenkins, 70s*)

Retelling this experience from decades ago still brings up feelings of confusion, indignity, and anger. Although no one else except the driver was there, this young man had to comply with the Jim Crow hierarchy. African Americans were under constant surveillance by ordinary whites who enforced white supremacy, often with terroristic threats. (Whites like the driver were also under the surveillance of other whites.) This is yet another example of the constant stress that African Americans endured as a reminder of their second-class citizenship. This experience had happened to him alone, yet his plural "we" signals he is keenly aware that such racial indignities were commonplace. Interestingly too, the respondent phrases "You see what we go through" in the *present tense*.

SURVEILLANCE AND CONTROLLING BLACK BODIES: TRAVEL RESTRICTIONS AND TRAINS

Jim Crow segregation had significant geographic boundaries that could be witnessed as one traversed the United States. As we have already seen, some respondents underscored the differential treatment they would experience as they moved about the country. As referenced in Harold Moore's account at the chapter opening, many military veterans commented that they were treated better in foreign countries than in the home country that they had risked their lives to defend. This treatment was often worse as they traveled farther south.

Respondent Millard Coleman, also a veteran, shares his experience on segregated trains in the Southwest:

> All I can tell you, [during Jim Crow if] you was black, [whites let] you know the whole time. I was in the navy, I didn't run into that stuff until me and my buddy, it was five of us, got discharged down there at Camp Wallace, that day. . . . So, he didn't know where the train station was in [town] to catch the train to go to [names town]. I knew where the train station was there to go to [names town] and also the one to come down here. But his train leaved before mine, I took him down to the train station in [town] and that was the first time I saw that damn ["colored"] sign, I didn't say nothing thinking, before we can even get the tickets to go to [town], "You got to go around here, with the colored people." Right there . . . that's the first time I had heard that thing, the whole time, I come plum across the United States, from Virginia to California, and never seen that damn sign, till we get right there. (*Millard Coleman, 80s*)

He recalls his ability to freely travel across the United States relatively unbothered by certain overt symbols of racial hatred, yet that changed as he traveled in areas of the Southwest. Before setting foot on the train, this paying customer and "defender of America's freedom" was stopped and told that he didn't really belong. In such cases, ordinary whites enforced the racial order. Like a reaction to a slap in the face, much frustration and anger are evident in his cursing of "that damn sign." The U.S. South has long been a symbol for blatant racial hatred and antiblack violence, both of which contributed to the great migration by black Americans to the North from the early to mid-1900s, including during and after World War II.

Several respondents noted that when traveling by train, some parts of their journey became more dangerous as they crossed particular geographical boundaries. Alice Carter, a respondent in the Southwest, recalls how bad things were on the trains that many people then rode between cities:

> When we rode the train, we would run into this situation on the train. Come through [names Texas town]. . . . You better put your shades down, close your windows down. You were in the coal cart.

You was right behind the engine. 'Cause white folks threw rocks at us. You know things like that. That's basically what happened. (*Alice Carter, 90s*)

This elderly woman recalls whites throwing rocks at railcar windows in which African Americans were known to be traveling—often in the cars in the loudest and most polluted part of the train. Throwing rocks shouldn't be dismissed as just juvenile pranks. White adults hurled stones as a terroristic warning to blacks not to get off in a particular town, as well as to cause physical or psychological harm. Significantly, Carter noted the importance of closing windows and pulling down window shades for protective reasons.

Throughout this book numerous respondents indicate that they have actively avoided interacting with whites, in the past and the present. Indeed, in conducting home interviews the first author observed that many of the African American respondents had their curtains drawn shut, sat in darkened rooms, or otherwise seemed to be in a protective mode. Although the overt signs of Jim Crow were long gone at the time of the interviews, the consequences of the racist hatred seen in the Jim Crow insults and assaults were still very evident. At times the respondents' nonverbal body language indicated physical pain as they recoiled at recalling traumatic memories. Some insisted that the tape recorders be turned off when revealing the details of some dramatic events, almost as if they still feared white retaliation. Other respondents needed reassurance that their confidentiality would not be compromised. As we discuss in a later chapter, many respondents used the present tense in their accounts of the past, in part because various forms of white racial discrimination still thrive today.

SURVEILLANCE AND CONTROLLING BLACK BODIES: TRAVELING BY CAR

In the Jim Crow era African Americans were subject to white surveillance not only when using public transportation, but also, as we have seen in a few previous accounts, when they traveled in their own automobiles. Herbert Parker, a retired veteran, underscores this reality as he remembers the filthy and unsafe conditions of rest stops in the Southwest:

> During my early years of service, there were places that I would go and couldn't get service and wouldn't allow us. Then we were traveling along the highway, and when we got hungry—there may be a truck stop—they always had some nasty place for us to eat. I experienced some of that traveling around. As I grew up, we were pretty much self-contained, so I didn't have to go into town. But the folks around us that had to go into town, they had it pretty bad; they had to put up with that. Like at my hometown, there was a bus station where they served all the white passengers in a nice area. Then they had this little nasty hole for the black passengers. There again they had in most public facilities that allowed you in there, they had would have a nice clean restroom for whites, and a nasty unclean one for blacks. (*Herbert Parker, 60s*)

This veteran recalls how basic bodily functions like eating and using the restroom led to many problematic situations for African Americans. Their movements were often restricted by overt "colored" signs or by making the conditions so terrible that there was a clear message of their presence not being desired. Like other respondents, Parker notes that his family was "self-contained" and often coped with Jim Crow segregation by actively avoiding interactions with whites.

Similarly, respondent Irene Jennings discusses the significant extra planning that was usually required for African Americans when traveling, in order to remain safe from white attacks:

> [What] I remember is that traveling from the North back down to [names town], back down to [names state] there were certain places we knew that we couldn't stop. You either had your tank full of gas, 'cause you knew that you couldn't stop in Mississippi 'cause they were already hanging people. And it was scary. So black people didn't want to be caught especially not at night. So you fill it with gas and never stop anywhere. You kept going. You could be tired and sleepy, but you couldn't stop at a motel. If you stopped at some little hole, you couldn't sleep 'cause you couldn't be able to rest. Because you didn't know if somebody was going to break into it because they knew black people were in there or not. It was an uncomfortable feeling. (*Irene Jennings, 60s*)

Not only were certain locations dangerous, but so were certain times of the day. This respondent notes that nighttime was often particularly scary. Being snatched out of your motel room and attacked in the middle of the night may seem today like the fictional making of a horror film. However, the *threat* of it happening was real for African Americans in the Jim Crow South. Individuals need not have experienced or witnessed traumatic events like violent assaults or lynchings to feel this antiblack terrorism's everyday consequences. Even the threat of a violent event, as expressed here, was a means of maintaining white dominance. Given recurring white threats, African American travelers needed to take extra precautions, such as carefully planning ahead for fuel and rest stops.

Shirley McKinney, a retired teacher in the Southwest, similarly recounts the numerous preparations that African Americans had to make to traverse the "land of liberty":

> Well, there are many times, when, we were traveling with our children in the early '50s, middle, early '60s during those days we did not have places for the blacks to sleep when we traveled. We had to sleep in our cars. And of course we always went to California to visit my husband's people, and we would go in the summertime and take us a little vacation. And we would travel in our little Ford car, and knowing that we did not have no place to sleep or eat we always—we had two children—we would fix our lunch, and we would have a lunch in our car. To carry us from [names state], at that time, to San Francisco, that's a long drive. And of course, we would take foods that we could eat along the road, then we would stop along the road to buy food to carry us along. (*Shirley McKinney, 70s*)

She continues her account with yet more travel-related actions that only black travelers had to take to make it across the United States:

> And for our sleeping we would stop at a roadside park, stop and let the children get out and rest, and play around. And then we would wash up and well of course, we always had our clothes, you know to change clothes in the [car], 'cause it would take us at least two days traveling in the car. And we would do most of the driving at night. And . . . my husband would drive so far, and I would drive so far. And sometimes we would see a place that we could stop at a café and go to the back door and get a cup of coffee or something at night,

especially to refresh us to continue to drive. But we always stopped
at a grocery store and bought our little food for the children to keep
us going to until we made it to California. [*You didn't really use
restaurants?*] We didn't use it 'cause we couldn't go in there. . . .
When traveling we would go prepared, 'cause we knew there were
some places that they would not let you come in, and we didn't
bother about that, we just went prepared. (*Shirley McKinney, 70s*)

The geographical boundaries within which African Americans could
freely and safely move about were often restrictive and dependent on
the whim of whites. McKinney describes the foresight required of black
travelers who couldn't count on the privileges and benefits routinely
granted to whites. Under Jim Crow norms, blacks were restricted in
how they moved about in white-controlled spaces. Traveling at night
and being cautious and creative in where to eat and sleep were meas-
ures taken to decrease the likelihood that they, or their children, would
be victims of unprovoked white hostility or violence. Throughout these
accounts we see that black Americans, whose ancestry in this country
goes back farther than that of many whites and who were then legally
full citizens, were constantly treated as second-class citizens.

SURVEILLANCE AND CONTROLLING BLACK BODIES: MAJOR DISCRIMINATION IN STORES

The foresight and preparation required of African Americans moving
about in supposedly public but white-controlled spaces was not limited
to traveling. When black shoppers went about their daily lives engaged
in such activities as grocery or clothing shopping, they also had to prepare themselves against potential racial indignities. They had to do this
mentally as well as in terms of certain material supplies. In contrast,
whites did not have to exert this mental energy, and thus could expend
such energy in other creative outlets.

Parents shopping with children had to plan ahead for bathroom
breaks and food. Caregivers for children might be tempted to claim that
this is a burden that all caregivers share, which is true to some extent.
However, black parents had to have an added layer of concern for their
child's safety, for they knew that physical violence might be a punishment if their child was caught drinking from the "wrong" water fountain

or using the "wrong" bathroom. (Under Jim Crow, ironically, blacks could only enter "white" bathrooms to clean them!) In addition, children also were forced to witness their parents and family elders treated with blatant white disrespect. In a later chapter we discuss how parents tried to protect their children in this era. Yet, however hard parents might try, they couldn't always shield their children from the harsh realities of white supremacy.

Respondent Gladys Jacob, in the Southwest, recalls witnessing her mother's racialized difficulties in buying a suitable dress:

> I used to go with my mother to the store—grocery, dresses—to buy dresses, but black ladies couldn't try the dresses on. They had to buy them. You couldn't try them on and if it didn't fit . . . you [could not] give it back to them and put it back. They wouldn't put it back on the rack because a black person had had it on. I didn't notice these things because I was little then, but I used to hear my momma and some of my aunties talking about it. And I think about that sometimes now, how things have really changed. Because sometimes she'd end up buying something that didn't exactly fit, then she'd have to go to a seamstress and get some more done to it because it really wasn't the size she needed. But . . . they wouldn't let her exchange it, 'cause she had already tried it on. (*Gladys Jacob, 60s*)

A senior citizen now, Jacob reflects on experiences in childhood. Although she claims that she was too young to notice what was going on, she was astute enough to know that something negative was being communicated to her. The literature on children's early sexual and racial knowledge suggests that adults often don't realize the full extent to which children actually do understand the cultural meanings in early interactions with other children and adults.[21] Moreover, like other African Americans in this era, Jacob's mother and aunts were viewed by whites as contaminating white goods like dresses and hats. The women surely paid a psychological price for being viewed as less than human compared to other paying customers who were white. We also see an economic cost to this discriminatory practice, as the women had to pay full price for the dress, and then pay an additional cost to a seamstress to fix an ill-fitting dress.

A retired teacher, Edna Bush, in the Southwest explains how difficult it was buying hats if you were African American:

Oh yes, in clothing stores, there are many clothing stores that my relatives and myself we would go in. And especially with hats, we always like to wear nice hats to church, to look nice. And of course we would go to the stores and look, we would see a hat. The first thing the clerk would say, "Oh please don't try the hat on 'cause you might have oil on your hair that will get on the hat." So you couldn't try on that hat, you just look at it. And if you thought it looked nice, it would look nice on you, you had to purchase the hat. Later on through the years, they would have these little plastic [caps] that you would put on your head . . . and then you could try that hat on. And that way, you know, if you had any oil on your hair it wouldn't get on the hat. And, of course, with clothing you couldn't try on the clothing because I guess they felt that you were not clean enough to try them on, so you couldn't try them on. You used to just go in and look at the dress and you would think, "Oh I think this is my size and I think I can wear it," so you would purchase the dress. (*Edna Bush, 80s*)

Repeatedly in the interview narratives, we encounter discussions of white actions that clearly signal the framing of African Americans as not clean. Bush discusses the acceptance that "of course" African Americans couldn't try on clothing, because they were viewed as dirty. The white clerk justifies not allowing black women to sample the hats for fear that their hair will contaminate them. In this period, as now, the use of hair oil was not restricted to African Americans; white hairstyles commonly relied on significant use of hair oil or pomade. Yet white women and men ordinarily had the opportunity to try on hats without interference. It was not the hair oil that was a problem, but the racialized stigma whites associated with black customers.

Several other respondents also noted the difficulties that African American women had when trying to buy a hat. Respondent Evelyn Dawson, living now in the Southwest, remembers her mother buying a hat during the Jim Crow years:

I know more about things going on during the civil rights years and how they beat and treat blacks than what I did when I was growing up. I just don't remember it. [But] it was there. I know that we didn't go to the formula [pharmacy] stores, we didn't. We had to know our place. We had to go in the back door. I remember that. But I really didn't have to go. My daddy and my mom and my grandfather went to the store. I didn't have to go. . . . My mamma wanted a hat from a store in [town] called "T's Brothers" and they would not let mamma try that hat on without putting a ton of paper in it because you know blacks have to put oil in their hair. A ton of paper. How did that hat look with all that paper on it? These are the kind of things—now, I remember that. And I thought that was silly then. To this day, I hate hats. Couldn't get me in a hat. [*Did she get the hat?*] Yeah, she got the hat. She was not like me and my daddy, my mamma went on and took the hat, but I probably wouldn't have even of bought the hat, had it of been me. She was very sweet. (*Evelyn Dawson, 80s*)

In this case, Dawson's mother faced the racialized indignity of placing physical barriers between the product she wished to purchase and her hair, but she was undeterred in getting this important purchase. Several scholars have emphasized the distinctive significance of hats in African American communities, particularly in churches, during slavery and legal segregation. These "crowns," as they were sometimes called, were a way to honor God. They also represented a dramatic break from the dreary uniforms of domestic servants and other service workers. Wearing a beautifully adorned "crown" in church on Sundays was one opportunity black women had to safely celebrate their individualism and break away from symbols of their subservient roles.[22]

In this interview quotation we observe different coping strategies evident between the two generations. The mother is determined to make her purchase regardless of the white shopkeeper's barriers, but Dawson suggests now that she wouldn't have allowed herself to be disrespected. This situation illustrates philosopher Marilyn Frye's concept of the double bind: No matter which option you select, because it takes place within the context of oppression, it benefits the oppressor. The white shop owner benefits financially if black women purchase their products. However, the shop owner benefits ideologically if black women do not purchase their products, for there is no longer a worry about their goods becoming "contaminated." As a result, and not surprisingly, the respondent notes that even today she hates hats. Based on the flow of the conversation, we can speculate that she is bothered less by the material fabric on her head, and more about the racialized associations she attributes to hats. Indeed, many respondents in their interviews noted that they hated or avoided numerous objects, from hats to water fountains and public buses, all symbols that still trigger their negative memories of Jim Crow's oppressiveness.

Note too Evelyn Dawson's difficulties in remembering some Jim Crow details. Although it's tempting to write this off as a common symptom of the natural aging process, we see evidence that for her, like many African Americans, collective forgetting is a critical coping strategy. While the specific details of the events may be deliberately forgotten, the emotions surrounding them are impossible to ignore. Psychological researchers have debated the relationship between negative emotions and increased memory recall, but it is clear that negative emotions can lead to suppression of such painful memories. [23]

Many African Americans who lived during the legal segregation decades have commented about how the feelings of pain and hurt have stayed with them during their entire lifetimes. On Sunday morning, September 15, 1963, four little girls lost their lives at the hands of white terrorists who bombed the Sixteenth Street Baptist Church in Birmingham, Alabama. The four girls—Denise McNair, Carole Robinson, Cynthia Wesley, and Addie Mae Collins—were just attending Sunday school. Collin's sister, Janie Gaines, describes the difficulty in recalling the events: "It's not easy because we had put so much of this behind us. And we don't remember. We just don't remember anymore. You know what I'm saying? But you know how you felt. You may not remember details or what—step by step—what I had to go through, but I do know it affected me. So bad." [24] Obviously, watching the murder of one's sister is highly traumatic, as compared with being denied the opportunity to try on a hat. However, both big traumas and little cumulative traumas need to be understood as taking place within the same terroristic and totalitarian context that severely restricted the lives of an entire racial group in the United States.

SURVEILLANCE AND CONTROLLING BLACK BODIES: MORE DISCRIMINATION IN STORES

Our respondents frequently reiterated this notion of "knowing their place" in regard to an array of segregating restrictions and barriers. African Americans were often perceived in the racial framing of whites as not only contaminated people, but also as potential thieves—a framing that has persisted to the present. A teacher in the Southwest, Nor-

ma Rivers, recalls being followed and suspected of shoplifting in the Jim
Crow era:

> Those were incidents that occurred on a daily experience that we had
> to deal with. We were treated in retail stores, you know, it's almost
> like they'd follow you around and there are some instances where
> they still do that even today because of your color. But even more so,
> you know, it's like we're going to pick something or steal and you
> know, we didn't do that. We were taught not to do that; and our
> parents watched us to make sure that we didn't have any problems
> with the law. We did every opportunity to make sure we didn't have
> an account with the law enforcement. We stayed out of trouble for
> the most part. (*Norma Rivers, 70s*)

African American children were under strict surveillance not only
from their parents, but also from white clerks who suspected them of
thievery. Indeed, adolescents in all racial groups have complained about
being watched in stores, yet white skin has not worked against white
adolescents. This has not been the case for black youth. During the Jim
Crow era the burden was placed on them to ensure that their behaviors
did not look suspicious, for their mere physical presence was looked
upon with suspicion.

Sylvia Grant, a respondent in the Southwest, recalls a specific event
of being watched in a department store for the simple reason that she is
African American. Although she followed the racial norms by not touching the clothes, she was still suspected of shoplifting. In anger at the
indignity, she physically confronted the white floorwalker:

> Yeah, she was a floorwalker . . . she was white. . . . I was there, going
> around looking at clothes and . . . she got too close behind me, and I
> took a silk dress and wrapped her in the face with it, and they called
> the police. . . . Mike [her brother] called back, "Momma, Sylvia done
> got into it!" . . . They called the police and the police and, and, and
> so . . . Mr. Hikes [the manager of the store] he say, "Well, she
> shouldn't of been following Sylvia." I say, "I told her in the first
> place, you know, I wasn't stealing nothing. Picking up nothing." . . .
> [The floorwalker] reported me to the white person which was Mr.
> Hikes. Well, well they had me leave the store and I told them I
> wasn't going to leave the store. Well, they didn't do nothing. They
> say, "You not leaving the store?" I say, "Naw." I say, "Well you can go

ahead and call them police, and I'll wait till the police get here," . . . and I waited there until they got there. The police say, "Well, uh, well what was she doing . . . was she picking up anything, was she stealing any stuff?" And they say, "No." They said, "Well then, why do you want her to leave the store?" Because I took that silk dress and wrapped that lady in the face with it . . . they already label you "blacks are going to steal, blacks and Hispanics gone steal, but blacks are gone steal more than anybody." And as soon as I walked in [the store] they'll put a floorwalker on me, thought I was going to steal, but I had money to buy. Yeah, every time I walked in [the store] down in town, or out there in [town], they'd put a floorwalker on me. (*Sylvia Grant, 60s*)

The respondent conforms to the Jim Crow hierarchy by monitoring her behaviors so she wouldn't be looked upon suspiciously, yet white floorwalkers still regularly monitored her. Following segregation rules did not protect her, for she was thought to be a shoplifter anyway. In one situation she became so frustrated that she lashed out, and the police were summoned. While this outburst may perpetuate the stereotype of the "angry black woman," from the respondent's point of view (one often invalidated and ignored by whites), it is a logical response to an illogical racist predicament.

Unfortunately, the negative experience with the white floorwalker did not end with that day in the store. Grant continued:

I was working . . . at the court. . . . That [floorwalker] lady got so, she came on my job that year. . . . She got mad I cussed her out, so she came on my job to report me. . . . [*She was the floorwalker?*] She sure did. She's a white woman, she came to the courthouse and told Mr. Mills. . . . Mr. Mills asked her, say, "Tell me what do you want?" "Well I come to, I come to report Sylvia." I don't know how she found out I worked at the courthouse. And so Mr. Mills said, "Well, what did Sylvia do? Did she pick up something? Did she steal anything?" "No, she didn't." He said, "Well, why are you down here on her job? Why you down here? If you come back here again I'm going to see that you go to jail." . . . And that's when he asked me, he say, "Sylvia, how well do you like [the store]?" I said, "Mr. Mills, they have what I like, that's the reason why." He said, "Well Sylvia, you should just stay out of there." . . . Yeah. She came round there, told Mr. Mills I cut up, Mr. Mills say, "Did you cut up?" I say, "I sure did." I say, "She ain't got nothing to do," I said, "whatever I do on the weekend is my business, Mr. Mills, and not hers." I say, "Yes I did curse her out." I say, "And I'll curse her out again." (*Sylvia Grant, 60s*)

In retaliation for the respondent not passively accepting her subordinate status as a potential thief in the store, the floorwalker attempted to get revenge. We can surmise that in the white woman's mind, the credibility of her whiteness would trump the relationship the respondent had with her boss. Her boss is certainly sympathetic and defends Sylvia (only after confirming that she didn't steal), yet his solution is for her to stay away from this white space, thereby upholding Jim Crow segregation. Grant concludes by indicating that what she does on weekends is her own "business." However, as she is aware, African Americans are under the surveillance of *all* whites at most places, whites who feel it is their business to keep people of color in their place.

SURVEILLANCE AND CONTROLLING BLACK BODIES: FRAMING BLACK DOMESTICS AS CRIMINAL

African Americans were not only presumed to be potential thieves in department stores, but also in the homes of white folks. Respondent Juanita Wilkins, in the Southeast, recalls how her mother was treated while working as a domestic in white homes:

> My mother, because she had to, when we were living in New York, she had to work in the white household as a maid doing the cleaning and the dusting and washing their clothes and taking care of the children. She said she never wanted, uh, she wanted us to get an education. That she never wanted us to have to clean somebody's house, because they could treat you very nasty in those kinds of situations. They were allowed to test whether or not you would steal. They . . . leave money laying around or leave jewelry laying around, and that was to find out if you would steal. And it wasn't accidental. So that's another reason she never wanted us to work . . . for white people cleaning their houses. Because then if something is missing they'd say you took it. . . . Oh yes, it was a well-known fact that that's the way they test to see if you would steal. I don't know, have you ever seen this [1983] movie *Trading Places* with Eddie Murphy? Do

you remember the [white] man accidentally lost his, supposedly accidentally lost his, money clip with money in it cause he expected Eddie Murphy to pick the money up and keep it. And Eddie Murphy picked up the money and brought it to him. Those are the kinds of things that my mother taught me that white folks would do in order to find out if you would steal if you were working around in their house and stuff like that. [My mom said] don't ever clean in a white folks' house. Get you an education. Go to school so you can do something else other than work in white people's house. [*How did it make you feel to know that?*] It made me feel like I was worthless. (*Juanita Wilkins, 70s*)

White employers frequently tested African American domestics, who whites assumed would steal. Consider the irony: African Americans were viewed as potential thieves, yet numerous scholars have shown that over many generations white wealth was secured through the stolen labor of African Americans and stolen land of Native Americans. Through means such as African American slavery and Jim Crow exploitation, as well as Native American genocide, collectively whites were able to secure access to many wealth-generating resources and thus to wealth.[25] In contrast, for centuries African Americans were denied access to wealth-generating resources, including in the Jim Crow era being paid a substandard wage for doing drudgery work for whites and then being tested to make sure they didn't resist and disrupt the racial hierarchy. While blacks struggled to secure necessities like basic food and clothing, whites often tested or mocked them by leaving money or jewelry lying around the house. Given this harsh reality, it's understandable why this respondent would note that hearing her mother talk about her dominant experiences made her feel "worthless."

Hattie Saunders, a respondent in the Southwest, recalls her experiences working in the homes of whites and echoes the previous respondent's comment about feeling worthless:

I was trying to work and go to school, and I worked in private homes. And my first bad encounter that really bothered me was when I would go to these homes to work. I was good enough to go into these homes, keep the babies, clean the home, wash and iron the clothes. But I was never good enough to sit at the tables with them and eat, and that always bothered me. Always bothered me so much, and I knew that I couldn't live like that. I couldn't feel like I was nothing. So then I left. (*Hattie Saunders, 80s*)

In the Jim Crow era, black women often worked as domestic workers in white homes, a primary source of income for most. Adults who care for children or aging parents understand how critically important, yet frequently undervalued, these jobs are in all families. However, to find someone who can be trusted with one's children, yet to not trust or want that person to eat at the same table, illustrates the irrationality of white racism. Like other respondents, Saunders notes the numerous times that the indignity of not being "good enough" bothered her.

In the book *White Men on Race*, the second author writes about the experiences of powerful white men who were raised in affluent white families by African American domestics. Many of these men recall with fondness their feelings for a black female domestic seen as a "second mother."[26] Indeed, many other whites claim that these black domestics in their families were treated as "members of the family." However, this was usually the case only when the black employee didn't dissent from or disrupt their racially subordinate status. Indeed, the tenuous relationship between white children who have significant relationships with their long-suffering caregivers is noted by Geraldine Richards, a respondent in the Southeast:

> We need their [whites'] money and they need our work. . . . They have to have somebody to keep their house clean. . . . Raise their children . . . the kids all hugged up with you. And then, they see you on the street when they grown, and they act like they don't know you. . . . You work for years and die on the job. It has always been that way. . . . But in the long run, we will never get to the top, but we can keep working on it. You see those children at that day care center. They all hugged up to me. A few years from now they will see me in the street and act like they don't know me. I have seen it before. I raise them from a baby, and when they get grown they ignores me. (*Geraldine Richards, 80s*)

The pain and sadness of being rejected by the very children she took care of is clear in her words. She was good enough to clean houses and raise white babies, probably at the expense of caring for her own children, yet not good enough to be acknowledged later on. She survived on the financial crumbs whites gave her. She is not only referring to the children for whom she has been the guardian, but also speaking more generally: Whites who once had intimate relationships with African American caregivers will usually internalize and enforce the old racist hierarchy as they grow older.

CONCLUSION

White surveillance and control of black Americans as they moved about public spaces were central to the Jim Crow system. Many forms of nonviolent and violent oppression of African Americans during this era were widely and legally sanctioned by whites, including white authorities. In contrast, violent crimes committed by whites against African Americans were usually not punished, or just weakly punished, under the law. Officially, the Jim Crow segregation laws often mandated separate-but-equal accommodations, but such accommodations, as we have seen in this chapter, were almost never equal. Even in the Deep South states, it was unlawful for black individuals to be raped, murdered, or terrorized. The white-run southern and border state governments had the responsibility to protect all citizens under their jurisdiction. White local, state, and federal officials were paid by the taxes of black Americans to protect them. Yet again, these white officials and a great many ordinary white citizens frequently disregarded the laws and committed individual or large-scale violence against African Americans, including for violating the informal norms of Jim Crow segregation.

4

MORE SURVEILLANCE OF BLACK BODIES

In this chapter we continue our examination of the extensive white surveillance and control of black bodies and black communities in all types of spaces and places. Even attempts to move about without any intention to have contact with whites could lead to very negative experiences. Just walking the streets could be a provocation for violent white actions. In addition, forgetting "one's place" was usually a dangerous thing to do, as whites would often retaliate and force recognition of that "place," or worse. Given the scale of these unprovoked public attacks, it is significant that African Americans even ventured out of their homes during this totalitarian era of Jim Crow oppression.

SURVEILLANCE AND CONTROLLING BLACK BODIES: NAVIGATING PUBLIC SPACES

In addition to white surveillance while traveling, shopping in stores, and working in white homes, African Americans faced much white surveillance merely walking on public sidewalks. Respondent Ray Lewis reports that in the 1940s he learned degrading deferential practices that regularly shaped interactions with whites:

> When whites were walking down the street, you had to get off the sidewalk. . . . Whites basically demanded it. . . . That was the whole process of racism. You had to get off the sidewalk, and you never addressed whites as nothing more than "Yes sir" or "Yes ma'am" and

you never look whites in the eye because that was a sign . . . that you were being belligerent. . . . An uppity "nigger," and you get challenged for that in a minute. . . . You were the powerless so you just said, "Yes sir" and "No sir." There were some blacks who used to voice their discontent but whites didn't know it. "Yes sir," you know [in a sarcastic tone] . . . allowing them to say it. But not because you've earned it, because I don't want no problems from you. (*Ray Lewis, 60s*)

Everyday racism is not simply a negative attitude or an inconvenience, but according to this respondent, it is an institutionalized process. Imposed by whites, this interactive racism was constantly re-created by Jim Crow practices and rituals. These frequently included avoiding eye contact with whites, stepping off the sidewalks as whites passed, and using formal greetings for whites such as "sir" and "ma'am." Violating racist rituals led to violence that was sporadic, uncertain, and often contradictory, and African Americans were usually powerless to resist actively. However, as Lewis notes, African Americans undermined white supremacy in subtle ways such as using sarcasm so they could maintain some humanity and still minimize possible violence at the hands of whites.

In the Southeast, Edward Harris remembers well the lack of agency that blacks often had in regard to resisting acts of humiliation in the Jim Crow decades:

If someone pushed you off the sidewalk, and that was a white person that did that . . . what were you going to do? Who were you going to fuss at about someone jumping in front of you in the line in the grocery store? We didn't have a recourse then, other than to speak up for yourself, and if you spoke up for yourself, then you didn't know what kind of retribution that you might face. You didn't know where or not rocks were going to get thrown in your window, or you might come out and your tires might be slashed, or whether or not there was going to be a cross burned in your yard. (*Edward Harris, 60s*)

He continues, noting the degrading deferential rituals in which his mother had to engage on a recurring basis:

My mother, when she encountered difficulties [with whites], she was very submissive . . . "No, uh, well, I'm sorry. . . ." And, you know, tried to appease whatever the situation was as best as she could, to make that situation a good situation, however it may be. . . . I have seen in the store where she was getting ready to purchase something, and she was there at the counter to be waited on. And another white woman would come up, and instead of them going ahead and waiting on my mother, they would go ahead and wait on them, and mother didn't say anything. She'd just step back and waited and let them do that. And then she took her turn. . . . I didn't understand what was going on. I didn't realize that this was wrong. I thought that that was just a way of life. It wasn't until later that I felt that that's not the way it should be. You're discriminating. We're humans and should be treated equal. I'm not a very aggressive person. I'm not going to let you walk over me, but I will acquiesce to you to try and keep the peace. Watching her, I think it's just kind of instilled in me and a part of my nature. (*Edward Harris, 60s*)

Everyday rituals of racism were backed up by the threat of punishment, including terroristic violence. Resisting even little injustices such as calling out a line jumper could result in aggressive warnings to not question white supremacy, or even acts of violence. Whites could usually retaliate with impunity against African Americans who tried to defend themselves. Although there were often witnesses—both whites and people of color—to discriminatory white insults and assaults, the criminal justice system offered little or no protection. It was institutionalized by elite whites to protect whites, even from a few whites who might stand up in sympathy with the plight of African Americans.

A retired service worker, Edith Dean, recalls learning from her parents how to interact with whites, yet even this lesson did not spare children or adults from the humiliation and anger that often occurred with their white experiences. She shares some of these experiences with violent white children:

Them children would jump us and hit us, and we [were] scared to hit them back. . . . We [would be] passing by in different places where they live and work. . . . Boy, they threw rocks at my brother. He was afraid. My brothers, they were scared. . . . Some of them [whites] got it in them *now*, but they try to keep it hid but if you round them long enough you can tell. . . . They were mean to black people. They were mean. I don't know what made them mean to black people but they were. . . . I know who was scared, we were! They didn't care for us. . . . I used to be so scared. I'd tell my children, I said, "Yes, ma'am. No, ma'am." . . . I told them in a way where they wouldn't be holding it against them now. They [parents] told us how to treat them. They were scared of them themselves. . . . I was little but I could tell. (*Edith Dean, 70s*)

At young ages, white and black youth learned appropriate "places" in the hierarchy of the total institution of Jim Crow. Like many respondents, she tries to understand the irrationality of white hatred for blacks, even black children. Many respondents echoed this sentiment of confusion over white cruelty. Indeed, when white adults let their children harass "little black children . . . white parents and the whole adult world of racial inequality had turned morality upside down."[1] Like numerous others, this respondent is painfully aware that her parents could not help their children fight back. Even as a child, she picked up the cues of African Americans' fears of whites, fears repeatedly generated by whites' maliciousness toward African Americans. Black children had to cope in defensive ways, also by using respectful titles like "sir" and "ma'am," yet they dared not actively defend themselves. In addition, she notes elsewhere in her interview that she has passed along these racialized messages of deference to her own children. In this way the impact of legal segregation has lasted well beyond its historical era.

Consider too that Edith Dean, like numerous others, makes note that some whites today maintain hidden animosity to African Americans that periodically seeps out in recurring interactions. She is warning that many whites today put on a temporary performance of non-racism around African Americans. Scholars like Bonilla-Silva and Forman argue that numerous whites have a racist perspective that they often try to cover up with a colorblind mask.[2] Similarly, Picca and Feagin suggest that whites will often interact differently depending upon the assumed racial identity of the persons with whom they are interacting. Thus, when whites are interacting with people of color in the social "frontstage," they often will present a non-racist and colorblind perspective. However, when whites think they are only interacting with other whites, in the social "backstage," they frequently drop the frontstage pleasantries and openly engage in racist joking and other racist commentary or actions.[3]

Respondent Mae Bridges somberly describes walking to school with her sister, when white violence presented itself at an unexpected moment:

> As a little girl, I used to go to Williams School, and we used to come down Wilcox Avenue. There was a white family living upstairs over a store, and that little boy come downstairs. And he spit in my face [lowers voice]. He spit in my face. . . . I cried all the way to school. . . . That thing hurt me so bad. I just cried, cried, cried. Because I understood he was doing it because he was white and I was black. We understood segregation. We knew white people would take advantage of us. Oh yeah, you knew that. [*Your mom and dad . . . ?*] Yeah, they knew it. But what could they do? They couldn't go back up there and fight about something that had happened. (*Mae Bridges, 80s*)

Some decades after the incident, as she poignantly remembers, her emotion is apparent. During the interview, her voice cracked, she lowered her voice, and she shook her head as she shared the painful memories. Bridges acknowledges that she and her parents understood the Jim Crow constraints well, and they too knew they could do nothing to protect themselves. As a child, her recourse for dealing with the humiliation was to cry. Like other respondents we have quoted, her parents were aware of her pain and doubtless had to wrestle with how to protect their children, suppress their rage, and hide their fears of a violent white reaction to any countering response.

Much social science research shows that repressing emotions of anger, pain, and rage usually has a detrimental impact on physical and mental health.[4] From the respondents' vivid accounts, we see the long-term damage that has occurred in the psyches of those who as children and younger adults endured Jim Crow but now are often fearful, hurting, elderly adults. As we consider the impact of this enforced racial hierarchy on the targets, we as scholars must also consider the impact on those who implemented and benefited from these oppressive racial structures. White children raised under Jim Crow are often today's older white adults—and often those who dominate in contemporary societal institutions. Children are not born with attitudes of white superiority; they have to be socialized by parents and the larger white society to be racially conforming and aggressively racist automatons.[5]

Throughout the legal segregation decades, African Americans of all ages had to be prepared for unprovoked violence at the hands of whites of all ages. The list of racially restricted public spaces was extensive— sidewalks, water fountains, public parks, buses, benches, swimming pools, restrooms, restaurants, and stores, to mention only a few. One interviewee, Rose Battle, recalls being denied a swim in a public pool:

> I know one time, my grandmother took me to go to [names park]. That was a park for whites. My grandmother decided she was going to take me to the park that day. There they had a little wading pool. I got in. She told me to get in the pool, and there sure enough I did. Finally, the warden came over and told me, "You gonna have to go." She said, "Why?" He said, "See because, this pool is for whites. You have to leave!" (*Rose Battle, 60s*)

We can speculate whether or not the respondent's grandmother was aware that the pool was for whites only when she told her granddaughter to get in. Everyday moments of resistance, even by children and the elderly, were attempts to chip away at the foundation of white supremacy. Recall that the role of black children and adolescents in the 1960s civil rights movement was especially prominent, yet that fact is often overlooked in much historical analysis. Children were then recruited to demonstrate in important civil rights marches and were prepared by adults for the possibility of incarceration. This was an attempt to advance the social justice movement with fewer disruptions to African American families and communities. Parents were thus able to continue working and earn a necessary wage while their children kept up the momentum for racial equality. Additionally, children were important in garnering national and international attention for the civil rights movement. These black parents should not be chastised for putting some children in harm's way. As all black parents would attest, their children were already in harm's way.

Another interviewee, Ellen Clay, recalls an incident with her grandmother and grandmother's friend at a park bench:

> My grandmother and her friend came, had an occasion to come to [names town] once and we were at the courthouse and the benches that were in the park were for the white people. Well, my grandmother's friend felt tired, and she sat down on the bench but my

grandmother said to her, "Ms. Frayshee, you know you are not supposed to be sitting on that bench, that's for the white people." Ms.
Frayshee said, "But I'm tired. Oh I'm just going to sit here a few
minutes." As soon as she sat down then a white man came along and
told her to get up, that she wasn't supposed to be sitting on that
bench. She got up and we left. (*Ellen Clay, 70s*)

Several respondents shared similar stories of how everyday whites—
without authority—would enforce the racial hierarchy. Children, the
elderly, even visitors were bound by the rules of white dominance.
Failure to comply was viewed as an affront to white supremacy.

SURVEILLANCE AND CONTROLLING BLACK BODIES: LEARNING YOUR "PLACE"

Given the intensive white surveillance that African Americans experienced in most facets of life—traveling, shopping, working, walking in
public areas—many respondents talked about the necessity of remain-
ing in "our place" and not threatening the rituals and spaces of white
supremacy. We have already seen numerous examples of this everyday
reality, but let us note a few more where our respondents underscored
this extreme normative aspect of Jim Crow. One respondent, Stanley
Brooke, in the Southwest explains that as a child he did not understand
the rigidity of Jim Crow and its consequences:

There was a large hotel called William Hotel. I never will forget this,
and this William Hotel had a lobby with an electric drinking fountain
where the water stayed cool. But they had a sign up there "White
Only," and this was on the other side of the tracks where we wasn't
even supposed to be. But me and my sister . . . we'd have to go to the
post office to get our mail. There wasn't delivery, we didn't have any
mailmen at that time. Instead of us going back home, we'd go across
that tracks and go over there to that hotel just to drink out of that
fountain. Nobody never said anything to us, but we'd go home, and
tell my mother about it and tell my daddy about it. He say, "Y'all
don't you do that, stay away from over there, 'cause some of them
over there, somebody over there one of these days will say something
to or do something to you. Then I become involved." He, my daddy,

was telling us this. Well, it didn't bother me any because we wanted that cold water [laughs]. (*Stanley Brooke, 70s*)

He then adds, with some strong emotion, comments on how he came to understand what had happened:

And I didn't really understand what he said until after I got grown. It would have involved him if they would have hit us or do something to us 'cause he would have to do something about it, about that for his kids. Being in a little small town like that, they would have did something to him, so he knew what he was talking about, but I didn't understand it. So, we didn't do it all the time, but every so often we'd get brave enough and we would do that . . . when we go to the post office to get the mail. We would just go a little bit farther over and . . . go in there and we drink water and this and that. Then we come out and go on home. They'd look at us, but like I say, had they said anything we just going to run anyway. We knew what we were going to do, so, but then after a while we'd get brave enough to talk about it at home. And that's how my daddy found out, you know. "Boy, y'all stop doing that 'cause if they say, they do something to you over there or anything, then I got to go over there and try to find out what, then I'm going to be in trouble, and we all going to be in trouble." Didn't mean anything to me then, but as I got older and wind up with kids, then I said, "Well, now . . ." So, but all and all and also in that little town *we learned our place*. (*Stanley Brooke, 70s*)

This respondent notes how such events became imprinted in his memory. As a child, all he understood is that he wanted a drink of cold, refreshing water, and he didn't realize the danger he put himself and his family in by violating Jim Crow's norms.

Small infractions of the white norms could have horrific consequences. An elderly woman, Gloria Clark, who lives in the Southwest, shared a story about when she witnessed a lynching:

The guy that was down there wasn't with us, but . . . just said "good evening" to a white girl, and she all freaked out. And things went from there. She went screaming and yelling . . . like somebody killed her. Some other white guys came along and asked what was going on . . . and they took him right then and there, took him away, and hung him. Got the rope off the truck, and just hung him right there in front of us and told us, "This is what happens to ninnies who get out of line and speak to people they're not supposed to speak—be spoken to." This happened a lot, throughout the South. . . . It was something that was just the norm back in those days. I had brothers during that time that we always, *always, always* begged them, whatever you do, do *not* speak to white women. (*Gloria Clark, 60s*)

Notice the irony here. While historical and contemporary media images have often portrayed black men as a threat to white womanhood, in reality white womanhood was a much bigger risk to black men.[6] The severe psychological impact of this experience is evident as the respondent recalls emotionally urging her brothers to protect themselves by not speaking at all to white women. As we note throughout this book, many lynchings occurred under the assumption that a black man had gotten too close to a white woman. As here, the presence of onlookers was not enough to deter criminal violence by a few white men. Instead, these men used this as an opportunity to threaten *all* African Americans. Again, too, we see much evidence of the segregation stress syndrome in these commentaries.

As evidenced in accounts we discuss in detail in the next chapter, the "trouble" caused by one African American stepping "out of place" could mean difficulties for an entire community. During the legal segregation era, black newspapers reported many cases of whites' assaults and attacks on innocent black citizens in retaliation for other blacks' violating the norms or laws of Jim Crow. One reason for such broad retaliation was (and still is) because black Americans "all look alike" to many white Americans. This reality is described as the other-race effect by psychological researchers. The homogenous view of individuals in another racial group has been attributed by some psychologists to a person having more experience looking at the faces of their own racial group. However, research also demonstrates that more prejudiced individuals are more likely to respond in this fashion and ignore significant individual differences.[7]

In his interview the previously mentioned respondent Stanley Brooke notes that he didn't fully understand the serious danger he was in or his father's realistic anger until he became a parent. This fatherly sentiment will ring true for many parents who would sacrifice their lives for their children. However, as we have seen several times in the interview accounts, a strong protective response by a parent was often impossible during the legal segregation era. Whites frequently used black children as a sort of weapon to keep parents in line. In his interview another respondent, Elmer Morris, explains that "If they [whites] wanted to get to your parents they would use you, their children." We will see harsh evidence of this reality in the next chapter in a case where a black woman's daughter was raped by a white police officer in retaliation for that woman hiring an attorney to appeal an arrest. Note too that Brooke suggests that not only would his parents not be able to protect his safety, but his actions threatened his parents' safety as well. Just as children suffered the consequences of their parents violating the racial norms, so too were parents held accountable for the actions, real or supposed, of their children.

Given the severe consequences for violating the racial order, numerous respondents underscored the necessity of constantly staying in "your place." A retired schoolteacher, Gordon Ross, explains this totalitarian reality in these poignant words: "Well, we for the most part knew our place or what had been assigned as our place and we stayed within those boundaries. Now we would stretch it to some extent, but not to the point to where it was going to cause serious harm or damage to your family members." An interviewee, George Jackson, in the Southwest, also remembers well knowing his place in the racial order:

> When you can't go to the store, into a café, and you can't go into the front, you have to go in the back. You know about it. . . . When I would go to [names town] with my dad and my grandfather whoever, there were certain places that were strictly the blacks' end of town. So we didn't try to go in on the other end of town. You just knew where your place was and so you didn't try to go. (*George Jackson, 80s*)

Respondent Grace Logan, in the Southwest, recalls that restaurants and theaters were sites of white-imposed, second-class citizenship:

> I remember them places where you'd had to go in that place, and they had divided the place where you had to go through the colored door over there and the white door over here. Yeah, I remember them places, yeah. You couldn't go in the drugstore and sit down at the counter and drink a fountain coke. Hell no, no you couldn't do that. You knowed you couldn't so it wasn't no need for you to go in there and try it. . . . Hell, because you couldn't sit there down where the white folk sat at, hell no! . . . . Discrimination. It's been that a

way, child, and it's going to be that way. They [whites] trying to give [blacks] a break now, but I'd tell you what, these young ones. Now they the ones that's going to mess up everything. They going to mess up everything. (*Grace Logan, 80s*)

She candidly describes in a straightforward manner the differential treatment for African Americans who weren't afforded the courtesy of sitting down in a public establishment to get a drink. It may come across to some readers that it was self-defeating to "not even try" to have resisted this racial order or to view racialized barriers, as a few respondents put it, as "our fault." However, we should not be quick to label these respondents as resigned to defeatism. These streetwise African Americans are underscoring the reality of surviving and coping under totalitarian Jim Crow's threats of white violence. She concludes, sadly, that even though some racial barriers have changed, she is afraid that young people will "mess up everything." This suggests that she feels racial change is not permanent, but can still be reversed.

As we have seen, young people were not always aware of the dangers of Jim Crow. Many respondents explained that they didn't realize the consequences of their actions, or inactions, until they got older. Consider a few examples of movie and theater settings. A retired teacher, June Bates, in the Southwest gives us another example of this reality:

We could go to the movies, but . . . we had to go and sit in what we used to call the "buzzard roof." And . . . as I said before, we went there we would see the movie, we were just glad and would enjoy it. We didn't realize this was something terrible. And of course, as time passed, we did. We were able to look back and say, "You know that was a shame!" But at the time we didn't know it was a shame. And we stayed with our friends, we stayed in our neighborhood and we enjoyed each other. (*June Bates, 70s*)

African Americans were forced to sit in the balcony, high enough up that they termed it the "buzzard roof." Although most of our interview accounts reveal sadness, horrific events, and blatant violations of human dignity, these are only one side of the Jim Crow story. We also see much evidence in the interviews of the great determination and remarkable resiliency of African Americans even in the face of such extreme everyday adversity.

Although black children may not have been aware of the reasons why whites treated them differently, they quickly realized that whites had it better. Marge Gray, a respondent in the Southwest, recalls going to the theater when she was around 12 years old. She recalls sitting next to her younger sister:

> It had to be, yeah, because at the time it was me, and my sister, and brother going to the show, mmm hmm. And my sister was little and momma always told us, hold her by the hand, 'cause you know, 'cause she wanted to go to the show with us, and we had to sit upstairs at the [theater name]. I mean they did have a black show. It, our show was called the "[names theater]," and momma and daddy didn't like for us to go down there. So, at the time, everybody started going to the [white theater] 'cause the [white theater] showed better pictures than the [black theater] did. They'd show any kind of pictures down at the [white theater], and so at the time we had to go upstairs with the blacks, the whites got to sit downstairs, I remember that. And . . . if somebody come up to the concession stand . . . if you were there first, I mean, you had to wait and let [whites] go and get their stuff and all that kind of old stuff. . . . I remember that. . . . I felt bad because you . . . had to sit upstairs, everybody couldn't sit down in the show together. (*Marge Gray, 80s*)

She continues by describing what happened when integration finally came to that historically white theater:

> It was a long time before they integrated the show, it was a . . . very long time. And then when they did integrate the show, the blacks still wanted to sit upstairs. . . . They had treated us, treated us so bad, [we] still didn't want to go downstairs, 'cause [we] didn't know what was going to happen. I mean, I mean, there was, I mean, they'd come in there and get to fighting in the show and somebody would get hurt. Yeah, yeah, it was always a fight in the show. I mean, you know, and then they started integrating the stuff little by little, little by little. They say, "Well, the blacks can go ahead if they want to." And a lot of them was still probably scared to go, 'cause they didn't know if somebody was gone go in there and come there and shoot and kill you. And they still wouldn't go . . . and didn't nobody want to get killed, so the blacks still stayed on they side of town. . . . Oh yeah, it's all right for them to come in a white restaurant and sit down, and then you didn't know whether you going to go in a white restaurant

and some white boys, Ku Klux Klan, will see you and go out there and start shooting, shooting and kill you. They were doing that probably back in the 60s. They didn't care nothing about blacks. (*Marge Gray, 80s*)

Certainly, the white fear of black men is well-recognized and discussed in this society, and that fear is regularly signaled today when whites cross the street or white women clutch their purses when they cross paths with black men. However, the reality of white terrorism directed against African Americans over centuries is very rarely discussed in white-controlled media and other settings in this society. Here Marge Gray notes the extremely common and necessary *black* fears of white assaults and other violence in retaliation for entering white spaces, even after legal segregation officially ended.

Consider too Gray's evidence in regard to white violence even as Jim Crow officially ended in the mid-to-late 1960s. That official end to legal segregation, brought theoretically in the major civil rights acts of the 1960s, did not actually bring full racial desegregation in many institutions until the 1970s and 1980s. For at least a decade, and in some cases several decades, black Americans did not feel truly free to act on the changes officially brought by these desegregation laws. As Gray states, whites "didn't care nothing about blacks." Indeed, to the present day, these civil rights laws have not been fully enforced, and thus have not brought a major dismantling of this society's racial hierarchy.

SURVEILLANCE AND CONTROLLING BLACK BODIES: NEGATIVE INTERACTIONS WITH THE POLICE

Our respondents often discussed the role of white police officers in enforcing legal segregation in many of its most oppressive forms. At best, the police were a possible resource to file a complaint of white discrimination, and even then, more often than not, nothing positive would result. At worst, the police instigated their own antiblack violence and assaulted black men, women, and children in public spaces or in jail, such as after an arrest for trumped-up violations of Jim Crow norms or for civil disobedience. Indeed, many white officers in the South in this era were active members in or sympathizers with white terrorist groups like the Ku Klux Klan.[8]

One older respondent, Pamela Malone, shares how her disabled brother had an experience with white police officers:

> My brother was at a place, and he said something. I don't know what it was, and he was crippled from that accident; it left him crippled. And the policeman . . . sheriff or whatever. He was at this place, and he said something. And they didn't like it, and they told him to come outside, and they put him in the car. And they beat him up. And . . . dropped him along the road. And it was nothing done, nothing was done. And he had not committed any crime or anything. Good thing I guess God took that man. It just hurt. We were all just so hurt that they would take a crippled man that did nothing. . . . I don't know what he could have said, but words, you not suppose to get beat up for words. But I can't remember what he said, something, and they told him to come outside and they took him outside and put him in the car and took him down the road and beat him up. He was, his eyes were all black. He was already crippled from that, and that's the worst. [*Did you report the beating?*] They did report it. It was just nothing done. Only God could take care of that. His wife died, and he committed suicide, I think. It just, that's just something that just hurt you so much. I almost didn't move to [this town] on account of that. (*Pamela Malone, 60s*)

Police officers are supposedly charged with protecting all citizens, yet white officers inflicted violence on the disabled brother. In southern and border states racist white judges also left African Americans with little chance of due process. Although blacks sometimes followed legal protocol by reporting acts of white violence, in most instances whites evaded any accountability or punishment. Pamela Malone searches for meaning and justification, yet can find no cause for the police violence. Often just challenging white dominance with words was justification enough for white retaliation. As is evident in numerous interviews quoted in this and later chapters, even looking the wrong way at whites could result in white violence. In her case religious faith is invoked as a source of comfort, as is seen in the comment that it was good that God took her brother. She notes too, multiple times, that it "just hurt," indeed probably for the whole family. This racialized pain may well have contributed to her brother's suicide. Historically, the topic of suicide in African American communities has been taboo, even though the rates of suicide for blacks have been much lower than for whites. Indeed, only recently have researchers and mental health practitioners begun to do research on the topic of African American suicide.[9]

Other respondents emphasized the often unnecessary and persistent surveillance by white police officers in their neighborhoods. One respondent, Alfred Richardson, states, "In our neighborhood it had got so bad that you couldn't hardly go out because the police was always on you. And you go to another part of the town and the police was just on you because of the times." Black citizens were frequently followed or under other close surveillance of white officers, as well as of ordinary whites, whether they were in white spaces or in their own neighborhoods. Most lived, worked, and played under constant white scrutiny to ensure they obeyed the norms of the white supremacy system.

Several respondents noted the differential treatment meted out by white police officers for white and black offenders. Ann Hart, a respondent in the Southwest, recalls incidents where the punishments for breaking the law were only applied to blacks:

> I know one evening we came from work, and there was a person out there that was drunk. And this person was white, and they called the cops, and the cops came out and sent him home instead of arresting him. He drove around the corner, into somebody's fence, into somebody's house. Just a few days before that one of my husband's subordinates had been stopped and he was drunk. You know what they did to him? They took him to jail. So there are some rules . . . of a town or a city, especially like [this town], [that] are made for you and I. They are not made for them. That may be everywhere, but rules and regulations we must abide by them, but they bend them for their own. . . . And if the law says you go to jail when you're drunk, that's what you should do. The white man—they sent him home and he ran into somebody's yard, tore up the yard and torn up somebody's house. The black man—they took him to jail. What does that tell you? (*Ann Hart, 80s*)

Criminologists have shown that, in the past and the present, white police, prosecutors, judges, correction officers, and paroling authorities have frequently used their discretion in discriminatory ways in deciding how to proceed in situations of lawbreaking. Of course, discretion is often necessary because policymakers can't create laws that encompass all conduct and because the prosecution of every law violation would overwhelm the criminal justice system. However, researchers have demonstrated that discretion is often biased in the direction of white privilege, of the unearned and invisible benefits that the dominant group takes for granted as normal.[10] Ann Hart is not angry that the black man was taken to jail; she is angry at the differential treatment. The expectation that the police will take an intoxicated white or black driver to jail is linked to the desire to maintain safety in the community so that no one gets hurt, as could have happened here.

Ida Barnett, a respondent in the Southwest, recalls the frequency with which white officers killed blacks, especially black men, and then justified their actions with often flimsy excuses such as self-defense or by claiming the black person was resisting arrest:

> In the community there . . . were several, a lot of black people getting killed. Black people just being killed like someone killing a stray animal. It happened a lot. The one that stands out the most. There was an older man, a black minister of sorts back in that time. He was known to everybody as . . . Reverend Jack. And he had a courtship with a lady, a black lady in our neighborhood. . . . He was in his late 60s or 70s. He had a girlfriend and he had a confrontation. He wasn't far from my house. She called the police, and they came there and gunned him down just like he was an animal. And they claimed he had a gun; there was no evidence of that. (*Ida Barnett, 60s*)

She continues with more details about these police malpractice events, which she emphasizes were commonplace:

> And that was just one of many, many cases of such. And a black could be having a squabble with his wife and they would go in and beat him up, brutalize him. He was just an ordinary man, he was angry and say something, and they would come up. And instead of talking to him like a man they would be like, "Boy, shut up." No man wants to hear this. Then they would beat him up and kill him and claim that he was resisting arrest. This happened frequently throughout the South in those years. And it kept happening for a time even after I left. And it kept happening until really the civil rights movement really picked up steam, and people started fighting back on large scales. Then it started to wane some, then the laws started to change, then folks started to be prosecuted for killing people. It hadn't been that long

since they were getting away with it, a white cop killing a black man, or a white person killing a black person, they were getting acquitted. There was no consequence and that's on a general scale, largely throughout the South. I don't know too many personally that it happened to. But I remember that because it happened down the street from me and I was old enough to remember. I think I was in my teens. I could understand all of that, what went on. I knew him; he would walk by our house every day. He had odd jobs; he would mow grass for people, trim trees. He was known throughout the community and it left a bitter taste afterwards. (*Ida Barnett, 60s*)

White police officers had the resources and authority to assault or murder African Americans, often like "a stray animal," with the excuse of them resisting arrest or of self-defense even if no weapons were found. This elderly man was compared not only with animals, but also with a child. Like most other black men in this era, he was referred to as "boy," verbal discrimination that served to emasculate and deny him the dignity of a real name. Whites had individual and collective control over Jim Crow institutions, including every aspect of the criminal justice system. African Americans usually had no recourse, except documenting the injustices in the few black-owned newspapers and, perhaps, hoping for national or international attention to their oppressed plight in the South.

Barnett explains that she didn't know the minister personally, yet was still impacted by the events. In the case of the segregation stress syndrome, black individuals need not have personally experienced discriminatory events to feel their impact. Moreover, knowing that such police brutality and murder took place in their communities was enough to send a message of warning: The police were not to be trusted and could bring more harm than good. There is evidence of this warning in other events during this legal segregation era. For example, in May 1954, in Little Rock, Arkansas, 12-year-old Melba Patillo, one of the "Little Rock Nine" who desegregated the local public schools, was chased by a white man who attempted to rape her in retaliation for the Supreme Court ruling. He ripped off her underwear as she managed to escape. Patillo's enraged father said, "We ain't gonna call the law. Those white police are liable to do something worse to her than what already happened."[11]

Let's be clear here. We aren't sympathizing with black or white perpetrators of intimate personal violence. Domestic violence has long been common in all communities and often has serious consequences for survivors of intimate personal violence as well as for the larger community and law enforcement responders.[12] However, the recurring problem in the Jim Crow era was that white police officers often took any opportunity to justify physical violence against black men and to rationalize their behavior with excuses such as the men were resisting arrest or the police would claim self-defense. Then as now, these police practices also have had consequences for black women who are victims of domestic violence.

Today black women experience intimate partner (husband, boy-friend) violence at rates higher than for whites, yet are still less likely to report their abusers, often because of negative interactions with white police. Black women often hesitate to call for police assistance because they distrust the police and they also know black men's vulnerability to police brutality. Black women are thus victimized by interpersonal violence and again by a white-run "justice" system that criminalizes black men and pathologizes black family relationships. Other contributing factors to black women's reluctance to seeking help services are the common negative stereotypes that black women are "strong, domineering, angry, and in control." In addition, in their communities black women have often been socialized to remain silent about domestic violence and to put their faith in God and the church. Unfortunately, this has created an environment where black womanhood and spirituality are pitted against each other and thus often creates significant internal conflict.[13]

THE ULTIMATE WHITE CONTROL: TERRORISTIC LYNCHINGS

As we have seen in numerous previous accounts, black southerners, young and old, were familiar with the white terrorism that took the form of recurring threats and realities of lynchings. Public displays of this type of white torture, dismemberment, and murder were part of a larger system of control to maintain white dominance. Like other respondents, an elderly woman, Viola Pryor, in the Southwest remembers her mother telling her about one such brutal lynching:

> My mother told me that at one time she saw a [black] man be lynched and they had dragged him. . . . They had tarred and feathered him I think. And they had dragged him behind . . . I forgot if it was a vehicle. . . . I don't know if it was from a horse or what. . . . She said that was the horriblest sight she had ever seen in her life. She didn't tell me what the person had done. (*Viola Pryor, 70s*)

Tar and feathering was one form of mob punishment against African Americans in this era, with the goal of great pain and group humiliation.[14] In this case, such bodily degradation was followed by the victim's flesh ripped off him as he was dragged to his death. African Americans were, in many instances, tortured before they were lynched. Their fingers, ears, and other body parts were often removed, and they were stabbed, beaten, and burned.[15] This horrific brutality and suffering almost always extended well beyond the victim to family, friends, witnesses, and those just hearing about the traumatic event in the broader community. A public lynching created "a poisoned atmosphere, one that permeated life far beyond those counties where a lynching had actually taken place."[16]

White mob lynchings of black men, women, and children were commonplace during the long legal segregation era. Recall our discussion in a previous chapter of some elderly respondents' painful recollections of local places called the "Hanging Tree" or "Lynch Hammock." In the latter case, respondent Ruby McKnight referenced an area in a state where at least half a dozen African Americans were lynched by white mobs in the early decades of the twentieth century. The brutal lynchings were so institutionalized that this particular area was named "Lynch Hammock."[17] In McKnight's larger interview she makes clear her fear in parenting a son, for simply being a black boy was all it took to create a risk of being lynched by whites. She also accents the normality of the fear of white terrorism for African Americans living in this Jim Crow era.

Respondent Flora Holland, a retired nurse living in a southeastern state, describes the actions of white supremacist groups and individuals:

They did used to hang people. . . . The last two, I know was [names two young men] . . . caught them with a white girl. I think they were fooling around with the girl all the time, and she just got caught. . . . They hung them . . . I don't know too much about it because they didn't put it in the paper, and I just heard mom and them talking about it in the house. [Whites] just went, broke into the house, and just grabbed them while they was sleeping. They say that, the girl say that they raped her. [*Was there a trial?*] No. . . . Those boys were teenagers, they might have been about nineteen, twenty. . . . They were young! (*Flora Holland, 70s*)

Holland shares with us that the two young black men were lynched because a white female claimed she was raped. This allegation doubtless fed common white notions that black men were a threat to white womanhood, and by extension to white racial purity. Official records of lynchings indicate that the raping of a white woman was one of the charges frequently alleged by whites as justification for these mob executions. However, many of these charges were fictional and just excuses for killings. In addition, white charges of "rape" sometimes included a black man merely looking at a white woman in a way whites charged as inappropriate. These alleged crimes were defined based on a varying white standard. Other such "crimes" included "attempting to register to vote," "annoying a white woman," or "testifying against a white man" and were also sometimes punishable by death.[18]

Being accused of a crime is certainly not the same as actually being guilty, and several researchers have found that black lynching victims were often innocent. Arthur Raper's study of nearly 100 lynchings convinced him that about one-third of the victims were falsely accused.[19] White mobs often misidentified the black perpetrator they were seeking, and it was common for whites to assault or kill a family member if the alleged perpetrator couldn't be found. Even though whites controlled the criminal justice system, white mobs still ignored the law and took matters into their own hands. They often broke into black homes or jails to capture their targets. As noted by this respondent, African Americans did not have the opportunity to defend themselves in a trial, although even if they did, the odds were never in their favor.

Holland explains that the white girl "got caught" with the black boys. In numerous documented cases the cross-racial relationships that led to a lynching did exist, but were consensual—a reality that few whites could publicly accept in the Jim Crow South. Scholars Danielle McGuire and Lisa Lindquist Dorr found that it wasn't uncommon for these white women to claim rape if they wanted to elude legal prosecution or informal punishments themselves.[20] For example, in March 1931 in Scottsboro, Alabama, two white women hitchhiked on a freight train and were found by the police. Fearing arrest, they claimed they had been raped by black men on the train. The white community stood behind the women, even after one retracted her charges and evidence surfaced that the women were prostitutes. With strong support from civil rights organizations, the nine men eventually were acquitted of the baseless charges.[21]

Not only did whites manufacture the myth that black men frequently sought to rape white women, but whites also overlooked the far more common type of rape in the South—white men raping black women. Compare this latter reality, very common since the Jim Crow era, with the white-framed stereotype that black men are particularly criminal and dangerous for white women. Some probing analysts have suggested that white men project onto black men the very desires and inclinations that white men are much guiltier of—that is, being criminal and dangerous for black women and men.[22]

One final note about the extreme brutality and extensiveness of the white-violence culture of the Jim Crow era: While black men were the most common lynching victims of whites, these terroristic crimes also included scores of black women and children. Consider the extreme white violence against one black woman, 20-year old Mary Turner, who was pregnant. In May 1918 in Brooks County, Georgia, Turner's husband was one of at least a dozen black men killed in a white lynching rampage. The lynchings were in revenge for the killing of an abusive white plantation owner by a black worker whom he had beaten. Turner's widow made the grave mistake of speaking out and arguing that whites responsible for the crime should be punished. Enraged at her courage, white men abducted her, tied her upside down, poured gasoline on her, and cut her stomach open. Following the murder of Turner and her fetus, hundreds of African Americans fled that town.[23]

Black parents sometimes suffered extreme white retaliation for offenses associated with their children. For example, in December 1915 outside Columbus, Mississippi, a black mother was taken to a police station for questioning because her son was accused of setting fire to a white man's barn. She told the police that she didn't know her son's whereabouts. Later that night, white men abducted her and savagely raped and lynched her from a tree.[24] Recurring white terrorism saw to it that a black person's "crime," alleged or real, was punished in a way to send a strong message to all African Americans—that whites had great control over them and their communities. These atrocities were typically not isolated incidents done by a few bigoted whites on the fringes of society seeking only retaliation on behalf of a specific crime. Lynchings were advertised, public, and often large social gatherings that included respected whites—men, women, and children—in the community.

As we have previously noted, from the end of the Civil War to present day, whites' use of lynchings as a repressive technique has brought death to at least 6,000 black men, women, and children. On average, a black man, woman, or child was murdered at least once a week just between 1882 and 1930. Note too that these lynching estimates do not include "legal lynchings" such as local and state executions by means of unjust trials. African Americans were frequently charged with crimes in which the process from arrest to trial to execution would span a very short time.[25]

BLOCKING BLACK ACCESS TO ECONOMIC AND SOCIAL CAPITAL

During the legal segregation era not only were the bodies of African Americans threatened with harm, but so were their property and opportunities to secure resources and assets for their families. Socioeconomic capital comes in many forms, sometimes in the form of property and businesses, and in yet other cases this social capital involves the opportunity to get important resources such as a good education. Numerous respondents noted that in the Jim Crow era they were denied numerous opportunities to build up human capital assets for themselves and their families, assets essential for escaping the poverty imposed on them by centuries of slavery and Jim Crow segregation.

One interviewee, Daniel Stewart, in the Southwest recalls and underscores the significance of inferior school resources for blacks:

And we had a separate school system. It was segregated, although they, the law, the federal government outlawed school segregation in 1954 but it went on for a long time. Because in . . . my hometown they built two . . . high schools, one on the east and one on the west side. The architecture on our school looked better, however inside the school the libraries and all them places, the equipment, the technical stuff like woodworking, all of that stuff was outdated. All of it was inadequate. Yeah, we had the big fancy building, but the books and the teachers and the curriculum we came up short. We came up short. (*Daniel Stewart, 60s*)

He then describes some specific racial barriers he encountered in trying to gain some human capital and learn how to be an auto mechanic:

We had the best instructor, he was a mechanical engineer. He was black, we had all black teachers. But we didn't have the modern equipment needed to learn to leave high school and hit the road running out there as a mechanic. One evening when school closed, we went over to the white school and looked through the window at the shop, and they had all the state-of-the-art equipment, all of it. We were lucky if we had jack. So consequently, when this white boy finished three years of auto mechanic school he would go out there, open a shop if he wanted to. He didn't have to go to trade school no more. . . . We didn't have any of the modern equipment, so when we finished high school, we needed to go on to trade school just to be on par with this guy. Now that's what he had, separate but not equal. The books that we were getting, even in elementary school had pages missing unless your folks bought you the books . . . the white kids had them first. Once the whites' kids were done tearing them up we got them. (*Daniel Stewart, 60s*)

Next he comments on the other ways that legal segregation sharply reduced the socioeconomic capital that black parents and families could develop in this oppressive era:

And our parents were paying the same taxes as everyone else, and what's worse, our parents were working much harder to get the money. Because they just had two pay scales, they were not allowed to pay a black person the same amount as a white person. It wasn't going to happen. White person side by side, was able to live as mid-

dle class, while the black person was in poverty. He couldn't afford
what the white man could afford, and they were doing the same job
every day, side by side. That was how difficult it was. That's how it
was at school; they made sure that it was that way, that we were left
behind. It was structured; they made sure it was that way. Then
when in the later years, what I laugh at, it was my home state, and I
don't like folks living on welfare. But then I look back, and why are
they complaining? They structured it that way, they didn't want them
to have education. (*Daniel Stewart, 60s*)

Elsewhere the second author has explained how a central feature of
slavery and Jim Crow segregation involved continuing and *unjust enrichment* of whites and continuing and *unjust impoverishment* for
African Americans. During long centuries of slavery and Jim Crow, and
continuing today with de facto segregation, African Americans have
long been denied opportunities for major socioeconomic resources like
a good education—resources necessary for generating intergenerational
family wealth.[26] As the "finish line" for one generation is the starting
point for the next, there is a transmission of wealth, or resources for
creating such wealth, across the generations. In this manner significant
assets are accumulated over time in white families, and far fewer assets
(or more debts) are created over time for black families. Centuries of
unjust enrichment for whites and unjust impoverishment for blacks
substantially account for the contemporary statistics of racial inequality.
In the 2010 Survey of Consumer Finances the median wealth of white
families was $124,000, about eight times that of black families
($16,000).[27] While many whites today justify this huge wealth gap by
arguing that their parents and grandparents worked harder than other
racial groups, many African Americans like this respondent recognize
the major impact of unjust structural barriers. The intentional racial
inequalities and supporting white violence of the Jim Crow era involved
more than the actions of a few white bigots, but were the result of white
group action and, thus, were well-institutionalized in government policies and laws.

Attempts at developing businesses were often destroyed or made
difficult by whites. African Americans were often told by whites, explicitly and implicitly through threats of violence, to stay in their segregated "place" and away from building up businesses. Clyde Baker, a re-

spondent in the Southwest, recalls a cross being burned on his front lawn in retaliation for a café his mother established:

> My mom owned a mom-and-pop café. At the time city ordinances said that you had to have light pole in front of such a place. It was just a light at the top of a pole. Well, where our property ended was some white folks living. . . . One of the white men approached my mother and told her that the light bothered him at night. She told him . . . , "You go inside your house, and pull your shades down. It wouldn't bother you." . . . Well the consequence of that was he got his plans and friends. Back in that day they would get in their cars and put on their brigades and ride into your property and burn crosses or something like that, that was their scare tactic. They burned a cross on our property. (*Clyde Baker, 70s*)

He continues with an account of black bravery in the face of these frequent white terroristic actions in communities like his:

> My mom, well she recognized the car that belonged to one of the neighbors . . . and she confronted him about it. She went down and confronted him with a gun and told him what would happen the next time he messed with her. . . . I was eight or nine. Later I asked her. She had a brown paper bag when she went down there. He came to his fence and she talked to him for about 30 minutes I guess. I asked her later and she told me that she had a gun in that bag. I wasn't close enough to see the gun, but several times I could see that she would move her hand in and out of that bag. She was showing the man her gun. She told me that if he was to come around again, she was going to let of those bullets pierce his skin. And there were no more, there was nothing else said about it. They didn't bother us anymore. She was one of those that they called "crazy." She was labeled as being a "crazy nigger." That was the only real confrontation I ever seen. . . . My mom actually called the cops, and the police came after that. They kicked down the cross. I guess they wrote some kind of report, whatever, but that was the end of that. Probably some of them were in the parade that night. Either they knew the people or were at the next meeting with them. But they knew not to come back. My mother told that man that if the Klan ever came back that she was going to shoot him first; he only lived two places down. She was going to get to him before she died. That was just the way she was made up. But they stayed their distance. (*Clyde Baker, 70s*)

The white man took issue first with the light, then with his mother's refusal to acquiesce to his request, as doing so would put her business in jeopardy for failing to comply with a city ordinance. Given the frequency with which whites attempted to destroy black businesses during the legal segregation era, we can speculate that the white man's complaint had more to do with the black business threatening the white-dominated racial order than only with his annoyance about a light. Whites used legal and informal strategies to force African Americans to submit to their will, and police authorities were often complicit in this process. Cross burnings were common symbols of white oppression and violence, and were often associated with the Ku Klux Klan, the oldest U.S. terrorist organization.

Clyde Baker was a child when he witnessed the burning cross in his yard. Research has shown that witnessing acts of violence as a child, particularly in one's home, which is usually perceived to be a safe haven, is associated with a greater likelihood of developing problems related to PTSD, including behavioral, social, emotional, cognitive, and attitudinal problems.[28] This is true as well for the segregation stress syndrome. This man's mother defended the family as best she could by threatening the neighbor with protective violence. This was a gutsy move, for it potentially put herself and her family in yet more danger of white violence. The gamble paid off in this case, for their family didn't face any further attacks by whites. Not surprisingly, the mother was stigmatized by whites with a label of "crazy nigger," a common white term for blacks who resisted Jim Crow totalitarianism. Instead of viewing the mother's actions as honorable and brave, she is written off as "crazy." Yet, such labeling was a small price to pay for protecting one's family. In many communities some resistance of this type was commonplace, and that courageous resistance has too often been left out of the histories of Jim Crow segregation.

Other black attempts to build up family assets, including property and lands, were not so successful. A retired nurse, Flora Holland, recalls how her aunt was living in a nice home at a desirable location, which led to white retaliatory violence:

> My aunt came here to visit us, and they set the house on fire. And they burned [my cousin] up in the house. When he tried to get out the window, they pushed him back in the house. They just nasty and mean. . . . Black people weren't supposed to live in no really nice

area like that. She was living on this lake, and they wanted it. . . . She was here in [names town], and so they went there. And he was, 'cause they left him home by himself. My cousin, he was a young man. . . . And they just burned . . . the house down and burnt him up in the house. She left that place. She didn't want nothing else to happen. . . . They know who did it, but wasn't nothing they can do about it. All the white people, they stuck together. . . . Back in the '40s. Just like Rosewood. They burned him alive. (*Flora Holland, 70s*)

With sadness in her voice and tears in her eyes, she describes how likely white jealousy turned her family's housing dream into a deadly sequence of events. Collective white jealousy often made the hope of attaining the American dream of a nice home dangerous, and in many cases impossible, for blacks. This was not an isolated incident of white violence, for several respondents shared similar stories to the effect that if whites wanted a property, they would cheat, assault, or kill to get it. Recall the 1923 Rosewood massacre mentioned in a previous chapter. In that case white mobs lit black homes on fire and shot at residents who emerged.[29] Our respondents' interviews strongly suggest that a large but undocumented number of African Americans throughout the South suffered similar atrocities and consequent material and psychological injuries.

In the Southwest, Ray Banks recalls similar accounts of African Americans losing their land and lives to jealous whites:

My grandmother said, "At one time a lot of blacks owned the land that is now owned by whites and that they were forced to sell their land." Those who did not sell lost their lives. Or the land was taken from them by means of taxation and indebtedness that they had incurred and they weren't aware that they were incurring. . . . Some of them were killed to take the land. [Whites] killed some of them to take the land. . . . Some drownings that were later said accidental, but they didn't kill them accidental. I wasn't supposed to hear it because I wasn't supposed to be around when adults were talking. . . . I overheard them talking about a lady who refused the advances of a white man, and how [whites] nearly destroyed her because she refused. I heard they mutilated her. [Long pause and look of disgust.] (*Ray Banks, 50s*)

Reflecting on the brutality routinely supporting segregation, this man cautiously describes the major material losses and severe psychological injuries suffered by many African American families. He recalls the land stolen by whites through an array of techniques: "legal" methods such as excessive taxation or debt and illegal methods such as killings. Much land and other property theft was often done in collusion with white government authorities. Analyst Raymond Winbush has described how African Americans lost significant resources for building up family wealth because of "whitecapping" during the Jim Crow era—that is, the actions of white "night riders who confiscated land from vulnerable blacks."[30] Countless lynching victims were also black landowners. Whites would often invent alleged crimes (such as "reckless eyeballing" of a white woman) against landowning blacks as a way to justify their exile or murder and then more easily acquire their land.[31] Social scientists Darity and Frank report that the destruction and "burning of courthouses, black churches, and homes were common ways of destroying evidence of black land ownership illegally obtained by white terrorists."[32]

Recall that in chapter 2 we also noted the loss of land suffered by numerous black families. Whatever its character and use of violence, this white land theft usually had long-term consequences for black families and communities. A recent Associated Press report found 406 documented cases of black landowners who had 24,000 acres of land stolen from them in just the three decades from 1900 to 1930. Indeed, in the early 1900s black southerners owned more than 15 million acres of land. Strikingly, a century later this number had dwindled to only 1.1 million acres.[33] The present value of the land stolen during Jim Crow decades is difficult to calculate, yet estimates of the lost value range into many billions of dollars. One National Public Radio report examined the dramatic story of Sandra Crawford's great-great-grandfather Anthony Crawford in Abbeville, South Carolina. Crawford was a relatively well-off black farmer who owned more than 400 acres of oil-rich land. Not surprisingly, he was lynched in 1916 after a dispute with a white storeowner. After his murder, Crawford's family was ordered to leave the town within 48 hours, leaving his valuable land behind. Several wealthy white oil barons have secured their wealth from just such stolen black land.[34] Contemporary projects such as the Reclamation of Southern Assets have attempted to reclaim some of this stolen property and other material assets of black families.

Forcing black Americans off their lands or denying them new land ownership also contributed to the emergence of "sundown towns" discussed in an earlier chapter. Between the 1890s and the 1960s many U.S. towns actually excluded all black residents. The term "sundown town" comes from signs posted in towns and cities stating, "Nigger, Don't Let the Sun Set On You In [name of town]."[35] Whites systematically drove African Americans out of many of these towns using economic tactics as well as deadly violence such as arson and lynching—in effect, an example of "racial cleansing."

Ray Banks also notes the mutilation of an African American woman for refusing the advances of a white man. This was a common occurrence during the Jim Crow era. Historically, under the cover of night white men raped not only African American women but also raped and sodomized African American boys and men—a reality of Jim Crow rarely discussed in the historical literature. The failure of state, local, and federal judicial agencies to prosecute whites for such racial violence clearly helped to sustain the formal and informal racist norms of the Jim Crow era.[36]

CONCLUSION

As we have seen in the last two chapters, the everyday surveillance and control of African American bodies in an array of public spaces and places had many severe and lasting impacts on individuals, families, and communities. This was true for individuals in all age groups, both genders, and all classes. For most blacks, recurring contacts with whites were unavoidable. White-racist surveillance was so extensive that blacks were not safe in any public spaces. The last respondent we quoted has communicated to us some painful childhood memories and lessons. In his interview he shook his head in disgust when recalling his hearing of news about vicious attacks on African Americans. Certainly, regularly hearing about white terroristic attacks on African Americans had a major emotional impact on African American children and adults. As we noted previously, social scientists have found that exposure to "second-hand information such as, hearing about rapes, killings, or racist crimes that victimize others via several methods including hearing may cause secondary traumatic stress, anger, sadness, and grief."[37] Black adults in all communities were certainly aware of the psychological damage that could arise from children hearing about such racial atrocities, and they often attempted to shield them from at least some of these negative effects. However, as we have observed in the interview accounts in several chapters now, it was impossible for African American parents to shelter their children from the hundreds of racial traumas that their children would face at the hands of an array of whites, even before they became adults.

In this totalitarian and terroristic Jim Crow system there was little everyday justice, either formally or informally. On most days, and almost everywhere, African Americans encountered an array of acts of formal and informal discrimination that were carried out by many whites in their racially segregated communities. They could not escape these actions, which were deliberate, enforced, extensive, and systemic.

5

RAPE AND RAPE THREATS

More Weapons of White Terror

There were rapes! The white man would rape *girls*. . . . If a white man see a halfway decent woman, if he wanted her, he went up and just grabbed her and start doing whatever he wanted to do to her. You know, she would fight, and say no, but he would beat her up, slap her, knock her down, and just, just take her. That was the norm back then for the white man to do. (*Bessie Bolden, 60s*)

This insightful respondent, Bessie Bolden, clearly underscores these commonplace experiences of many black women during the Jim Crow decades. White men often sexually attacked black women, and usually with impunity. Black Americans endured violence at the hands of white men that was not only racialized but also sexualized and gendered. Yet, today, this dramatic societal reality is typically unremarked or ignored, including by almost all white historical analysts and media commentators.

Utilizing a sociological perspective, we focus in this chapter on individual and collective black experiences with this type of severe racial-sexual trauma. Decades of research on rape and other sexual assaults have demonstrated that these are not about an individual male's compulsion to lust and eroticism. Rape and threats of rape are usually used as a form of social control and power to ensure that subordinate groups remain "in their place."[1] Here we outline the seldom discussed frequency of attempted and completed rapes of black women and children at the hands of white men, and some reasons why such horrific events were common. We discuss the stark disparities between the punishments for black men and white men in regard to such criminal actions, real and alleged, against women of the other racial group: Black men were often attacked or lynched at the mere allegation of their looking the wrong way at a white woman, yet white men often savagely and sexually attacked black women with impunity. Historically, the real story of the extensive rape of black women has mostly been ignored, and the emphasis has been given instead to the imagined or feared possible rape of white women by black men.[2]

CENTURIES OF SLAVERY AND THE RAPE OF BLACK WOMEN

In order to better understand the reality and prevalence of the sexual assault of black women during the decades of legal segregation, it is useful to understand the background history of interracial sexuality during the previous centuries of white enslavement of Africans and African Americans. From the earliest years after enslaved Africans were brought into the colony of Virginia, interracial sexual relationships were aggressively opposed by whites, and several colonies punished such relationships—with the black partner in them receiving the greater punishments. In 1664 the colony of Maryland was the first to legally ban interracial relationships, and was soon followed in this by Virginia.[3] In colonial Virginia, moreover, children from interracial sexual relationships, mostly those involving white male slaveholders and those they enslaved, were defined racially based on the mother's racial status. Some scholars argue that defining the racial status of children based on the mother's racial status further encouraged coercive sexual actions by white slaveholders targeting enslaved black women, as those white men often materially benefited by getting an enslaved child.[4] Colonial laws thus ensured that the institution of slavery would be protected despite, or because of, this sexual coercion of enslaved black women by white men. Recurring sexual assaults by white men of black women were fully legalized and thus encouraged.[5]

When the United States outlawed the importation of enslaved persons in 1808, the system of slavery did not end, and the number of those enslaved still increased. There was a continuing but illegal slave trade, but in many areas there was little need to import enslaved workers when new ones could be made by white rape of enslaved black women or by the forced breeding of enslaved blacks.[6] Some scholars have argued that the goal of the widespread laws against white-black sexual relationships of the colonies, and later of the U.S. states, was not "to prevent sexual relations between White and Black," but rather "'to de-base to a still lower status the offspring of the blacks . . . , to leave women of color without protection against white men,' and to prevent the growth of a free Black population."[7] While the laws clearly banned interracial marriages, they did little to protect enslaved women from white men's unwanted sexual advances.

During the slavery era the widespread rape and other sexual violence imposed by white men on black women is well-documented.[8] In *Slave Life in Georgia*, John Brown recounts an example of the brutality that one black woman endured for resisting a white man's advances:

> [The master's] second son had cast his eyes on a handsome young negro girl, to whom he made dishonest overtures. She would not submit to him, and finding he could not overcome her, he swore he would be revenged. One night he called her out of the gin-house, and then bade me and two or three more, strip her naked; which we did. He then made us throw her down on her face, in front of the door, and hold her whilst he flogged her, the brute with the bull-whip, cutting great gashes of flesh out of her person, at every blow, from five to six inches long. The poor unfortunate girl screamed most awfully all the time, and writhed under our strong arms, rendering it necessary for us to use our united strength to hold her down. He flogged her for half an hour, until he nearly killed her, and then left her to crawl away to her cabin.[9]

Terroristic sexual violence and violent punishment for noncooperation are often reported in the autobiographies of blacks enslaved before the Civil War. Rape, or the threat of rape, further ensured domination and social control over white slaveholders' human "property."[10] White slaveholders also enjoyed an economic benefit as children conceived would be enslaved and boost profits.

Some of the white male slaveholders who engaged in the sexual coercion and rape of enslaved women were most prominent founders of the United States. Consider these four enslaved black children: Ann Dandridge, William Costin, West Ford, and Jack Custis. They were relatives of the first "First Family," George and Martha Washington, because of sexual coercion and rape. Ann Dandridge was Martha Washington's black half-sister. She was born to a black woman (name unrecorded) who was enslaved and sexually coerced by Martha's wealthy slaveholding father, John Dandridge. Later, Martha enslaved Ann as a servant at the large Washington slave plantation, Mt. Vernon in Virginia. There is also strong circumstantial evidence that Martha's son from her first marriage, Jacky Custis, raped Ann Dandridge. The child of that coercion was an enslaved child named William (later, William Costin). Earlier, Martha's first father-in-law, the major slaveholder John Custis, raped an enslaved woman named Alice, who bore him a son named John. Moreover, West Ford's mother was an enslaved servant of Washington's brother John's wife, and his white father was either John Washington himself or his son Bushrod Washington.[11] Most slaveholders, including very powerful white men like these, typically enslaved the biracial children resulting from their sexual predation. During the long slavery era, hundreds of thousands of white slaveholders and other white men sexually attacked and raped black girls and women. Note, thus, how extensive and well-institutionalized these rapacious practices were.

Although the regularity of these sexual assaults and rapes during slavery is well-documented, some sexual assault scholars have been criticized for excluding this extensive racialized rape pattern. For example, Susan Brownmiller, author of the pioneering *Against Our Will: Men, Women, and Rape* (1975), has been criticized for ignoring the recurring rape of black women during and after slavery and for relying on racist stereotypes of black men posing a supposed risk to white women.[12]

Significantly too, during the slavery era numerous laws also sought to prohibit white women from having consensual sexual relationships with men of color. White women were subjected to the harshest of punishments for violating these laws.[13] For example, the original seventeenth-century Maryland law, the Act Concerning Negroes and Other Slaves, "held that if white women, forgetful of their free condition and to the disgrace of our nation, married slaves, they would serve the slave's master until her husband's death."[14] This and similar laws made no mention of white men. Thus, these racial laws were meant to control the sexual activities of white women, whose interracial children were seen as tainted and thus a threat to white "racial purity," which in fact did not exist.

RAPE DURING THE JIM CROW ERA

White hostility toward black male and white female sexual relationships was also extraordinarily strong in the Jim Crow era. As we have seen previously, the mere insinuation that black men were looking in the direction of white women was often enough to justify violent punishment, including death by lynching. Lynchings had been relatively uncommon during slavery, as they destroyed whites' "property." With emancipation, however, whites in the South were free to lynch, and they did so with alarming frequency. Moreover, the rape of black women and girls after emancipation also continued the subjugation of the black community. Sociologist Patricia Hill Collins notes how the reality became more dangerous for black women:

> No longer the property of a *few* White men, African American women became sexually available to *all* White men. As free women who belonged to nobody except themselves and in a climate of violence that meted out severe consequences for their either defending themselves or soliciting Black male protection, Black women could be raped.[15]

Collins's point here is critical. In the case of black women, white supremacy trumped any patriarchal protections that normally extended to (white) women. This threat of rape, with its physical and psychological trauma, was recurring for African American women and girls. Historians have documented rape attacks on black women who simply went about their daily routines, such as working (particularly as domestics in whites' homes), walking down the street with friends, using public transportation, and relaxing in their home.[16]

In the legal segregation era white rapes of black girls and women were frequent, but were significantly underreported, or not reported at all, in white-owned newspapers. Even when they were reported, the long-term consequences for black victims were almost never mentioned. However, black-run newspapers such as the *Atlanta Daily*

World, Chicago Defender, Baltimore Afro-American, and *Philadelphia Tribune* frequently documented the details of these rapes of black women, including providing the testimony of the victim, the perpetrator's information, and the (lack of) criminal justice system responses. These newspapers often detailed a clear, undeniable, and painful picture of the recurring white rapes faced by black women and their families. Newspaper reports often made clear that these black women were law-abiding and from upstanding black families (thereby reflecting concern for the stereotype of "deviant" black women). Such reports also frequently emphasized the black communities' efforts to get justice from a racist criminal justice system. It is clear from our interviews that the incidents that were reported in all newspapers, white and black, represent only a small proportion of those that actually occurred in and around black communities—not only in southern states, but in border and northern states as well.

RAPES OF BLACK WOMEN: JIM CROW'S VIOLENT SEXUAL REALITY

Given the culture of silence and the common feelings of shame surrounding sexual violence, it is not surprising that only a few of our respondents were willing to speak openly about recurring rapes and attempted rapes in their communities. This pain of re-telling violent events has been noted by other scholars. In her important book, *Surviving the Silence: Black Women's Stories of Rape,* Charlotte Pierce-Baker notes that a recounting of rape and its impact can be re-traumatizing for those who experienced it.[17] A few of our brave respondents shared painful stories of family members, neighbors, and friends being raped, or of their own rape or near-rape experiences. Although the events took place decades ago, some still sobbed and cried out at the memory of this horrific violence. Social science and medical research on rape attacks shows that they are so traumatic that they almost always result in a lifetime of serious psychological problems. Not surprisingly, thus, black women who were sexually assaulted or whose close friends or relatives were assaulted have typically suffered from some aspects of the segregation stress syndrome.

Herman Griffin, a respondent living in the Southeast, recalls a rape case in his community and its outcome:

> This lady's name was Elizabeth Smith and she was going to the sanctified church around the corner from Mt. Carmel Church. And she got kidnapped by a white guy, and he took her out in the woods and sodomized her and raped her. . . . He never served a day in jail. (*Herman Griffin, 60s*)

Note again the lack of punishment for the white perpetrator, a typical result for this era. By invoking the church connection of this victim of white violence, the respondent insists that the victim is a good person with upstanding morals. Griffin thereby challenges the white narrative that black women were then "promiscuous" and thus deserving of assault. In his interview he also adds that the woman was unmarried, perhaps suggesting she was a virgin.

Recall the time period. During this era it brought disgrace on a family for any girl or woman to have sexual relations before her marriage.[18] Another interviewee, Lester Martin, likewise accents the upstanding character and virtuousness of the black women:

> Back in those days, [black] women were not promiscuous at all. My granddaddy used to tell me that the only time he could see a lady's ankle, is when . . . she would step in a car, or got on a bus or something. . . . [There was] the whole value system. . . . If a young girl messed around and got pregnant, she was ostracized. The child wasn't. But that was a black eye to the family. That was a black eye to the girl. Shame. For the child and the family, because it was a reflection on the family: I didn't do a good job. And that was the standard back then. (*Lester Martin, 70s*)

The emphasis on the virtue and morality of black women is deliberate, an attempt to circumvent the prevalent white framing of black women as loose in sexual morality, a view often used by whites to rationalize sexual violence.

This respondent underscores the "whole value system," a reality missing from most historical narratives about black families, then as now.[19] It was shameful to the family if an unmarried female became pregnant. A few respondents noted that black women were often forced out of the community if they became pregnant, even if the sexual intercourse was not voluntary. Indeed, black-run newspapers periodically urged women to marry and achieve "true womanhood," often as a means of negating harsh white stereotypes about immoral black women.[20] While this urging revealed that black people held the same conventions of sexual morality as whites, it also entrenched the patriarchal notions that are still evident today. One message sent to black women by black newspapers and by organizations like the National Association of Colored Women was often "get a husband to protect you." Moreover, by calling out the Christian morality of the rape victims, our respondents also convey the point that "moral" women did not deserve rape— which implies that immoral women might deserve it and ostracization. Although we criticize such a perspective, we should remember that it was a calculated resistance strategy against the recurring white rapes in and around black communities.

Black newspaper reporters understood the importance of emphasizing the morality and innocence of black victims. White rapes of black children in particular warranted attention. For example, on October 23, 1915, the *Chicago Defender* reported the rape of a little girl in Kansas by a 62-year-old white man and called that child one of the "best citizens of the race." The white rapist admitted "that he lured the young girl by offering her a quarter," and that he was drunk. A white doctor verified the rape, noting, "There was not a question as to what had been done, and someone was guilty."[21] We can only imagine the extreme and lasting trauma such young people, and their parents, thereby experienced.

Vivian Simon, a respondent in the Southeast, boldly shares a personal example of how she was sexually molested. She begins by sharing the lessons she learned from her elders about surviving Jim Crow oppression:

> The only thing . . . is not to be caught out nowhere by yourself and different things. The one time . . . my mother let me went to pick some peas with a white man, one morning. . . . I got on in the truck, and we went on down the road and, ah, all of a sudden he's reached over there to grab me. I was just beating that man like I was crazy. He yelled. "Stop! Stop!" I said, "You keep your hands where they're supposed to go 'cause they don't go on me!" I said, "You leave me alone!" I got out of the truck and . . . walked back to my house. (*Vivian Simon, 70s*)

She continues with many details on her father's response to the attack:

> So as I was going back, my daddy and my mother, and the [white] man's brother was standing right there talking. They said, "What, you back? I thought you was going." . . . And I went over there and told everybody. . . . And my daddy got so mad, he said, "I'm going to kill that cracker! I'm going to kill him!" [His white brother] said, "No you ain't. You ain't going to kill him. I'm going to kill him!" That was his brother saying. His brother saying, "You know not to touch no girl like that. That is a little young girl!" . . . I was more mad than I was scared! 'Cause I ain't wanting no man to touch me. . . . [His brother] said [to the man], "How would you feel like if you had a daughter and a black man was caught with her? You would, you would be ready to hang him, wouldn't you." And he say, "Yeah, I reckon I sure probably would have." "Well, that's how he feels about you. He feels like killing you right now." . . . My Dad was ready to kill him. And he say, "You wouldn't want me to touch your child. *That's right.* Well, I feel about mine just like you feel about yours." [My mom] said [to me], "You did right by coming to tell. A lot of people would try to make like they scared and don't come up and tell it right then. You told it right then. And you done good." I said, "That's what I'm gonna do [to] anybody touch me that's don't supposed to touch me, I going to tell them. I'm a good girl, my mama raised me." (*Vivian Simon,* 70s)

Vivian Simon shares her experiences with assault at the age of 13. Her father was outraged, yet the police were not summoned, and the white man was never held accountable. We also observe the role that other whites sometimes played. The man's brother serves here as an intermediary between the white attacker and the black family and appears to appease the family. Note too that the respondent ends her narrative by pointing out that she is a "good girl." While she does thereby accent the problematical narrative of black respectability criticized above, she also strongly shows that a brave young woman could have agency in resisting white-racist myths about young women like herself. In the Jim Crow era (as is still true today) the burden often fell on young victims to prove that they were not at fault. Her resistance was also powerful. While it ended well, this was not always the case in an era when blacks were frequently punished for even reporting white atrocities.

In the research literature the term "second rape" is sometimes used to refer to rape survivors' experiences of victim-blaming by people in the criminal justice system or social service and medical agencies, which blaming can significantly increase the victims' suffering.[22] During the Jim Crow period, black rape victims who reported an assault ran great risk of being blamed and having their sexual history aggressively scrutinized.[23] In addition, black victims often had to worry about retaliation from the white attacker or the broader white community. They ran the risk of future violence. The rape victims' feelings of fear, hyper-vigilance, and uncertainty about what might happen are again aspects of the segregation stress syndrome.

Consider the experiences of Recy Taylor, a 24-year-old wife and mother who is heralded as one of the early "organizational sparks" for the civil rights movement against legal segregation. In September 1944 in Abbeville, Alabama, she was walking home from church and was abducted at gunpoint by white men in a car. They drove to a remote spot where she was gang-raped and left for dead. Although the men admitted to the crime, they only had to pay a modest fine. The black community was outraged and appealed to the NAACP, which sent their best field reporter to investigate, the later famous Rosa Parks. A trial was held, yet after a five-minute deliberation by an all-white jury, the case was dismissed. Following the trial, Taylor received multiple death threats, and her home was firebombed. The white sheriff also accused Taylor of "being nothing but a whore around Abbeville."[24] Such tactics of victim-shaming were a common tactic to silence those who challenged white hegemonic supremacy. Taylor noted, "I felt like if I tried to push it, to try to get them put in jail, I thought maybe it would be bad on me, so I just left town."[25] Once again, there was no justice for a black woman who was a victim of extreme white violence.

In October 2010 the Associated Press did a phone interview with Mrs. Taylor from her Florida home about the brutal attack that occurred over 60 years previously. Her words offer insight into the lives of all black women who have endured the mental anguish and psychological consequences of assaults like this one. At age 90, she reflected, "They shouldn't have did that. I never give them no reason to do it." She still recalls her great fear after the white attack: "I didn't go out at night. And then I got afraid of living right there after that happened too, 'cause I was afraid that maybe something else might happen." Throughout her interview, she insists that "I was an honest person and living right." Again, Mrs. Taylor is urging the listener to see her not as a stereotypical "loose" black woman caricature, but as an upstanding citizen worthy of dignity and respect. In addition, her brother was interviewed. He commented on how his sister's rape still impacts him today: "I still don't like what happened. . . . It has never been a week that went by where it didn't cross my mind. . . . It made me feel terrible." Clearly, black family members also endured extreme racialized traumas, whose effects can be seen to the present day in various forms of the segregation stress syndrome.

Like the overwhelming majority of black women assaulted in the legal segregation decades, Taylor never received justice. In the recent interviews she stated that her "desire for closure is still there, more than 60 years later."[26] Asked about an apology from the state agencies that were involved, even after six decades, Mrs. Taylor said, "It would mean a whole lot to me."

RAPES OF CHILDREN AND PROTECTIVE SOCIALIZATION

Scholars and other analysts have long argued that sexual assault is not about an individual man's desire to fulfill sexual urges, but is about maintaining male power and dominance. Nowhere is this better demonstrated than in the many white male attacks on black children in this era. Black parents had a difficult time protecting their children from these white rapists. They usually socialized their children to be on their best behavior around whites, to listen to them, but not trust them. Unfortunately, too many also had to endure the tragedy of helplessly listening to horrific details of violence that their children sustained in interactions with whites.

Recall from the first page of this chapter Bessie Bolden's comments about rape being extensive in the Jim Crow era. She is a retired service worker who in her interview shares yet more details about life under constant assault and rape threats when she was growing up. Listen to her additional comments:

There were rapes! The white man would rape *girls*. . . . If a white man see a halfway decent woman, if he wanted her, he went up and just grabbed her and start doing whatever he wanted to do to her. . . . That was the norm back then for the white man to do. If you just happened to be in an area where they [whites] were, it could happen to you. We were basically homebound people, so, we didn't get out much. We would have to walk to school when we were kids coming up. We walked for two miles just to get to school so it wasn't any area to where it was predominately white. . . . It was predominately [a] black area of town. . . . My dad was . . . an overseer, him and my grandfather. And when it came to us being out and about, they always forewarned us to be on the very best behavior, no matter what that white person would say to us. Always "yes sir/no sir, thank you sir" or whatever . . . never show any attitude or any animosity for all that would lead to was either a beating, rape, or killing. (*Bessie Bolden, 60s*)

This remarkable woman articulates the overt socialization she received from her family: listen and defer to whites. This African American strategy involved much difficult emotional labor. Indeed, throughout the interviews we find respondents noting that they had to manage their emotions in settings where whites were present. As this respondent explains, blacks could "never show any attitude or any animosity," lest a lack of deferential treatment lead to white violence. In effect, African Americans had to put on a "mask" in daily dealings with whites, a masking that could have negative effects on their health over time.[27] Note too that the white threat of sexual assault was used to keep her "in her place," which was in her predominately black area of town. Importantly, this respondent takes it for granted that whites would look for lack of deference as an invitation for such violence. At the end of her narrative, she links physical assault, sexual assault, and murder—all powerful white tools of systemic racial subordination.

To defer to whites or to suffer violence, that was often the challenge for African American children. On the one hand, they were taught to obey and show deference to whites. Yet, they also were taught that whites cannot always be trusted. For example, in April 1916, the *Chicago Defender* ran a story about a 13-year-old black girl. The child was living with her grandfather, who was out working. A white man asked her for a glass of water, which request she obliged. The man entered the house and raped her. When the grandfather returned to home, the white rapist was still there and begged for mercy. The child was examined by doctors who "found all the evidence of virginity and of rape." Nonetheless, no charges were brought against the man. According to the paper, "the girl had took cold feet and was afraid to prosecute the man."[28] We see a pattern of children surviving a racially traumatic event, yet still suffering from the psychological consequences of the segregation stress syndrome, such as in this case fear of what might happen if they do testify.

Our respondents frequently discussed the messages they received from black elders about how to defend themselves from white threats. Wilma Oliver, a respondent in the Southeast, recalls the diverse strategies her father used to protect his daughters:

> My dad use to have his gun by his side. He didn't allow white men to see us. If a white man came to our house to sell something or pick up payment for a bill, my dad would tell us girls to go in the house and stay out of sight. He knew about the bad things that happened to girls, and he didn't want it to happen to us. We would stay out of sight and hide. (*Wilma Oliver, 60s*)

Knowing the frequency of white sexual assaults, this father tried to shield his daughters from some painful realities of Jim Crow. In addition, Oliver indicates that young girls were often homebound because of the intergenerational transmission of savvy knowledge about whites. Young girls were frequently encouraged to be invisible and avoid white men, and even then they were not truly safe, even in their own homes.

Attacks on girls and women could happen at any moment, even in one's private home. Nighttime was an especially dangerous time for all African Americans. Under the cover of night, whites often collectively imposed racial violence. Blacks who were thought to have violated the dominant racial norms were frequent targets. Recalling his first memories of whites, a former professor, Phillip Bailey, recalls his mother's warnings about the sexual violence that could happen to black boys as well as girls:

> My mother used to insist that I always be in the yard before the sun go down. I could not understand that. Until one day, they call them night riders, they kidnapped a black kid. And they sodomized him

and castrated him. My mother said, "Now you see why I want you to stay in the house." . . . Night riders would come, white guys would come to the black community in trucks and cars and kidnap black kids and stuff of that nature. . . . That happened in other communities. . . . I'm sure the adults knew who these people were. But who could they turn to? There was nobody. The NAACP would send people through as representatives but you had, that was a hush-hush thing. And it was held at a church. And people were very quiet about where they were going to have these meetings because the church could be burned to the ground. It happened in other communities. . . . Black people just disappeared. (*Phillip Bailey, 60s*)

Reflecting on the routine brutality of white "night riders," this respondent describes the severe physical and psychological injuries suffered by racially targeted black families. Although females were the most frequent targets of sexual violence, males were also targeted for rape and castration. Blacks did sometimes resist, such as by threatening whites with a weapon, as was alluded to in the previous narrative of a father who keeps a gun at his side. However, even this defensive strategy always risked retaliatory violence on a larger scale, including lynchings and the burning up of black churches.[29] Moreover, black adults (and their children) who were perceived by whites to be community organizers or who attended civil rights meetings were especially at risk, as this respondent notes.

RAPES OF GIRLS AND WOMEN: ECONOMIC DIMENSIONS

Jim Crow institutions offered few opportunities for economic stability or mobility for African Americans. White perpetrators were aware of black impoverishment and sometimes used it to manipulate children and their families. In their efforts to obtain employment to secure the economic stability of their families, black girls and women became more vulnerable to sexual advances, abuse, and rape at the hands of white men. This was particularly true when they worked as domestics in white households, but it was also evident in public streets. One of our respondents in the Southwest, Pearl Ward, recalls such a white rapist:

I have . . . a cousin, I called her Aunt Bell. . . . She told me that this white prostitute across the street, Ms. Ann, my auntie worked for her [as a domestic worker], and she was over there working one day and this [white] man that owned a store a block up the street, came to see Ms. Ann. . . . He was married. Ms. Ann wasn't there. He raped my aunt and my aunt got pregnant and when she got pregnant she told [her family] what happened. She told them that he had raped her that day. And they went to talk to him, and you know what they [whites] did? They made her leave town. They said you have to send her out of town, and my aunt said that is what they did to blacks. The white men would rape the black girls, and if the black girls got pregnant, the families would have to send them out of town to have the babies. (*Pearl Ward, 70s*)

The raping of black women was a frequent occurrence in much of the South and in some border states, a part of U.S. history usually covered up today in white histories. African American women can often still identify the white male criminals, including prominent members of the community, who participated in such racially targeted violence. This young woman experienced a racially traumatic event, attempted to get justice from her attacker, and was forced to leave town, thereby also losing support from her family and community. Much violence that occurred during legal segregation was sanctioned, witnessed, or assisted in by law enforcement officials and other prominent whites. That societal reality makes it harder even now to get to the historical truths about such violent racial oppression.

All too often, white men lured black girls and women into unsafe spaces for the purpose of sexual exploitation. For example, the *Chicago Defender* profiled an attack on a 14-year-old girl on November 1, 1947, in Goldsboro, North Carolina. A 35-year-old white man convinced a black girl who had previously babysat for his family that she was needed to work at 4:00 a.m. because his wife was ill. According to the girl, he "drove to a secluded spot outside of town and threatened to kill her if she didn't submit to his advances." The mother, suspecting something wrong, called the police who found the partially naked white man and girl on the outskirts of town.[30]

THE PLACES AND PERPETRATORS OF RAPE

In some instances, the rapes of women and children occurred in their own homes. Although one's home is usually viewed as a safe space, that was not the case during the Jim Crow era. It was common in numerous areas for whites to enter African American homes without permission, often with the goal of committing rape, assault, or murder. Many of these atrocities were enacted by or ignored by white authorities, including the police. If reported, they were only in black newspapers. For example, in the border state of Missouri, on May 31, 1919, a *Chicago Defender* headline read, "White Man Rapes Six-Year-Old Girl." A 35-year-old white man raped a six-year-old in her home while her mother was visiting friends. The rapist followed the six-year-old home from school, then "gave her a nickel, forced her to sit upon his knee, and attempted to assault her." The mother returned to find the 35-year-old in the bedroom with her daughter, and the child's clothes "were badly torn and blood stained."[31] The white man didn't deny that he raped the child. The mother chased him from the house and called the police.

The white men who committed such extreme violence against black girls and women were not necessarily psychopathic individuals or individuals on the margins of their communities, even though their behaviors suggest that. Many were husbands and fathers, and ordinary—even upstanding—members of their white communities. Moreover, in these reports of white rape, the role of white women was variable. Some even assisted their husbands in sexual assaults. For example, in August 1955, in Greenwood, Mississippi, a black girl was asked to babysit for a wealthy white man. While she was playing with the white child, his wife summoned her and took the girl to her naked husband, who raped her. In this case, a white woman was an accessory to the raping of a black girl.[32]

The social science and medical literatures on child sexual abuse provide overwhelming evidence of the short-term and long-term consequences of such abuse, including psychological, physiological, and social injuries.[33] While there were no rape trauma or psychological counseling centers for these black victims in this era, there was also no guarantee even that basic medical assistance would be available.

DISSENTING WHITES: INDIVIDUAL DISADVANTAGES
AND SOCIETAL ADVANTAGES

In numerous cases some white wives or other white women did intervene on behalf of the black girls and women who were attacked by
white men. For example, on July 24, 1920, the *Philadelphia Tribune* ran
a story about an African American girl who was raped by her white male
employer in Charleston, West Virginia, a border state. In this case the
wife of the rapist risked physical injury by fighting off her husband and
offering the girl assistance. [34] In our interview study there were numerous respondents who spoke about some "good white folks" in their
communities, particularly certain white women. One respondent in the
Southwest, Wilma Pittman, describes how a white woman intervened
when her sister was threatened with rape:

> My sister [and I] were heading to my grandfather's house, and my
> grandfather . . . was a minister. And he had one of those big wash-
> tubs, number five, with a scrub board and stuff on it. We was going
> up there to my grandfather's house. And my sister . . . she always had
> a mouth on her. . . . There was a white man who did say something to
> her one time and, she talked back. [The guys] got out and, hemmed
> her up, and they were gonna rape her if it hadn't been for a [white]
> lady that had came out with a broom. And this is what it was like in
> the, I think it was about '66, '67. I stayed up there until my dad came
> and got her. . . . I knew what my father and my grandfather always
> said, "A steel tongue makes a wise person," and, and just watch what
> you say. And that's what I did. (*Wilma Pittman, 70s*)

As in previous interviews, Pittman recounts how she was socialized
to understand the power that whites had in local communities. The
development of the "steel tongue" suggests that, regardless of how you
felt, silence and deference were the wise lifesaving strategies. Women
who stood up for themselves risked being assaulted. Again and again,
sexual assault was a weapon of terror used to keep black residents in
their very segregated "place" in southern and border state towns and
cities.

Even whites who challenged the racial hierarchy might face mocking, ostracization, or violent punishment. Another respondent in the

Southwest, Beverly Copeland, recalls how there were whites that sometimes wanted to help, but were forced to remain silent too:

> They are much better in that those who wish, that see the injustice of
> the whole thing can act on it without fear of being hurt. Now I might
> have been a white person back there, and [said] about [this black
> man] over here, and "you're not treating him fair." He would imme-
> diately become labeled as a "nigger lover." That's dangerous, that
> was more dangerous than being a "nigger." So [laughs] what were
> they supposed to do? They kept their mouths shut, but today they
> can speak out against it. (*Beverly Copeland, 90s*)

Individual whites who wanted to assist African Americans were often
labeled as "nigger lovers" and could suffer significant consequences.
Caring whites were frequently forced to be silent about the social injustices they witnessed. It may be tempting to assess this situation as "See,
whites had it tough in Jim Crow, too!" However, there is a huge difference between a few individual disadvantages that would accrue to these
more caring whites and the collective, cumulative, and structural disadvantages faced by all African Americans in the same communities. Significantly, the white dissenters usually kept many white privileges even
when speaking out occasionally against Jim Crow patterns.

As is evident in these interview narratives, white supremacy reigned
in every major institution during these long Jim Crow decades, including in the criminal justice, health care, educational, family, religious,
economic, media, and military institutions. In various settings whites
played a variety of social roles—as instigators, supporters, passive by-
standers, passive resisters, or active resisters. Just as African Americans
should not be viewed as a homogeneous group of "helpless victims" in
this era, neither should whites be viewed as a monolithic group of racist
extremists. Certainly, not all whites were responsible for *causing* the
major injustices of the long Jim Crow era, but all did *benefit* from white
privileges. Then as now, white privilege refers to the unearned, often
invisible racial benefits that those in the dominant group take for
granted as normal. Racial privilege is not individually determined, but is
a cumulative and collective societal reality. It is deeply embedded in the
social structures of racial oppression and power of this society.[35]

THE CRIMINAL "INJUSTICE" SYSTEM

Newspaper reports often indicated that the whites who attacked black women and men were important members of white communities and/or had friends in local law enforcement agencies. Not surprisingly, thus, they were seldom seriously prosecuted for these racial crimes. For example, in Kentucky on April 11, 1931, the *New Journal and Guide* reported the rape of a 16-year-old black girl by her white employer. After the child reported the rape, the police still allowed the man to leave town. Similarly, in Birmingham, Alabama, a 12-year-old black girl was raped by a white man who had hired her as a domestic, and in this case the police refused to arrest him. In August 1947, in Meridian, Mississippi, a white oil dealer lured a young woman from her home with the promise of a babysitting job. He drove her to a roadhouse, beat and raped her, and dragged her body behind his car. Nonetheless, an all-white-male jury recommended mercy for the rapist.[36]

In addition to the sympathetic actions or inactions of the police and juries, white judges also intervened to protect white rapists. In July 1960 in Grenada, Mississippi, a white man hired a 16-year-old African American girl as a domestic. When she got into his car, he attacked and raped her. The all-white jury handed down a verdict of "guilty as charged," which made the death sentence mandatory. However, a circuit court judge sentenced him only to "guilty with mercy," sparing his life.[37] In the commonplace white racial framing of this Jim Crow society, white men were fundamentally good and deserved to receive the mercy from other whites if they committed crimes against black people. In the case of these crimes, white criminals were often viewed as "good men who made a mistake." This double standard has long been in operation in the U.S. criminal justice system, including in the present day, as Michelle Alexander has demonstrated in her book, *The New Jim Crow.*[38]

The white judges and other government officials were part of the white male elite that played a central role in implementing the white racist framing and meanings of this Jim Crow era. Late in the slavery era, the chief justice of the U.S. Supreme Court, Roger Taney, declared in his 1857 *Dred Scott v. Sandford* decision that blacks were "beings of an inferior order, and altogether unfit to associate with the white race, either in social or political relations; and so far inferior, that they had no rights which the white man was bound to respect."[39] Nearly 40 years later, this sentiment was echoed in the *Plessy v. Ferguson* case that legitimated the massive spread of "separate but equal" segregation across the South. In that decision Supreme Court Justice Brown stated, "We consider the underlying fallacy of the plaintiff's argument to consist in the assumption that the enforced separation of the two races stamps the colored race with a badge of inferiority. If this be so, it is not by reason of anything found in the act, but solely because the colored race chooses to put that construction upon it."[40] Given this dominant perspective, white southerners had the constitutional right to set up racially segregated facilities as they saw fit. Black women and men still had no rights that white men needed to respect. The sexual assaults of women at the hands of white men were much more than the actions of individual whites, for they were in part a consequence of an institutionally sanctioned criminal justice system that allowed, even encouraged, horrific racial crimes to go unpunished. Whites created and enforced two systems of criminal justice. If the victim of a serious crime was white and the accused black, then lynching and dismemberment were a real possibility. In stark contrast, for the same type of crime, if the victim was black and the accused white, white men usually did not have to fear serious imprisonment, much less execution.

In the legal segregation era whites utilized various strategies to elude serious prosecution. To avoid being placed in a predicament where they might face jail time for kidnapping, assault, rape, and murder, an accused white man commonly used such strategies as these: (1) claiming that he was with a willing partner who had a history of "loose morals" or (2) he was temporarily or permanently insane. For example, in 1932 the *Atlanta Daily World* reported on the rape of a black child by a 58-year-old white storekeeper who "was caught in bed with the tiny tot after doors had been broken down." Rather than holding the rapist criminally responsible, a white jury judged him to be insane. An insanity plea was periodically used by white lawyers in cases where the white rapist and his lawyers apparently thought that the evidence was overwhelming.[41] In Lexington, Kentucky, in 1926, a white man abducted at gunpoint two black sisters (aged 11 and 17) who were walking home one evening. He raped the younger girl while her older sister watched and was unable to assist her sister. After the attack he forced the girls to walk through the streets. The older sister escaped and got help. The *Chicago Defender* reported that the 11-year-old "is in a sanitarium in a serious condition, due to the assault, and her sister is at home suffering from exposure and severe nervous shock." With the help of the NAACP, the white rapist was charged with the crimes of kidnapping and rape. Throughout the trial there were outbursts of sobbing from family members as the older sister explained to the all-white male jury and judge what had happened.[42] Again we see the extreme psychological trauma that black girls and their families suffered as a result of racial assaults. However, even after the convincing testimony of intentional action, the all-white, all-male jury took less than an hour to find the white rapist to be "of unsound mind," and he was sentenced to a mental hospital.

At the time a black newspaper editorial entitled "Color and Crime" compared the treatment of this white man and a black man who was accused of a similar crime in the state of Kentucky. The black man was accused of raping a white woman and was sentenced to death after a pseudo-trial. During his quick trial and immediate state-sanctioned execution, he had to be protected by armed guards to prevent a white mob from lynching him.

> The white man was given a trial by a jury of his peers and it took three days, not seventeen minutes, to find him insane. [He] thereby does not dangle from the end of a murderous rope, but is committed to an institution for the insane and we have no doubt his sanity will soon be restored and he will be permitted to go scot-free while [the black man] lies rotting under the bluegrass of Kentucky and the two little violated girls of dusky hue can find no balm in Gilead for their defiled bodies. It will take a weird imagination to reconcile these two flagrant cases. To Kentucky and the South, however, a philosophy is ever-present that can explain those matters with surprising simplicity. . . . It is not a matter of crime but a matter of color.[43]

Some decades later, the *Philadelphia Tribune* noted on July 4, 1950, that a South Carolina judge sentenced both a white man and a black man to death by electric chair for committing rapes. The white judge noted that the "verdicts should establish beyond all doubt that any person, regardless of race, color or creed, can get justice in South Carolina." However, this decision may have had less to do with seeking justice and more about countering complaints of northerners who were growing less tolerant of southern racial violence. According to this southern judge, there is "very limited news coverage of any and all crime incidents that might be considered unfavorable to the north. . . . Those people up there hate us."[44] Additionally, the severity of the crime committed by the white man was not equal to that of which the black man was accused. The black man, a 19-year-old, was accused of attempting to rape a white woman and received the death sentence. The white man confessed to kidnapping and raping a black woman and confessed to being a serial rapist who had "over-powering desires to force women to do his will."[45]

After the first white man was executed for rape in South Carolina, there was an outcry from some black leaders, such as those in the influential civil rights organization the Congress of Racial Equality (CORE), to halt all executions for rape. For most black leaders this was a civil rights matter because black men were very disproportionately those who were executed for rape. Another reason that black leaders fought to halt all executions was to appeal to the dominant group for the "greater good." By halting all rape executions, white men too would not face this extreme punishment.[46]

IMPACT ON BLACK GENDER RELATIONS

The sexual assaults of black women by white men impacted the relationships African American men and women had with each other. Indeed, black men were often severely punished for trying to protect black women from physical and sexual assaults. One African American commentator has put the matter thus:

> When black men are prevented from defending their women and their children, they are symbolically castrated and assaulted in their essential dignity. Black women, in such a situation, are doubly instrumentalized—as objects of forcible rape and as instruments in the degradation of their men. In this sense, the sexual assaults on black women are part of the reinforcing structure upholding a system of racial and economic exploitation. Physical terror against black men who defend their women is one aspect of this reinforcing structure. . . . Every black man must learn two lessons, if the system of oppression is to survive. "Defend black women—and die!" is one. "Touch white women—and die!" is the other.[47]

In spite of these warnings, black fathers, sons, and brothers frequently risked their lives in trying to protect the girls and women in their families. In most families there was unwavering devotion between women and men.

Although black women were frequently targets of white sexual violence, they often sacrificed their safety, even their lives, to ensure the security of husbands, brothers, and fathers. Consider the brutal violence suffered by a black teenager in Muskogee, Oklahoma, in spring 1914, as recounted by a relative to a black newspaper:

> The young man's sister was but 17 years old and of respectable parents. Two half-drunken white men walked into their home during the absence of the mother and found the girl dressing, locked themselves into her room and criminally assaulted her. Her screams for help were heard by her brother, who, kicking down the door, went to her rescue. In defending his sister, he shot one of the brutes. The other escaped. Later in the evening the local authorities, failing to find the brother, arrested the sister, who was taken from jail by a mob at 4:00 in the morning and lynched. From his hiding place the brother, who is 21 years old, could hear his sister's cries for help, but he was powerless to aid her.[48]

This teenager was a victim of white intruders. The violent injustice was racialized and extraordinarily brutal: She was an innocent victim of home invasion and rape. She was imprisoned, but the laws, police, and courts did not protect her. Her brother had to intervene to protect her, and then flee. Once again, white vigilantes took matters into their own hands and viciously murdered her because they could not find her brother.

One of our respondents in the Southeast, Elise Rowe, tearfully shares her horrific experience with an attempted rape:

> I remember one Sunday afternoon . . . a white man came to our house. I must have been about 15. . . . This man knocked on the door. My mom was sleeping. . . . My brother was in the next room sleeping. I answered the door. The man looked like he was spellbound. It frightened me, so I started backing up and he started following me. He went straight through my mom's bedroom and my brother's bedroom. I ran . . . he was following me. My brother sat up in the bed, to see what was happening. . . . He came behind him. I

can remember . . . my sister saying, "Oh, no, no, Richard. No, no, no." He was going to hurt him. . . . I ran up under the house and hid. He walked in the yard looking for me, and eventually he went on and got in the car. My dad wanted to know who he was. . . . I was never able to tell him who he was. I couldn't remember telling him what he looked like. It frightened me. I was young and it frightened me. I knew that these things happened and I didn't want that to happen to me. . . . It was terrible. . . . It was very frightening. My brother wouldn't have been able to do anything about it. (*Elise Rowe, 80s*)

Although this attempted rape took place several decades in the past, Elise Rowe described in much detail that terrifying day. Such events from long ago are more than "mere history," for many of the participants are, as is quite evident in her weeping, still suffering significantly. These events could have been taken from a Hollywood horror movie: An intruder breaks into your home when most of the family is sleeping. This home is supposed to be your sanctuary, but a strange white man chases you in and around your home. Your loved ones are awakened and consider aggressively resisting. As a savvy teenager, you are aware of the regularity of whites invading black homes and you flee for safety.

In Rowe's interview, much of her discussion of this attempted rape event wasn't focused on the near attack, but on her fear for her brother and father. The female members of the family knew that intervention by male relatives could have terrible consequences, even leading to their death at the hands of a white mob. In the last line of this interview excerpt, the respondent indicates that her brother was powerless to help. In fact, Rowe indicates that her brother was active in the civil rights movement, and it was difficult for him not to interfere. Indeed, later in her interview she recounts that her brother was murdered, perhaps for his outspoken views against the Jim Crow system. She recognizes the white-dominated institutional structures could literally trample on her—and all African Americans'—rights, privacy, and dignity. Note too that the feeling of uncertainty about what might happen next is another important dimension of the segregation stress syndrome. That feeling doesn't end when the racially traumatic event is over, for it very probably continues throughout the lifetimes of all those involved.

Black men who were not relatives also tried to protect girls and women in their communities, often at great cost. An elderly interviewee, Beulah Craig, painfully recalls witnessing a black man lynched primarily as punishment for attempting to defend her:

> There was a man, a black man. He was a janitor, he cleaned up the place, and he went and told this white man that was so mean to me. . . . That he didn't have to treat me the way he was treating me. [The white man] took and pushed me over one of the tables. . . . He got tired of him doing that, before I know it he leaned back and hit that white man and beat him up. It scared me so bad because I didn't know what [the white man] was going to do to him. When the police come, [the white man] had almost beat him to death. You know. So anyways, my parents raised enough money to get him out of jail. [Pauses, then starts to cry.] Somebody, back then, you could go up and down the highway and see the black boy hanging from the tree, and he was dead. They killed him on the tree. . . . I didn't think that I could live to see somebody beat somebody like that man did and not [have anyone] do anything about it. [Cries harder.] (*Beulah Craig, 80s*)

Craig described the penalty her coworker bore for defending her. As was evidenced in her frequent pauses to weep, it was an arduous task to describe such brutal and bloody events. To live during this era was clearly a constant nightmare that required great personal and collective strength and resolve to survive.

She continues with a description of how this black man was horrifically punished for his bravery:

> The white man, they took hot water, they boiled that water, and they put him in the water, and cooked him. How could somebody treat somebody, a human being, and just threw them in the pot! They had a big old pot they use to make soap out of it. And they just throw them in there [the pot]. Whenever you use to do stuff, you were dead. You couldn't do anything, you had to just stand there and watch them do him like that, and every time his head would come up like that, they pushed him right down in the pot. God brought us through all of that, he sure did. He brought us, God made for that person down there to die that day. When we got down there we pray, and we ask God to forgive them, because they didn't know what they was doing. It didn't help his family to see him tortured down there . . . it was a black pot, a cast iron. . . . they rejoiced. Can you

believe that they rejoiced about what they did to him in the black
pot? They rejoiced! (*Beulah Craig, 80s*)

The vivid details of an African American man being boiled in a pot
while his family watched *epitomizes the atrocities of racial violence*
during legal segregation. The racial violence is collective and physical
and inflicts great psychological trauma on blacks who witnessed it and
heard about it. This respondent's frequent crying decades after the
event demonstrates the long-lasting and extreme symptoms of racial
segregation trauma. The woman reports that they prayed for forgiveness for "they didn't know what they were doing." As we observe elsewhere in our interviews, religion and prayer serve as powerful coping
mechanisms when faced with this extreme white viciousness and violence.

She continues in her interview and transitions to the widespread
character of this racial violence in the Jim Crow era:

> When you walk back into your backyard and see your grandfather
> hanging from an oak tree. [Cries harder] Those were some hard
> times. . . . Back in those days, you could be standing back there, in
> your backyard, and see your grandfather and grandmother, and any-
> body in your family, hanging on a tree. And when you saw one
> hanging on a tree, they would come to the church real soon. And
> they would set the church on fire, and kill all of the black people that
> was in the church. That wasn't nothing! To white people that was
> fun. And all you could do was stand there and look. (*Beulah Craig,
> 80s*)

Craig alludes to other white violence connected with her family by
discussing her grandfather hanging from an oak tree. While she did not
share the details, it is clear that she recognized the widespread and
systemic nature of white violence and its constant negative impacts on
blacks individually and collectively.

Consider too the psychological and social impact on whites. Several
of our respondents note the glee with which whites engaged in these
atrocities. Here Beulah Craig mentions several times the delight whites
took in this extreme torture. It's common to read in the historical literature about a lynching by an "angry" white mob. However, while whites
were clearly motivated by hate-filled racist framing, their ritualized

lynchings were often joyous occasions at which significant numbers of white men, women, and children would gather, celebrate, and even picnic. Many lynchings were the result of coordinated organization that was advertised in advance with many whites in attendance. This was an important social gathering, as well as a crime scene. Whites sometimes printed postcards or created other photo memorabilia that depicted white crowds enjoying picnics and games for children under swinging black bodies, parts of which were often taken home by whites as souvenirs.[49] Almost no social scientists have studied the long-term impact of Jim Crow on these whites and their descendants. One rare scholar, Kristen Lavelle, has interviewed elderly whites about their memories of Jim Crow. She found that most denied or significantly downplayed this extensive racial violence—and their passive or active involvement in its perpetuation.[50]

SUSTAINED SEXUAL COERCION: MORE COMMUNITY COMPLEXITIES

Not all sexual assaults were isolated incidents involving white strangers. Some were grounded in sustained oppressive relationships—which, yet again, black family members were usually powerless to stop. In one interview, Maurice Willis, a prominent business owner in a local black community, described the precarious position of all black women, including those employed in professional positions:

> Influential white men would stay in the homes of black women three days out of the week while their wives knew about it. Black women's husbands knew about it but there was nothing they could do. They learned to live with it, and they would argue about it. But the women would say, "He forced me to do it." And the husband could do nothing about it. Black teachers would be forced to have sex with principals and the superintendent. . . . If you didn't want to have sex with the superintendent, then you would not be able to get a job in that county. (*Maurice Willis, 70s*)

After this response Willis requested that the recorder be turned off as he further recalled the frequent rape of black women locally. This hesitancy to discuss sexual assault on the record helps to explain the lack of information on this topic, even in black communities. Long before the term "sexual harassment" became popularly discussed in recent decades, during this segregation epoch black women were frequently sexually harassed and coerced into relationships with powerful white men, often just to secure employment. Black husbands often knew about the coercive arrangements, but were usually unable to do anything about it. Some husbands left, sometimes arguing their wives enjoyed these relationships. Others silently endured, grateful for the wife's job security yet greatly tormented by a forced relationship that breached their marital relationship. Such an intimidating ultimatum to black wives from influential (and other) white men "traumatized black family systems."[51]

Women workers in various types of jobs were at risk of forced sexual relations with white supervisors. In his interview, Rudolph Byrd, who is a custodian, hesitantly discusses how black women, including his mother, had no protection from such sexual assault:

> My mamma was a maid. She used to work with a lot of white folks. . . . My mama had gray eyes and red hair. . . . So, when [my brother] come out with blond head, they ain't no goodwill where he come from. . . . He come from a [white] man who'd . . . been dipping into my family a long time ago. . . . White folk, they love the [black] women especially. . . . Bring them in, and their wives couldn't say nothing. . . . And so you know about these kids, coming up with the light skin, you know. They know where they come from. (*Rudolph Byrd, 60s*)

In this poignant excerpt Byrd uses the term "dipping" to signal how common rape was. Further on in his interview, he mentioned that he had brothers with blond hair and that his dark-skinned father left his mother when he was young. He did not realize what had actually occurred until he was older and understood how the coercive Jim Crow context explained why his family included different physical aspects. With hesitation, he suggests that black women were forced into sexual relations with white men.[52] Like most others in our sample, he recalled these horrific rapes with great pain, anguish, and shame.

As these detailed narratives suggest, white wives were frequently aware of their husband's extracurricular sexual activities. However, they too were constrained by the oppressive racial and patriarchal systems, and thus were often unable to end the "dipping." When told by others, these wives might plead ignorance of their husbands' actions or just chalk them up to "boys being boys." Indeed, several scholars have documented that during both the slavery and Jim Crow eras some white wives seemed to prefer husbands to have "affairs" with black girls or women—so that the husbands could perform their sexual perversions with the latter, and maintain sexual "dignity" with their white wives. Reportedly, some white wives preferred the affair to be with a black woman who posed no threat, as opposed to a "legitimate affair" with a white woman.[53]

LONG-TERM WHITE-BLACK RELATIONSHIPS

Frequently these white male/black female relationships became long-term. Several studies of this historical era have documented the fact that in numerous communities influential white men had a white family, their public family, and also a black family that might, or might not, be kept secret in the community. In one historical study a black nurse reported thus: "I know at least fifty places in my small town where white men are positively raising two families—a white family in the 'Big House' in front, and a colored family in a 'Little House' in the backyard."[54]

According to the available data, including that from our respondents, most of these interracial relationships involved white men's coercion of various forms in regard to the black women who were involved. Given the oppressive societal contexts of Jim Crow, it is difficult to know if any of the more long-term interracial relationships reported here and elsewhere did involve some free choice on the part of blacks. Some long-term relationships reportedly did take on aspects of mutual respect, although they may not have begun that way. For example, one of our respondents, Geneva Hodge, a relatively light-skinned African American woman in the Southeast, noted repeatedly throughout her interview that her grandparents had been an interracial couple and that their relationship was one of genuine love and not sexual coercion. Giving the first author a tour of her house, she showed a picture of her grandfather, an elderly white man with a white beard. She said, "This is my grandfather. He and my grandmother were married. He married her, they were married." Geneva Hodge's insistence that her grandparents were married is an indication of her seeking validation that the relationship was authentic. However, given the legal banning of all intermarriage in this part of the South during Jim Crow, her assertion of a legal marriage is probably inaccurate.

Another respondent, Sidney Mack, now living southeast of Atlanta, reported that his ancestors included a white great-grandfather and a black great-grandmother. Although the two never married, his white great-grandfather maintained two households (one white, one black), and he provided economic support for not only his white family but also his black family. As an added complexity, Mack's formerly enslaved black great-grandmother was also married to a formerly enslaved black man. He suggests that he has two great-grandfathers: a black great-grandfather married to his great-grandmother, and a white great-grandfather who had a sexual relationship and biracial children with her—and provided the latter with some economic resources. Mack discusses certain benefits his biracial grandfather gained from their interracial relationship:

> And [my grandfather] had an advantage in the sense that his mother and father came out of south Atlanta when they freed the slaves. They came down here with their white family. You see what I'm saying? And as a result of that, [my grandfather] was a protected kind of individual. I'll have to show you a picture of him one time, and you might see why he is protected! [Laugher] But anyways, he was a mixed-blood. Okay. Just that simple. Connected by blood. The "yellow" blood. Now [my grandfather] was born here, but could never find out whether his mother came here pregnant or not. (*Sidney Mack, 70s*)

In the interview it became evident that Mack's grandfather was biracial, which during this rigid segregation era was sometimes referred to as being "yellow" or "high yellow" in black communities. Remember, too, that in this era the "one drop of black blood rule" aggressively used by whites in racial classifications dictated that any amount of known black ancestry meant a black classification. Although his biracial grandfather's black parents had been enslaved, after slavery they followed the well-off white family to the Southeast.

Mack knows that his great-grandparents were enslaved. Too often many whites write off slavery as just "ancient history" without recognizing that slavery still directly impacts contemporary black people and their families, in psychological well-being as well as economic viability. In his interview Sidney Mack hopes that the listener will understand the complex interracial and coercive relationships of the oppressive Jim Crow era, as he frequently used phrases such as "You see what I'm saying?" He continues his detailed account:

> So, my great-grandmother and great-grandfather worked for the [white] family. [My grandfather] was born here [in the Southeast], and he grew up and everything. The house that ended up being [my grandfather's] home, [the white great-grandfather] gave that property to [him] to build that home and everything. . . . This was just a decent white family. The [white family] ended up and got [him] a job at a [local office]. Then after that he decide to work on the train, he worked on the train, and he did that for a period of time until he hooked up with Mr. Blair, who was kin to [the white] family, and he had a [business] in Oklahoma. Mr. Blair met my granddaddy and liked my granddaddy and everything. And so [Mr. Blair] hooked up with granddaddy and opened up a [business] here. So [my grandfather] was always kind of in that slightly protected class, so he never really talked about the situation. (*Sidney Mack, 70s*)

Mack's account is telling in many ways. It illustrates how some whites, both after the emancipation of enslaved persons and during the Jim Crow years, treated African Americans with significant respect. According to the respondent, his grandfather did not suffer for his lighter complexion, but that served him well as he was in a "slightly protected class." However, it is noteworthy that he ends this passage with a note that his grandfather did *not* talk much about this complex historical background.

He benefited economically from the intergenerational connection to a white family that his biracial grandfather had. Significantly, he was one of very few people we interviewed who was financially well-off. Still, even with the economic resources provided to the respondent's ancestors, we will never know how the respondents' black great-grandmother felt about her relationship with the white great-grandfather. In the interview, we see no signs that the sustained white-black relationships were aggressively or violently coercive like in most other cases. However, even if this relationship were more consensual, that still does not mean it was wanted. Several scholars have shown that black women sometimes voluntarily agreed to sexual relations that were unwanted if that meant their families could secure access to (usually, white-only) resources, such as better education or more protection against police brutality, and thus access to a better life.[55] The binary framework of "violent coercion" or "free choice" in regard to sexual relationships is incomplete, for it denies situating some interracial relationships within the complex social reality often faced by black women in this era. Clearly, no black woman freely chose to live under the totalitarian conditions of Jim Crow, but once born into those conditions she usually made the best of the situation that she could. Thus, the societal choices available for these women were always severely restricted and socially pressured and forced in one way or another. Still, in some cases what likely started as clearly coercive relationships seem to have grown into more respectful and humane relationships with at least some whites. Some whites clearly came to see blacks as real human beings like themselves. Such more humane relationships, unfortunately, did not force major changes in the larger societal context, the still highly coercive and totalitarian system of legal segregation.

As Jim Crow segregation slowly began to crumble, some of these interracial relationships became much less coercive and more freely chosen and respectful. During the last few decades of the Jim Crow epoch (1940s–1960s), and occasionally before, there is documentation of mutually respectful and loving relationships, such as that of Mildred Loving, a black woman, and Richard Loving, a white man. In 1958 they married in Washington, D.C., but when they came back to the state of Virginia they were arrested, convicted, and sentenced to prison for violating the state's law banning racial intermarriages. They were, however, allowed to leave Virginia. Later on, with the help of the ACLU, they became central figures in the key Supreme Court case about racial intermarriage, titled *Loving v. Virginia* (1967), which struck down Virginia's law (and effectively sixteen other states' laws) against intermarriage.[56] The Lovings went to great efforts to be legally married and were in a non-coercive relationship with all signs of mutual love and respect. Long years of such human resistance to Jim Crow were essential to its eventual demise.

RAPE'S IMPACT: THE BLACK CHILDREN OF WHITE MEN

Of course, the number of African American women who gave birth to the child of the white men who forced them into sexual intercourse is unknown, but likely to have been very large in racially segregated towns and cities. In black communities, unfortunately, the black women who were pregnant because of coerced intercourse were often not viewed favorably. With few exceptions, we see evidence in the interviews of the suffering of biracial children who were innocent victims in the forced circumstances of their conception. One respondent, Sarah Benson, recalls how she was stigmatized as a result of her mother's rape:

> I was ostracized by the black community. They chased my mother out of town. . . . My mother was ostracized because she was raped by a white man. I only met my white father once, he gave me a coat. I never saw him again. My mother left town, and I was raised by my grandmother. Throughout my life I was treated differently for being mixed. I was just a little girl. It wasn't my fault. I lost my mother and my father. I had to fight to get respect from blacks. (*Sarah Benson, 80s*)

The respondent didn't have the benefit of being raised by her own mother. In the present day, she poignantly expresses the pain she has felt at being stigmatized throughout her life.

Another respondent, Stella Weaver, remembers the significant challenges faced by a childhood friend who was considered "too light" because of interracial sex:

> I remember this little boy [sighs] across the street named Charlie. He was one of my friends. . . . His mother looked white but she was black, and she married a black man, and they had a daughter who was about my complexion. Then Charlie came here with blond hair and snow white just really, really white. The daddy said, "I'm outta here." He left and said, "That's not my baby." Charlie went to school with us through about the first or second grade and his mother got such flack. You know in the neighborhood, they said, "He was the ice man's baby." They used to deliver ice to the house and come in and put it in your icebox wrapped in those burlap bags. . . . You didn't have refrigerators then. It was iceboxes, and they said, "That Charlie's daddy was the ice man." (*Stella Weaver, 60s*)

She continues with a detailed account of the boy's reactions to being light-skinned:

> His mother . . . reared him as a white boy. . . . He never accepted the fact that he ever had any black in him, but his mother reared him that way. And when his mother died that's the only time he ever came back to [this place]. His sister was living there and the mother was there. He came for the funeral. His sister said he got there just in time for the funeral, went to the funeral, and when it was over he told her good-bye and that was it. . . . She never heard from him anymore. He was a little boy and it wasn't his fault, but the kids teased him and everything. (*Stella Weaver, 60s*)

As a result of some type of coerced sexual assault by a white man, the consequences were severe: The child left and was in effect disowned by his family, community, and local networks.

BLACK RESISTANCE TO WHITE RAPISTS

As we have frequently observed in these extraordinary interview accounts, black women were under constant threat of assault by white men of various class levels. Nonetheless, they oftentimes challenged and fought back with their physical actions or quick wits. One African American newspaper reported on June 27, 1959, the attempted rape of a woman at her Florida home. The white aggressor, at gunpoint, forced some people to drive him to her home, where he was determined to rape her. As was evident in the planning involved, the rape was not a private incident, and the presence of white witnesses was not enough to deter him from the crime. He took off his clothes and forced the pregnant woman to disrobe. Using her wits, the woman convinced him that she knew of another woman that he might prefer. Clearly feeling like he had control of the situation, he drove her to that woman's home where she had the opportunity to call the police.[57]

Throughout this book we witness many black resistance tactics to sexual and other physical assaults at the micro-level, such as the victims screaming, fighting back with their bodies or weapons, escaping, or tricking their assaulter. Reporting their experiences to the white police agencies also took bravery, given the risks of white retaliation on them, their reputations, personal property, or their families, as well as the improbability of getting real justice. These recurring sexual assaults were also resisted at the community level. In some cases civil rights, church, or newspaper leaders helped to organize communities to raise awareness about sexual assaults and to demand justice. One example of community organization followed the assault of a black teenager in 1951 in a very Jim-Crowed southern town. A white grocery store owner hired her to babysit. One night after babysitting, he was driving her home. He stopped the car on the roadside and raped her. Her parents pressed charges, yet an all-white jury deliberated only five minutes before returning a not-guilty verdict. However, his grocery store was located in a mostly black community, which then boycotted his store because of the verdict and forced its closure. Although it was a financially painful consequence, it was minimal compared to the violent trauma that the young woman had experienced. According to her mother, she died of "shock" a few years after the attack, as she had "never recovered from the ordeal."[58] Once again, we observe the continuing and accumulating impact of racial trauma and, thus, *revictimization*.

Retaliation was usually the white response to such black resistance. Not only did the victim of rape often suffer, but so too did members of the broader black community who got caught in the middle. For example, in May 1959 in Tallahassee, Florida, two black female university students were abducted at gunpoint by four white men while on a date after a dance. The presence of two black men did not deter the white men, who reportedly wanted to "go out and get a nigger girl."[59] One black woman was gang-raped at gunpoint by the white men. The other was able to escape and report the crime to local police. A sympathetic white police intern agreed to look for the missing student, and he found her bound and gagged on the floorboard of the men's car. The white men were arrested and admitted to the crimes in taped confessions. However, in the courtroom they pleaded innocent. In an unusual verdict, one of the first in the South, the white men were found guilty, although with a recommendation for mercy. Given a life sentence, one of the men was still released from jail just four years later. (In contrast, those black women targeted by these rapists *always* got a "life sentence" of continuing pain and trauma.) Enraged, he tracked down and murdered a black woman who had nothing to do with the events. The murderer thought she was one of the students who had reported his crime. In addition, several respondents mentioned in their interviews that white rapists warned their black targets that if they told on them, the rapists would come back and kill them. These later acts of violence against women who reported rape were a warning to all blacks to keep silent.

Family members were at risk of retaliation for exposing violent white criminals. In April 1946 a black newspaper reported on the arrest of a black woman in Montgomery, Alabama, who worked at an air force base. She had refused to give up her seat on a public bus. After her arrest, the woman hired an attorney to help on her case, which angered some white police officers. As a form of revenge, one officer kidnapped the woman's teenaged daughter, drove her to a cemetery, and raped her. No charges were filed against the officer, whom the police chief allowed to quietly leave town.[60]

As we'll discuss in the next chapter, a common resistance tactic used by African Americans, like this woman, was to knowingly violate the unjust Jim Crow laws. Unfortunately, such resistance tactics often came with a heavy price, such as punishment of innocent family members. Additionally, under arrest, many black women and men put themselves at the mercy of white prison guards who periodically used sexual or other physical assaults as a retaliatory technique. For example, two black women and a 16-year-old girl were arrested in June 1963 in Winona, Mississippi, for attempting to desegregate a bus terminal lunch counter and then were sexually assaulted by Winona police jailers.[61]

Unfortunately, there were countless examples of white officers who used their position as a "bully with a badge" to satisfy their often sadistic inclinations. Consider another such event in August 1928 in New Orleans: A white night-watch guard reportedly raped a 12-year-old black child. Two years later in the same city, a 14-year-old was shot and killed in a restaurant by a white police officer because she resisted his attempts to rape her. In 1945 in Memphis, Tennessee, two black girls were forced into a police car and taken to an isolated spot where two uniformed officers assaulted them. Moreover, in October 1946 in Richmond, Virginia, a black waitress accepted a ride from two white police officers. They drove her to a remote location and sexually assaulted her at gunpoint. The officers were sentenced to seven years in prison, yet served less than a year. In March 1949 in Montgomery, Alabama, a black woman was walking home, and two white officers stopped her and accused her of public drunkenness. When she refused to get in their car, they pushed her in and repeatedly raped her at gunpoint. Her minister organized a protest, and charges were eventually filed, yet no one was indicted. In May 1956 in Mississippi, another black woman was making preparations for her wedding when she was ordered from her home by a white man with a gun who was posing as a police officer. He and other white men took her to a remote spot where they gang-raped her. Although four men confessed, only one received a serious prison sentence.[62]

In July 1942 in Little Rock, Arkansas, a teenaged high school student was walking home from church when she was approached by white uniformed police officers. The police officers threatened to arrest her if she did not get in their car. They drove her behind a railroad embankment and raped her. She eventually escaped by "promising to get them another girl."[63] Clearly, throughout much of the South white law enforcement officers felt uninhibited in raping black women as punishment when they were jailed or by luring them under false pretenses to remote locations. The scale of this sexual oppression of black women by these white men who represented "law and order" is quite remarkable, and the fact that it is little analyzed and usually covered up in white society's recalling of the Jim Crow era signals just how much truth-telling is necessary for white America to even begin to deal with the continuing legacies of this country's centuries of extreme racial oppression.

Fear of retaliation from whites, including police officers and many others, was quite general in this era. One respondent, Arleana Stanley, provides us with memories of the consequences for African Americans who spoke out on white killings:

> I don't remember when it happened . . . 'cause they had the Ku Klux Klan all around. I mean they didn't want you around these places, I mean, like they, down in town. They still say blacks can go in there to eat, but blacks didn't want to go in there and eat, 'cause they didn't know if . . . a white man would have killed a black person, wasn't going to be nothing did about it. It was always like that. If you black, you stay on your part of town. . . . One year, they found [a girl]; they never did know who killed that girl. . . . They never did know who killed [her], at the time they say she was going with a white man. . . . They just said a white man killed her and left her on the beach, and

they never did pursue it or nothing, sure did. And I remember a long time ago, they say it was a white man going with a black girl . . . and wasn't nothing done about that, and I remember that. You see, you got to be careful where you go. . . . [*How did this affect the community?*] I mean, you know, it made them mad, but what can they do? At the time, if you was a black person and you told on a white person, you better be for sure. And if they do it, they didn't know if they were going to come back and kill you and blow your house up at that time or what. So you had to be really careful. . . . And black people don't hardly go on no beach. Black people didn't go on the beach at that time. (*Arleana Stanley, 70s*)

Whether this black woman's involvement with a white man was coercive or consensual, it certainly did not end well for her. Although we do not know the details of the woman's death, we learn again that blacks were not supposed to divulge information about such events involving whites. In our interviews there are numerous examples of white retaliation against blacks who did so. Notice, once again, the lack of a white investigation or interest in punishment for the white man who was thought to have killed the black woman.

CONCLUSION

The physical, psychological, emotional, and spiritual damage that was done to the many thousands of black survivors of white rapes who are still alive today is irreversible. For some, like the just-noted black teenager, there was no apology, amends, or restitution that could ease her suffering. Although many of these white male assaults took place decades ago, many assault survivors are still alive. However, many white assailants are likely now to be deceased, and the statute of limitations for prosecuting certain sexual assault cases may have expired in southern states. In some areas, still, a case could be made for criminal or civil prosecution if there are living black victims and white assailants. Importantly, too, many rape victims seek validation of their violent experiences, an apology for inaction (or worse) by the criminal justice system, and for personal and family closure. Sadly, for most still-living black victims of these white rapes, this closure will never come. They will never get the justice that they certainly deserve.

For some readers, this Jim Crow segregation and the experiences of these elderly African Americans may seem like "ancient history." However, as we write, Jim Crow segregation ended less than a half century ago. It is very important to recognize that this Jim Crow era, and the preceding slavery era, laid the foundation for the contemporary white-racist framing of black women and men, as well as of black communities generally. Thus, a recent interview study of many mostly well-educated white men by sociologist Brittany Slatton revealed that their often very negative racist framing of black women is still grounded in the white-racist framing of black women that emerged so vigorously during the slavery and legal segregation eras.[64] While women of all racial groups have long been plagued with patriarchy and an array of gender stereotypes, black women have long been viewed by whites in the most extreme terms—as hyper-sexualized, domineering, absent, or matriarchs.[65] From the medical community to pornography and everything in between, the bodies of black women and other women of color have always been portrayed as more sexually available or ugly, as contradictory as that seems, compared to the positive white framing of white women. In contrast to the cult of white women as embodying "true womanhood," black women are often portrayed very negatively, indeed usually as just the opposite. The foundation of these negative black and positive white images stems directly from the long eras of slavery and Jim Crow, when collective and individual white supremacy dominated all major aspects of African American women's and men's everyday lives.

6

COPING AND RESISTANCE STRATEGIES

The rule of thumb was you never tell white folks what you thinking. Because they are going to use it against you, no questions about it. There was this whole coping skills that black men had. They call it "shuffling." Shuffling around, scratching their heads. White folks got—Lord have mercy. [To] white folks, "I don't know." I saw them doing it, "I don't know. Yes, sir. I don't know. I don't know, sir." You know, but the white would come to you because they thought you had something to tell them. So the first thing you do was to deny it. . . . You had to take on the role of a buffoon to get this guy off of you because he could make life difficult for you. So, that's what you did, and it worked. Once the white person left, you laughed. You know, it happened all the time. "Do you boys know so and so, and so and so?" "No, sir, never heard of him." (*Bob Shaw, 60s*)

In studied detail Bob Shaw reflects on the savvy shuffle that African Americans consciously adopted as one long-term strategy to survive Jim Crow oppression. To borrow the language of Audre Lorde, African Americans commonly used some of the "master's tools" to resist systemic racism. That is to say, to survive they often had to play into the controlling white racial framing of African Americans as ignorant, shuffling, head-scratching buffoons. Deceiving whites was one type of everyday resistance strategy.

This daily coping strategy is one that suggests philosopher Marilyn Frye's concept of the double bind: Oppressed groups are damned if they do, and damned if they don't. In a system of oppression and subordination, even certain coping and resistance strategies can further one's subordination.[1] In the legal segregation era African Americans faced trouble if they complied with white demands for information because, as this respondent notes, "they are going to use it against you, no questions about it." However, they would have been stigmatized or punished if they did not comply with white demands and provide information. By claiming ignorance, they usually could safely remove themselves from certain dangerous situations.

In the slavery era white-created minstrel shows depicted a mythical "happy slave" who was racially stereotyped and imaged as a dim-witted, ignorant, or lazy buffoon for comic effect. This racial framing persisted throughout the Jim Crow era as well. Although African Americans knew they were putting on an act and could laugh privately at white ignorance, pretending to shuffle perpetuated this negative racial framing by whites. In the short term, blacks benefited by getting away from whites who might cause them great harm. However, in the long term this strategy had very negative consequences, as African Americans have been plagued to the present with this racist framing. Indeed, one recent national opinion survey found that 14 percent of Americans still openly agreed that "lazy" characterizes blacks "extremely well" or "very well." More than half agreed with various other types of antiblack racial framing.[2]

In this chapter, we examine the strategies that African Americans had to formulate and use during the long legal segregation decades to cope and survive, as well as to thrive and resist. We begin this chapter with the experiences of light-skinned African Americans and the strategy of "passing" for white as a coping mechanism. Then we describe the coping stratagems that most African Americans used to maintain their sanity and sense of dignity. These coping and contending approaches involved tactics repeatedly used just for daily survival. Next, we discuss the overt resistance strategies that many employed to resist and dismantle elements of legal segregation. Numerous history books emphasize the organized civil rights movements of the 1960s, but equally as important were the smaller-scale, everyday moments of resistance used by black Americans to chip away at segregation's norms and institutions. Finally, we consider how black children were socialized to deal with the harsh realities of this oppressive segregation era, and the impact of that socialization on the intergenerational transmission of both the countering strategies and the negative elements of the segregation stress syndrome.

COLORISM AND PASSING FOR WHITE

White-created racial categorizations typically only differentiate among a limited array of racial groups such as white Americans, African Americans, Asian Americans, Latinos, and Native Americans. However, many researchers and other analysts have long noted the differentiation within each racial group, sometimes termed "colorism." Much of this colorism is the result of white men sexually exploiting black women during the slavery and Jim Crow eras. Frequently, greater access to some societal resources and benefits accrued to those who looked more like, or aligned more with, whites. Often in the slavery era the often lighter-skinned "house slaves" had greater benefits and endured less physically demanding labor than the usually darker "field slaves." Lighter-skinned house slaves were frequently the children of white slavemasters or overseers, and by state law they had to be treated as enslaved persons.

These socially constructed skin-color distinctions continued to be noted and have significant impacts during the era of legal segregation. In our interviews some respondents noted certain benefits, as well as some challenges, for lighter-skinned African Americans. One respondent in the Southwest, Georgia McNeil, recollects her employer's wife's orientation:

> Mr. Price's wife was real prejudiced. And she always would try to pick issues with us. If anybody came in and said, "Oh, you are so pretty." And she would say, "I beg your pardon, she's colored." You know, it would just really, they wouldn't ask her, you know. It's like you couldn't be colored and be pretty. . . . I found out why [Mrs. Price] was so prejudiced, because her grandmother was prejudiced. In the afternoon when we would get in our homework, and the other little kids, children came in to meet the little girl, her grandmother would tell them, "She's colored." And they would look at me like, huh? . . . Anybody came in, the grandmother would have to go and announce I was colored. (*Georgia McNeil, 70s*)

Because racial identities were not always distinguishable, or as here were ambiguous, it was important for whites to aggressively maintain the society's racial boundaries so that the "colored" child wasn't accidentally associated with whites. (Other scholars have recently examined these socially constructed colorism and racial "visibility" issues.)[3] Note too that the definition of real beauty was controlled by whites, for this white employer contended that it was impossible to be both "colored" and pretty.

Jim Crow's segregation laws and informal norms generally required that a person's socially constructed "race" be agreed upon by all concerned. Therefore, it was critical for whites to identify the racial category of each person, and racial ambiguity resulted in discomfort or confusion in everyday interactions. One light-skinned respondent in the Southeast, Bonnie Waters, observes that her restaurant employer hired people of different racial groups and the patrons needed to know how to classify people:

> At the theater we would go to the back. And we had to go in the balcony, the colored had to go up in the balcony and, you know, whites down. By working at the restaurant . . . we were light-skinned and they didn't know we were colored. But Mr. Jefferson, he knew we were. Well in fact he had . . . all different races. He had an Indian girl, a Mexican girl, my sister and I, and then they had a black-skinned girl was there. And everybody that would come in thought it was just so, you know they couldn't believe that. And they'd come in and try to say, you know, bet who was who. And a lot of times they would ask me who was the colored girl working here. And they'd [say], you know, it would be me. And a lot of times they would ask me out on a date and I would tell them, "You know we gonna have a hard time holding hands. I'll be on the balcony and you'll be downstairs [laughing]." (*Bonnie Waters, 70s*)

Although it was often difficult for whites to tell that she was black, this woman was still expected to follow the Jim Crow protocol of black subordination by relating that she was indeed black and had to sit in inferior seats. She sometimes used humor in telling white "suitors" that she was black. This humor was an important coping mechanism that hid the stress of being between two socially defined worlds, one privileged (and white) and the other unprivileged (and black).

PASSING AS COPING

Another respondent in the Southeast, Emily Webster, calls up the challenges of being light-skinned, including how the perks were often at the expense of darker-skinned blacks:

> By being light-skinned you [were] sort of like a double victim. Your own, black people don't want to be with you because you too light, and white people don't want to be with you because you're so close to [them], they can't tell. And it's just sort of like you're in the middle of the road. . . . And you have to pick your friends real careful and . . . it's so hurtful if you with a white person, and they say a black joke . . . [and] you don't know what to say, whether you should speak out or what. So it puts you like in the middle, on the fence, you don't know which way to go. It was just the way it was. When things get a certain way you just, you know, if it's not hurting you, you just keep on going but the people that's being hurt by it, that's the ones that really speak out. . . . So it was just, the worst part is seeing other people being treated unfairly and that you couldn't do nothing about it because . . . they thought you was white. (*Emily Webster, 70s*)

Webster relates the recurring trauma of being torn between two racial worlds. As a fair-skinned person, she is able to pass as white, which gave her access to certain privileges of white-only spaces. However, this passing also came with significant costs. The fear of being "caught" was one source of great stress. Webster is also a firsthand witness to whites treating African Americans unfairly and reports feeling torn as to what to do. As can be seen in other interviews, this uncertainty oftentimes led to feelings of shame, guilt, and sadness—again, symptoms of the segregation stress syndrome. This ability to pass and receive, at least temporarily and conditionally, some white privileges led to resentment on the part of some darker-skinned African Americans who were not allowed the same benefits.

One light-skinned respondent in the Southwest, Lillie Chandler, remembers certain privileges when she went to the store:

> Because I would go in a store . . . you could get your dress and go and try it on, and I had gone in. And I had tried on a dress and something else. And this black lady was in the store . . . looking at some stuff and she was picking it up and the man that owned the store came in and

said, "Don't be touching the items, you gonna get 'em dirty." Ah, that
just hurt me so much, and here I am. . . . I can't remember . . . if he
knew that I was colored or not. But here I am trying on the dress,
and the girdle, and all that stuff . . . you know, intimate stuff. And
here's this lady that's just touching it. And he told her she's gonna
dirty it. Look like that lump got in my throat, and it just look like I
couldn't go back in. It just would hurt so bad. It just got to me. [*Do
you remember the reaction of the woman that was there?*][4] She just
acted nonchalant like if it didn't hurt her and just walked out. . . . But
I was looking at the dress that I had put on and it just hurt to know
how they had spoke to her. (*Lillie Chandler, 70s*)

We noted in a previous chapter that in white-run stores the clerks,
employers, and whites generally framed African Americans racially, as
dirty or potential thieves. Chandler notes that the other black woman
acted nonchalant, but likely felt degraded and embarrassed as a result
of the racially traumatic events. Undoubtedly, both were experiencing
these feelings. In this case Chandler is light enough to pass, but that
does not protect her from the pain of watching another woman experiencing racial trauma. As we have observed before, a witness to a racially
traumatic event who cannot intervene often feels pain too, as well as a
sense of helplessness. As she has noted, it "hurt so bad."

Numerous lighter-skinned interviewees noted their emotions of anguish and pain in witnessing the harsh treatment that whites directed
toward darker-skinned friends and family members. One respondent,
Violet Pitts, reports on interactions with whites when she was with a
friend who was darker:

She was pretty, you know. She's the youngest in the family so I guess
she must have been about . . . seven or eight. But . . . [whites would]
tell you that they didn't have a bathroom. And somebody light-
skinned would come in, and they'd have a bathroom. And that really
did hurt, it would make you both feel bad. Because a lot of light-
skinned people are colored. And a lot of . . . times you would [be
with] a dark-skinned person. And they'd tell you, you could do something and then they'd tell the dark-skinned person that they can't do
it, not knowing that you two are together. (*Violet Pitts, 80s*)

Similarly, a respondent in the Southwest, George McNeil, recalls
passing as white to eat at white-owned restaurants:

> We were hungry, and we went out. . . . You couldn't go in the front of
> a restaurant, you had to go to the back door. . . . You know, I didn't
> want to go to the back door and [my wife] was pregnant. You know,
> you just don't want to get your feelings hurt. The restaurant that I
> worked at—anybody that was colored would come in, and, oh, they
> would usher them out. They'd put you out. Even though I was col-
> ored in there, it just hurt to see them talk about other people be-
> cause they didn't know that we were black. (*George McNeil, 70s*)

The emotions around the recognition of differential treatment are
often powerful, especially for these veterans of the legal segregation
era. Numerous respondents used words like "hurt," frequently multiple
times, to describe the experience of being lighter-skinned. Lighter-
skinned African Americans were sometimes able to access white privilege, such as using public restroom facilities or eating at restaurants, yet
that came at some cost to their sense of fairness as they witnessed other
blacks being humiliated.

While whites have long been socialized to racially frame African
Americans as "inferior" in many ways, these light-skinned African
Americans knew that such framing is racist and thus often experienced
inner turmoil in their passing. Another respondent, Muriel Baldwin,
recalls her shame in passing:

> The bus was the worst. Because you had to go to the back of the bus.
> And if you didn't, being light-skinned, if you didn't go back and
> somebody knew you, you'd be passing and you would be shamed. So
> we just run on to the back of the bus. (*Muriel Baldwin, 70s*)

Baldwin struggled with where she belongs in segregated public
transport and noted the stigma associated with passing for white. The
danger in passing was the potential that they would be "outed" either by
a white person or by someone in the local black community. This fear
explains why leaving town was frequently the best option for many
African Americans who decided to pass.

PASSING AS RESISTING

A number of scholars have explored the variable boundaries of whiteness and blackness in various historical eras, including the utility and costs for black Americans of attempted "passing."[5] Variation in phenotypical characteristics did have positive and negative effects for some of our respondents. Light-skinned African Americans periodically used their color privilege to resist the racial hierarchy and challenge white supremacy. One older respondent, Lillie Chandler, who in a previous excerpt reports watching a woman being called dirty, continues in her interview by noting a visit to a department store with her darker-skinned daughter Anita:

> I had Anita with me and she had [picked out] a few items in the junior department. And we went to the women's department, and we asked the lady if it was all right if she takes the clothes from one department to another. And when I would pay for my stuff, I would pay for hers. And so we went in, and I found some clothes. And I was trying them on and when I came back . . . she didn't have anything on her arms. . . . I said, "Well where's your things?" She said, "The lady came and took them off my arm and said that I couldn't take clothes from one department to another." [I said] "Didn't you tell her the lady said it was all right and that I was gonna pay for it?" So when we got to the thing. . . . I was gonna go pay for it. And [Anita] said, "No, I don't want it. . . . You can give them to Goodwill. I'm not wearing them." But she didn't tell me that until after I had paid for it. . . . I don't know what was the [sales] lady's idea, that . . . because she was colored that she couldn't, that she was gonna steal the clothes? (*Lillie Chandler, 70s*)

Again, Chandler was a witness to another black female experiencing a painful racial traumatic event—except this time it was her daughter who was apparently assumed to be a potential thief. Anita was humiliated and did not want to possess the reminders of this traumatic experience. Undeniably, as we have observed in previous accounts, active avoidance of certain things and places associated with Jim Crow discrimination is one of the unsurprising symptoms of the contemporary segregation stress syndrome.

Lillie Chandler also noted in her interview that she should have contacted the store manager, which is what she did in another experience while shopping with her daughter:

> We'd spend, you know, over hundred dollars just on paper, just little things that they needed for school. We went in and had the buggy all loaded, and Anita needed to use the bathroom. . . . So I said at the lady, "Could you tell me where's the restroom?" She said, "We don't have a restroom. If you want to go the restroom you have to go to the courthouse or to a filling station." . . . I said, "Leave the basket. Leave that." . . . We went on and go to the filling station [to use] the bathroom. . . . That next weekend we went to [another town] and bought all the school supplies. I happened to go in [the first store] by myself one day, and the manager was there. And I told him what had happened. I said, "You see my children spend their allowances in here buying all the little necklaces and little jewelry. . . . If you saw that basket with all that school supplies in it, that was mine. And we walked out." And . . . he said, "Well if that ever happens again, just let me know." (*Lillie Chandler, 70s*)

The initial bathroom incident happened before the beginning of the school year. Later in her narrative, Chandler notes that she had an opportunity months later to speak forcefully with the white manager on behalf of her daughter. The white clerk may have easily forgotten the traumatic racial incident but clearly it had weighed on the respondent's mind for these months. The psychological anguish of witnessing unfair treatment of a loved one doesn't soon go away. We also observe the light-skin privilege too in a situation where the manager reportedly spoke with her in respectful terms, likely more so than if she had been a darker-skinned African American.

Other respondents recounted using their light-skin privilege as a strategy of resistance to white racism. Clarence Martin, a respondent in the Southwest, explains that his wife sometimes got away with speaking her mind because of her light skin color:

> No, I don't see how me and my wife [might confront] a situation that I cannot handle, I could handle but it would mean fighting, and I would get put in jail 'cause my wife is aggressive. And sorry to say, she's not only aggressive, she's lighter in skin and that is another problem we've got going, you see. 'Cause the lighter black person got

it better, and so if I'm going to have a trouble with white folk, that's
going to be an argument I send her! [laughs] Now if the thing get too
rough, then I'm there for the physical confrontation. But she can
holler and shout and cuss and get by with it. (*Clarence Martin, 90s*)

Martin felt that his light-skinned wife could get away with more
argument and assertiveness than he could. Passing as a white person
could sometimes be a resistance strategy, one that might forestall possible racial discrimination. However, this was often not possible. While
it's tempting to conclude that black women, whatever their skin color,
were granted greater freedom in resisting the Jim Crow oppression
than black men, not only our data in previous chapters but also the
historical literature strongly indicate that black women likewise suffered an enormous amount of white discrimination, pushback, and violence, including in cases of their overt resistance to Jim Crow's harsh
realities. Both black women and men faced very serious threats from
whites (women and men), and thus in the Jim Crow era, as today, both
groups have been racially vulnerable and victimized, to the point of
extreme violence.

OTHER COPING STRATEGIES

Relationships with Whites: Avoidance Strategies

Probably the most frequent coping strategy cited by our respondents
was to stay in "their place" and as far away from whites as possible.
Respondent Gene Hicks, living in the Southwest now, recounts his
childhood working on a white plantation and how his father coped with
oppression:

> But they wasn't his cows, they was on the farm, plantation. I remem-
> ber that. [*Was it your farm?*] No, whites. White farm. . . . We didn't
> own nothing. . . . Got grown and bought our own. My dad . . . didn't
> like the city. No way. He moved far back in the woods as he could go.
> Yes, he did. He said he didn't want to be around nobody, especially
> whites. You couldn't raise anything. He just got off by himself. He
> just never was the kind that want to, I guess, mix [pause] with, um,
> [lowers voice] them. [Talking louder.] Black people and Spanish, just

like I said, that's all we know. He had some white friends. I guess my mom had some white friends 'cause she worked long years ago. She worked all the time. (*Gene Hicks, 70s*)

The content of Hicks's narrative is telling, as is his voice inflection. Even though the interviewer and respondent are the only ones in the room, he lowers his voice when indicating that his father didn't interact much with whites. Such whispering has been noted in other studies of past and present contemporary racial settings and usually indicates a hesitation to discuss difficult or dangerous racial topics.[6] To compensate for this, the respondent discusses some white friendships that his parents had. Throughout the interviews, these older African American respondents even today show fear of negative repercussions for speaking out in any way about whites. Numerous respondents asked for the tape recorder to be switched off, or to speak "off the record."

Hicks notes that his father did not own land and worked on a white man's farm. During this era most black southerners lived under the near-slavery conditions of farm labor, tenant farming, sharecropping, and debt peonage.[7] Just as in the slavery era, most were engaged in generating white wealth by the expenditure of much hard labor. In order to harvest crops such as cotton, black tenant farmers incurred significant debt in purchasing from whites the seeds, tools, clothing, food, and livestock they needed. Interest on these debts usually led to a cycle of black poverty and debt, from which most could not escape without risking arrest by local white authorities.

In the Jim Crow states the local and state criminal justice systems were set up by powerful whites in part to criminalize many black workers. The purpose was to facilitate the generation of yet more white wealth. Being in public without proof of employment or just being "uppity" to a white person often led to felony crime charges, convictions, and imprisonment or hefty fines. False accusations of these "crimes" were common, but still led to imprisonment or fines for those accused—which in turn reinforced the stereotype of "criminal" in the white-racist framing of black men. White landowners and other employers would pay the fine or debt in exchange for securing black laborers, and local governments would outsource black prisoners to white employers for a profit. Despite the passage of the Thirteenth Amendment to the U.S. Constitution abolishing slavery in 1865, scholarly estimates suggest, even decades later in the late 1800s and early 1900s, nearly 40 percent of black workers in the South were held in labor involuntarily—so as to enable white employers to profit unfairly from their hard labor.[8]

In the late 1800s it seems that the practice of white employers "buying" this black labor by such means as debt peonage was the most common, but by the early 1900s it had become common too for local prison systems to outsource their black prisoners as profit-generating laborers. The system of convict leasing has been deemed by many researchers to have been worse than slavery in some ways. Whippings, chain gangs, and food deprivation were so widespread that the prisoner death rate was often 30–40 percent annually.[9] Ironically, under slavery African Americans had usually been considered valuable "property" and were thus protected to some degree from deadly abuse, especially from whites who were not slaveholders. Under Jim Crow segregation, however, they were not even protected to this degree. They could easily be made into "criminals" under discriminatory Jim Crow laws and thus face either extreme labor exploitation from an array of employers or, especially if they rebelled, violent beatings or lynchings.

Given this context, a frequently reported coping strategy was a studied avoidance of whites wherever possible. As we have witnessed in previous chapters, the avoidance of whites was particularly critical in certain dangerous contexts such as at night or places where much alcohol was consumed. Recall this commentary from chapter 5 by a former professor, Phillip Bailey, about his mother's warnings: "My mother used to insist that I always be in the yard before the sun go down. I could not understand that. Until one day, they call them night riders, they kidnapped a black kid and they sodomized him and castrated him." In his account we observe evidence of the intergenerational transmission of racialized trauma and of the coping strategies that children were taught, in this case the strategy of avoiding whites (especially at nightfall). African Americans of all ages learned the importance of being as invisible as they could be when around whites. Given the totalitarian segregation context, the desire of most blacks to avoid whites cannot be equated with the desire of many whites to avoid blacks. The first type of avoidance was based on a long history of collectively documented and personally witnessed white discrimination, assault, and violence. The second type of avoidance was based mainly on whites' negative stereo-typing and other racist framing of subordinated black southerners.

Relationship with Whites: Turning to "Good" Whites

For our respondents and other black southerners, there was generally a *low threshold* for whites to be considered "good whites." That designation usually meant just the absence of whites doing harm, rather than the presence of white assistance and support. Unmistakably, whites played multiple roles during the legal segregation years: violent instigator, active supporter, passive bystander, passive resister, and/or active resister. As part of their survival strategies, black men, women, and children quickly learned which whites were relatively trustworthy and which were to be carefully avoided, and they usually passed this information along to many others in their communities. A respondent in the Southeast, Mabel Manning, remembers her first encounter with whites as relatively positive:

> The first interaction I had I think was good. There was a store in our community that was owned by white people. You were always in-debted to them though, 'cause then you would buy stuff on credit. They have a book with your name. . . . And we would go down there and say, "My momma wanted a pound of sausage," and this and that. And they would write you up. So you could say that they gave you food even though you got it on credit, and you never finished paying. It still was a good experience. You looked at them as good people. They let us have food. (*Mabel Manning, 70s*)

She explains how there were good whites who allowed blacks to buy food on credit. However, this narrative illustrates the depths of black poverty as most had limited resources to secure adequate food and were thus subject to a continuous cycle of debt that they "never finished paying." Depending on the white person's attitude, the impact of that debt dependency could vary dramatically. As we have already discussed, that debt was often used to significantly increase the subordination of black individuals and families in numerous southern communities.

Remarkably, being a "good" white person might include just ordinary kindness such as allowing black families to have food. It could also mean an *absence* of white violence, as was noted by Walter Frazier, a retired teacher in the Southwest:

> My grandfather always told us that he had never had a bad encounter with white people. He was always cordial to them because he didn't want to get in trouble with them, because during those days they would invade the black homes and take the black man out and beat and kill him. And my father didn't want that to happen to him 'cause he had seen all of this in Atlanta, Georgia. So he would always keep himself in a position where he would not have to, you know, meet with them. . . . He never had a bad encounter with the whites, he always was cordial, and they were nice enough. Just like I had said before, this was a nice place for the blacks to live because there had not been lynching, beating, and killing the blacks. And I had not had that experience either when I was going to school. Because we were always separated and we were not trying to push . . . for integration at that time. We didn't know too much about it. But we always wanted a better way of living, but we did that from the sweat of the brow. We just worked hard to progress as far as we could go without having to, you know, fight and get our way through what we were . . . trying to do. (*Walter Frazier, 80s*)

This respondent notes the normality of antiblack violence, night riders, and home invaders in the Deep South, and the apparent improvement for his father and the family in the Southwest. As a common coping mechanism across the South, however, most African Americans obeyed the strict racial norms, did not push hard for integration, and avoided whites when necessary. Even in the respondent's contemporary interview, he appeared rather uncomfortable discussing racial integration, as was suggested by his frequent pauses.

He continues his interview, citing a specific example in which some whites did come to the rescue of a well-regarded black man in the community:

> How the conversation started I don't know, but I do know that the man that started the fight was a white man with a black man, and he told him that "you think you are a smart nigger but you are not." And when he called him a nigger and of course this man told him, "You come off of this porch and I will show you what kind of nigger I am." So when the black man started off the porch, this was a little store,

the white man kicked the black man and of course the black man beat the white man up. And immediately they took the black man and put him in jail. That was a bad disturbance here, and of course the white man that did the kicking to the black man was not an outstanding white man in the community. But the black man was an outstanding man. Therefore the white people . . . came to the rescue . . . and told them to let the black man out of jail because he is an outstanding black man in the community. . . . And of course the blacks were all getting geared up to come to his rescue, but the blacks got together and they all came to an agreement that we do not want the disturbance in this community, we want to always have peace and harmony. . . . This has always been a community of trying to have peace and harmony among the whites and the blacks. But the blacks never received the best of anything during those days, like brand new books and things that would help the blacks. (*Walter Frazier, 80s*)

Frazier shares a specific example where some powerful whites came to the rescue of a respectable black man, who had a bad encounter with a less respectable white man. The respondent emphasizes African Americans' desire to have community peace, even though they were regularly treated as second-class citizens. Many whites shared this desire for racial peace, particularly if African Americans there didn't push for racial integration. In spite of possible backlash from other whites, some did what they could to assist certain African Americans, but mainly because of the convergence of white and black group interests in community peace.

As we frequently observe in these astute interviews, African Americans had to learn to differentiate between whites who were trustworthy and whites who meant to cause them harm. This strategizing imposed yet another stressful burden on them, for an error could be very costly. Respondent Leona Kelley, in the Southeast, remembers her grandparents teaching her to be in a relationship with good white folks:

My grandmother was the one who, you know, would make the choice of what type of white people we would work for. And because we lived on the farm, we didn't work in white people's, inside the house. We always worked in the fields. [. . . She created] good relationships with those white people who were open to our respectable and decent behavior toward one another. So she had a good rapport with the good white folks she knew. She taught us to stay away from the bad white folks regardless of what kind of excuses you had to make. You didn't go out there doing things that would cause you to . . . create this favor with the bad, mean white folks who were looking for some reason to abuse you anyway. You just stay away from those people. You know if they come and say, "Well I want you to work in the field today," well you got an excuse. (*Leona Kelley, 70s*)

Kelley discusses important survival strategies. First, assess which whites could be trusted and which whites were abusive; secondly, be prepared for difficult interactions with bad whites. This grandmother taught the respondent to have an available excuse when interacting with untrustworthy whites. In certain instances, she could claim to be unavailable for labor in their fields. By conjuring up this ruse, she was saved from interacting with unpredictable whites, yet she also did not risk disrupting the racial hierarchy by disobeying those whites.

Although the vast majority of the respondents reported feeling most comfortable in their own social networks, a few respondents who were domestic workers recalled certain positive interactions with white families and networks. One respondent in the Southwest, Eunice Blackwell, recalls how she was more like a family member in the home of one particular white family:

I worked for one family; in fact he lived near the mall. I worked for them folks for eighteen years. . . . They had three girls, three girls and one boy. I raised all those kids. Lived with them until they got married. Went to all of them weddings and then I started to babysit their kids. So, like I said, yeah I even raised the grandkids. I just am still in the family. Birthdays they bring me . . . the mother may come out and bring me some money or she will mail it to me. I will get a card right now. Yep. Nice. Nice. They is some nice peoples out there. . . . No problems. I worked for them from eight to five. I worked from eight to five for eighteen years. (*Eunice Blackwell, 70s*)

For nearly two decades Blackwell raised the white children and grandchildren, and she considers them "family" because she was integrated into their activities. In her interview she recalls how she left the town after the white children were grown. She moved away and remembers crying when her husband decided that he wanted to move back:

He wanted to come back to [names town], and I cried for two weeks.
I cried because I never wanted to come back here [voice low and
sad]. . . . We come back here and I [have been] back here ever since.
He didn't have a job. [*So why didn't you want to come back to the
town?*] I just didn't! No. I didn't want to come. (*Eunice Blackwell,
70s*)

Although she considered herself to be part of the white family, she
was upset when she had to move back. Her strong feelings signal that,
in spite of her positive comments on her relationship to the white family, there were significant negative aspects to her experiences in the
family and the community there. Eunice Blackwell had moved out of
that town in a search for something better than that negative experience. This contradiction reveals the complex relationship between employer and employee in a caretaking relationship under Jim Crow conditions. Although the relationship involved much nurturing by her of
the white children and some respect for her, it was still a hierarchical
and paternalistic relationship where one person was financially compensated (but severely underpaid) for her services.

Other research on affluent white families and their black domestic
workers has shown that these paternalistic relationships were common
in the South and the North, and the black workers experienced a variety
of working conditions, some more positive and some quite negative. In
any event the black workers and the young whites who depended on
them both learned that the black caretakers could easily be replaced or
punished if they stepped out of "their place."[10]

Destructive Coping Strategies

In discussing their everyday coping strategies our interviewees talked
not only about their relationships with whites, but also about their relationships with other African Americans. Additionally, not all these coping strategies involved healthy life choices. Margie Boykin, a respondent in the Southeast, explains that her life changed when she moved
"out of the projects" and her parents engaged in some destructive behavior:

So when I look back I had desired myself to be a good person. Now,
the reason I said that, my background is from parents that drank, a

lot. . . . When I was nine years old we moved from the projects to a home . . . My dad got it from these people at a white church that he worked with. But it seems to me that when we made that move my mother was drinking more. My mother would send us to Mrs. Mary's on the next street to go get [alcohol] for her. . . . My mother would get drunk . . . [sighs]. I never lost respect for my mother, but I was ashamed because sometimes she would be cursing, then my dad would be cursing. My dad was a peaceful man. He would drink, but then he would go in bed and sleep. When my momma was [drinking], she would go in and pull the cover off and just aggravate him, then they might start to fight. . . . I wanted to be a good person, which I am, a very good person. I had two brothers and a sister, now I am finding out that I have another brother. He was around occasionally, whenever he did come around he and my mother would always get into a fuss because he was supposed to belong to someone else. But . . . he belonged to her, but she never really admitted it to us. So I can't really get real close to him, but I'm trying. But he is just . . . different. (*Margie Boykin, 70s*)

Boykin's mother drank more heavily when they moved out of mostly poor black dwellings to living closer to whites in a home. As an adult, she speculates that her half-brother, who is biracial, was a source of some of her mother's stress and anguish. As noted previously, black women were often raped by white men and usually suffered the consequences alone—such as psychological trauma or an unwanted pregnancy. The respondent didn't share with us where her half-brother grew up, yet black women commonly sent children conceived because of rape, coercion, or an affair to live with family members out of town.

Given the taboo nature of revealing alcoholism, few of our respondents cited using alcohol as a coping strategy to numb the recurring pain of legal segregation. Many more respondents noted the tactic of avoiding whites who were especially prone to discrimination and violence when they drank too much. A respondent in the Southwest, Rachel Polk, discusses these difficult situations:

We did not go in any place where they sold liquor or . . . you know anywhere where they had anybody [with alcohol]. . . . And so sometimes they [whites would] stop and ask us [to come in] on our way back from lunch, but we never would go in. We were afraid to go in. . . . We didn't want anything to happen. (*Rachel Polk, 60s*)

The racial norms of Jim Crow were firmly grounded in African Americans' knowing "their place" at the bottom of the racial hierarchy. Interracial gatherings where whites, blacks, or both groups had impaired judgment could be very dangerous for blacks.

Another respondent in the Southwest, Otis Miles, recalls a similar sentiment of avoiding all people who drink too much alcohol: "When people get to drinking, they say things that they wouldn't, and I don't care about being around them. . . . That's the reason why I don't fool around over there. I don't go anywhere, hardly. Trouble is too easy to get in." He continues to describe his avoidance of alcohol and men carrying guns:

> When I was a little boy . . . I wouldn't walk down a sidewalk that the law [police] was on. I'd get on the other side, if I had to pass him. Or he was meeting me, I'd get on the other side, the other street and go. . . . I just couldn't stand that [white] man with that gun on. And he used to come down to my grandfather's house every Sunday. My grandfather made that ole bootleg beer, sit up there and play that ole hillbilly records, and drank that beer. But I didn't give a damn to see that man with that gun on. . . . God damn, I couldn't stand to pass that man with that gun . . . I was just scared of that man with that gun on. Ain't done a thing, but I just can't stand to pass him. That man use to come down to the house every Sunday morning 'cause my grandfather had two 10-gallon crocks, had something ready for him every weekend. And they'd come down there and sit on the porch and just drank that shit and talk. (*Otis Miles, 70s*)

The respondent reports that nothing bad ever happened in the interactions between his black grandfather and the white officer. Yet, the presence of an armed white officer drinking his grandfather's home brew was a source of stress. Indeed, he underscores the point multiple times in his interview that he avoided crossing paths with any gun-carrying white man.

Actually, some black southerners coped with white violence by keeping a weapon nearby. Recall from the previous chapter, the respondent, Wilma Oliver, who noted that her "dad used to have his gun by his side. . . . He knew about the bad things that happened to girls and he didn't want it to happen to us." It was common knowledge in black communities that some white men preyed on black women and children for sexualized violence. Unfortunately, however, guns were not just used for protection from potential white attackers. Some black southerners unleashed their frustration on one another, as Leones Peacock, a 78-year-old respondent, explains in his interview: "And it was always a confrontation or fighting going on. It wasn't the old folks, it was the youngsters. And the police wouldn't do nothing, they would just say, 'Well, those "N" words, they can kill each other off.'" Without consideration of the difficult and very stressful Jim Crow context, such black-on-black violence—excessively highlighted then as now in the white-controlled mass media—might suggest a serious sociocultural flaw in black communities. From a sociological point of view, however, there is much more to this social reality. In this Jim Crow era black-on-black anger and violence were among the safer expressions of built-up personal frustrations. Although not all black coping mechanisms were salubrious, they all should be understood within this extraordinarily oppressive racial context. Oppressed persons often cope by fighting others who are oppressed for the crumbs of social rewards and power, rather than attacking their more dangerous and powerful white oppressors.[11]

Pro-Active Coping Strategies

As we discovered in the interview excerpts in chapter 3, Jim Crow's informal norms and laws took a toll on the geographical mobility of black southerners. They faced numerous racial restrictions in most areas of public life, including in traveling, shopping, and public accommodations. They were required to know these informal norms and laws and to be prepared and equipped to handle racist barriers they encountered. Several respondents explained in their interviews that their mothers would be diligent in numerous ways, such as by packing sack lunches for long car or train rides.

Irving Cox, a respondent in the Southwest, talks about the recurring stress of traveling in Jim Crow situations:

> When you are in grammar school, you don't be going to trips and stuff like that and to games. And in high school we [would] go, you know, we would take part in things like that. And when we went . . . you were not allowed to use the restroom. When they'd stop at a filling station you could get a soda because they were out front in a

box. But you couldn't use the bathroom. So you would wherever you were going, you had to be prepared to hold it from one place to another. Well at the time, when you're young and you need to go to a bathroom . . . that's the time when it really hurts. (*Irving Cox, 60s*)

Cox shares the memory of physical pain in not being permitted to relieve himself in the most basic of bodily functions. We can reasonably speculate that this pain was not only physical, but also emotional and psychological. He knew that bathroom facilities were available, but his presence was deemed by whites to be inferior and contaminating of these amenities. In his interview he discusses the pro-active strategies regularly required of black travelers, such as limiting one's liquid intake to reduce the need for bathroom breaks.

Other pro-active coping strategies involved preparing a defense against expected white allegations of theft. Katherine Bonner, living in the Southeast, reports on how her parents taught her to always get written documentation for any purchase:

I would let my kids go to the store without me. And I always taught my children, because I was taught, never come out of the store with anything in your hand. Always ensure that you get a receipt and a bag. And that's me today, because that's just what my parents told me. Today I tell my grandkids: "Don't go in the store and buy you a package of gum and let the sales clerk give it to you in your hand. If they can't give you a bag, ask for your money back." My dad told me the same thing; I didn't know why. That's probably why. That's why. We could not go to the store unless our parents were with us. And so my children, and my grandkids are forever hearing "Don't you come out of that store without that product in a bag and having a receipt for it." (*Katherine Bonner, 70s*)

We observe here the intergenerational transmission of skills needed to resist white accusations of theft. Bonner learned from her father and passed the lessons along to her children and grandchildren. Removed from the context of white-racist framing, she might be perceived as "paranoid" for insisting on a bag and receipt for small purchases. However, African Americans were often falsely accused of crimes for the slightest of oversights or normative transgressions. These could bring steep fines, incarceration, or even a lynching. Therefore, deliberate attention to even the smallest of details could be a lifesaving strategy.

Compare the experience of Katherine Bonner to that of Frank Wilson, a man in his 80s in the Southeast. He describes his first significant encounter with whites when his mother bought him a bicycle:

> She had bought me a bicycle on time . . . I paid [the white clerk] 15 dollars. . . . I didn't get a receipt. . . . When my mother went there to pay the next time we were a month behind on the bicycle. . . . He told mama that I didn't pay him. I said, "I paid you.". . . He said, "Nigger, don't you never call me a liar! I said you didn't pay me!" I said, "Oh yes, sir, Mr. Ray, I paid you and I am not telling no lie." . . . [Mother said] "Come on, son, let's go." . . . He didn't too much like what I had said, and the police come up to my house after this was all over with. The police ask, "Where is this boy they call Frankie?" I told him, "My name is Frank Wilson but they call me Frankie." "Nigger, you being smart with me!" I said, "No, I'm not being smart.". . . He said, "Pull your hat off your head." I said, "For what?" He said, "Don't no nigger stand up and talk to me face-to-face with no hat on his head. You get that hat off your head!" My mama said, "Take your cap off your head, son. Take it off! Take it off!" . . . He told mama he didn't want to have no more trouble with me. Because if he do, he was going to send me off for a long time. So that night my mama and my daddy talked to me and told me the way the white man thinks, and the way the white man do and the best way to get along with him. . . . Say "yes sir," and "no sir." . . . White man was something else when I was coming up. He would hit you. He would kick you. He would beat you. He would kill you, and there was nothing your parents could do about it. (*Frank Wilson, 80s*)

We observe why there were often strong lessons for black children about getting a receipt for payments. Wilson remembers this traumatic event as a turning point in life and his first hard lesson about white supremacy. The child is called the English language's most demeaning racist epithet. As we have observed in previous accounts, children were early on taught coping strategies such as conforming to the racist norms and laws without question and that all whites were authority figures and potentially dangerous. Most children soon understood that they had little recourse in recurring difficult interactions with whites.

Being pro-active and prepared for problematical interactions with whites was thus required for African Americans of all ages. Some respondents noted the importance of learning the wisdom and strength in trusting one's own judgment in choosing which racial battles to fight. Recall our respondent Delores Fowler, in the Southwest; she remembers how African Americans sometimes used silence to cope in interactions with white people:

> Oh yeah, you're going to hear people telling you different things about what to do. But I think that your best experience is what you learn for yourself, because sometimes following some other people, it might, not be the best thing on certain things. . . . Well you can start some violence by expressing too much, you know, when you don't got no voice. That's how I feel about it. [*Can you give me an example . . . ?*] Well you know, if you're talking with someone and . . . what they say [is], "Oh well I wouldn't take this" about such and such a thing. And "I done did such and such a thing." Well if you did that, you ain't doing nothing but making it harder on yourself because you know you don't have no voice. And if you tried to take it to court, or whatever, or go see a lawyer, well you're still going to their [white] color so . . . you can't win the battle. . . . I try to teach [my kids] that everything come up sometimes, and you can't let it have its way, or you're hurting yourself . . . but it's time for all things, and there's a place for all things. (*Delores Fowler, 80s*)

It is tempting for those outside a difficult social situation to suggest, "I would have done this" or "You should have done that." Yet these remarks, no matter how well-intended, place an extra burden on disadvantaged persons and don't always consider the limitations on choices available to them. Members of racially subordinate groups often must consider a social cost-benefit analysis when confronting unjust interactions. Given the limits on human energy and resources, one cannot fight in every "battle," so then as now African Americans have needed to strategize *in advance* about the best courses of action. In this era major civic resources available to whites to protect life and livelihood—for example, police officers, lawyers, and judges—were typically immersed in white supremacy and thus unavailable to black Americans.

Coping strategies included the wisdom and strength to remain silent, and being obedient to the racist norms and laws for survival's sake. Again, these everyday strategies were ordinarily thought out well in advance of interacting with whites. The previous interviewee explains multiple times during the interview that African Americans had "no voice" in this era. Other respondents' comments echoed this forced silence as well. Another respondent, Bernard Campbell, remembers silence as a coping mechanism in keeping a job:

> You kept your mouth shut whenever you interacted with white peo-
> ple because you had to. . . . Blacks were brought to that level of
> humiliation . . . Their job depended on it. It was a process or you
> could be fired in a minute off the job if, you know, for being uppity
> and those kinds of things. There was nothing you could do about it.
> So, you got a family to feed, you got a life to live, so it was a bitter pill
> to swallow but you have to do it. (*Bernard Campbell, 60s*)

Respondent Frank Wilson similarly explains the lack of having a voice in this era as a way of protecting one's family and community:

> You see everything was bottled up for so many years that I could not
> say what I wanted to say. "Yes sir, no sir, yes sir, no sir, Mr. white
> folks.". . . Back then I didn't have no voice. Back then you had to be
> humble . . . very humble. Because you didn't want them to come
> along and try to burn the house down and your family on account of
> you. . . . A whole lot of them. You couldn't prove it. You just couldn't
> prove it. If you try to live big, they would destroy you. . . . You better
> not live too high. [*Why didn't the community come together?*]
> Scared! Scared. You want to know the truth. Scared. They could get
> hurt. Definitely, get hurt! (*Frank Wilson, 80s*)

For many African Americans daily survival required a life of humil-
ity, deference, and being invisible and silent around whites who had the
potential to cause great harm. This tactic of survival created a double
bind: Whites often claimed that African Americans were content in
their racially subordinate position because they didn't actively fight
back. Such a racist framing, however, denied the institutionally enforced white dominance operative in every corner of societal life in this
era.

Residing in the Southwest, Leroy Watson discusses his durable insistence on self-worth and his not aspiring to the unattainable white standard of success:

> Because I'm tired of chasing that dream of being really equal with
> them, with [white] folks 'cause I ain't going to make it. I'm doing all
> right. I'm not rich, but I'm doing all right. . . . When I joined the

army in 1941, I wanted to be a pilot. But you know what they told me? They said, "Naw, you can't be no pilot. You got to have at least five years of college, plus some more years of like flying a plane." Anybody can fly a plane! But you know what, I had a buddy that knew how to fly a jet, and one day he invited me to go in the plane. And I asked him if it was easy, and he said yes. And on the spot he showed me how to fly a helicopter. And I flew a helicopter. But they tell you they don't want no black people—ain't got sense enough. That's what the white folks wanted to input in your mind, that we couldn't do it. But we know better. We can do whatever they do and we can do it better. We have proved it. (*Leroy Watson, 80s*)

Watson explains that the standards for flying a plane then included years of training and years of college, standards that did not explicitly exclude African Americans. However, until the 1960s many historically white colleges and universities had explicit rules against admitting African Americans, and those that did—in northern and border states— had tuition and fees that made college attendance out of reach for most African Americans. On the surface, it appears that Watson accepts second-class citizenship by not pushing for a career in flying planes. However, upon closer inspection, that goal was for most of his life impossible because of racial barriers in the military and airline industry. In addition, he does not internalize the dominant message that he is inferior to whites. He has proven to himself that he is capable of flying, but makes a conscious choice not to chase after the "white dream." Observe too that there were "good whites" who, as here, assisted African Americans, but they too were often limited by systemic racism.

Caring and Coping in the Community

Other frequent coping strategies for discriminatory situations involved personal hard work and turning to the collective wisdom of African American communities. In his interview, Michael Cooper discusses survival tactics, echoing in part the previous respondent in redefining success away from an abundance of material possessions:

My daddy worked, worked, worked. We never saw him. My father would do [work] all day, every day, and then when it hit 5:00 in the afternoon . . . he had a side job feeding the mules. So when he got home at night it would be 9:30 or 10:00. We already be in the bed, me and my sister. . . . I'd just hear him 'cause he'd leave home in the morning to go feed the mules and to harness them up, and get ready to go to work at 8:00. Then he'd feed them at night . . . he needed those two jobs to make enough money to keep us in school, and . . . that went on for quite a while, 'cause they wasn't making any money. (*Michael Cooper, 70s*)

Then he shifts his commentary to his own hard work, from the Jim Crow era to the present day:

I got grown, and got able to get out on my own, and I worked on two jobs for forty years, and my mother and daddy were both living then. My mother used to tell me, "You're working too much. You're going to kill yourself. You're going to be just like your daddy. You're going to work yourself to death." Yeah, yeah, yeah. But . . . knowing at the time that he was working on two jobs. I think that had a little effect on me, because [people ask], "Why you working as old as you are?" I say, "I need the money." . . . "I may not spend it on myself, but I spend it on my grandkids." . . . Me and my wife, we eat one good meal a day, but I got great-grandchildren, great-great-grandchildren, and some of them, some of their parents are hurting, just like my parents was. So, whatever they need, that I can do, I do it, for the little kids. And I don't feel like I would be happy having a great big bank account and a little grandkid running around needing some shoes. (*Michael Cooper, 70s*)

He then adds some comments on a hardworking uncle and certain family relationships:

I had one uncle that, my daddy's brother, and he used to pick cotton, go out on these fields in West Texas and all around. We lived in [names town] at this time, and he'd go pick cotton all the year, until around December when it would get too cold and cotton picking was over. Then he would come back to [names town] and live with us. . . . And my momma would take care of him, wash his clothes, and all of that. But all through the year when he was picking cotton, he would send money home to her, to keep his insurance up. (*Michael Cooper, 70s*)

This respondent recalls the intergenerational transmission of the value and necessity of hard work. His father killed himself working so much, and he seems to be doing the same. As we have observed previously, over most of the long Jim Crow era black men were often incarcerated if they couldn't prove they had regular employment, so hard work was not only necessary for family survival but also for them to even remain free. Documented accounts of hard labor in the fields as sharecroppers or in white homes as domestic servants stand in stark contrast to the commonplace white framing of African Americans as "lazy." Clearly, few workers in U.S. history have worked harder as a group. Moreover, African American families heavily relied on each other for financial as well as emotional support, and many members endured great personal sacrifices to ensure that their extended families were adequately supported.

Other respondents noted this importance in relying on one's local community for individual and collective survival. A retired teacher in the Southwest, Jane Townsend, remembers the collective response to extreme racial challenges:

> There were incidents where they were lynching people in Mississippi, Alabama, and there were some cases in [this state] where they had done the same thing to blacks for apparently no reason. All that we thought was that it was simply an unnecessary reason. So it caused us to be a closer-knit community because everybody was aware of what everybody was doing—[so] that you really would cover and watch each other's back. . . . We knew the ramifications and the boundaries, so we tended to group together. . . . So we knew what the dangers were and we were given strategies to overcome them. (*Jane Townsend, 70s*)

Similar to this teacher, in the Southeast Sidney Mack recalls how African Americans had to stick together to deal with problematic whites. He recalls a conversation with his grandfather when the 1950s–1960s civil rights movement was getting national attention:

> [My grandfather] never really talked about the situation but when we started the [civil rights] movement, this is the only thing he said to me. He said, "I think I know what you're doing, I think I understand what you're doing." He said, "Now I'm not saying what you're doing is wrong," he said, "but what you need to be looking at is jobs." That

was the only thing that he said to me. You need to be . . . fighting for these people to have some jobs . . . There wasn't no social security, there wasn't nothing. . . . Black folks raising white folks' children is what it boiled down to. . . . [*How do you think people coped during that time from what you saw?*] I'm back to this community now. A communal type of thing. That is when everybody looked out for everybody. . . . I mean everybody knew everybody, everybody knew all the children. The morals and the conduct and behavior were standard. . . . The core value system was just there. . . . Discipline was a community thing, it wasn't just a family inside your house thing, that was a community thing. . . . Church was important back then. . . . When you walked outside that church, walking back and forth to school, we had no buses back then, walking back and forth to school, people sitting on their front porch. . . . So, everybody just shared everything. . . . Those who were a little bit more fortunate than the others all got shares. . . . That was how they made it. . . . So they worked for it. And I can tell you, I wonder sometime myself how in the hell they made it. (*Sidney Mack, 70s*)

Conversations with his grandfather illustrate the wisdom of elderly African Americans before him: The civil rights movement wasn't just about sitting next to whites in restaurants and on buses, but it was about the fundamental right to one's livelihood. Access to jobs provides the economic capital to provide for one's family and to increase the tax base, which can mean better neighborhood schools and other community amenities. Looking back on the horrific experiences with systemic racism, he wonders how African Americans coped with that daily white oppression. Mack cites numerous contending and coping strategies already noted, including hard work and turning to the black community and church.

Conflicting Memories and Denial

The majority of our respondents shared broadly similar memories of the difficult Jim Crow decades. However, a few reported memories that were internally inconsistent or inconsistent with the many negative reports of their peers. For example, Agnes Howell, an elderly respondent in the Southwest, shares her memories in this way:

> We rode buses with them [whites] and they never told us to go to the back of the bus or when you buy a hamburger go to the back door or to the back window and get your hamburger. No. I did not experience that 'cause they never—I never lived with that. I never was told that. I will say it like that. I never was told that. I guess coming up my dad and my mom, probably, but not none of us kids. We never, we never experienced that fight. So I couldn't tell you nothing about white people 'cause we never—we drank out the same, yeah, we drank out the same fountain. Never experienced that other stuff. No, we didn't. (*Agnes Howell, 80s*)

However, a few minutes later in the interview she does note that the 1950s–1960s civil rights movement brought some major changes in segregation:

> Yes, I remember Martin Luther King. . . . Yes, they got to be some nice good white people. They had to be nice 'cause they combine the schools. White peoples and working together in the same offices, all that kinda stuff. You could ride anywhere on the bus you wanted to ride. My dad use to tell us that he had to go to the back before this happened. I think that all the blacks had to go to the back of the bus, and white people had to sit to the front. But when they changed this over, then you could sit anywhere you want on the bus. You could sit beside one of them. If they didn't want to sit there, they could move. . . . I remember when it happened. . . . It was rough till then. (*Agnes Howell, 80s*)

We see internal contradictions in Agnes Howell's interview where she reports not personally experiencing racially segregated buses, even though her age and geographic location of growing up would strongly suggest otherwise. In addition, she remembers here that there was much bus and school segregation and that "it was rough." Possible interpretations of her inconsistencies would include some age-related memory loss, for it can be difficult to recall events that took place nearly 50 years in the past. Additionally, her comments may reflect some denial of the painful and traumatic racial events that she likely experienced. Denying or forgetting some of the past is one way to cope with its great pain, a common symptom of the segregation stress syndrome.

A second respondent, Julia Rose, also stands out as suggesting an alternate reality for African Americans in the Jim Crow era. She was asked about the presence of the Ku Klux Klan. Although other respondents of her southern town confirmed a significant Klan presence, her tone in the interview immediately changed as she replied:

> No. No, not here. [The respondent's voice gets louder and agitated.] No, ain't no Klan here. No. I ain't heard about it. If there had been some Klan I am sure we would have heard it. [*What about when you were growing up?* The respondent responds even louder.] No! I ain't heard nothing about no Ku Klux Klan. I heard about the Ku Klux Klan, I think I was sitting here one time looking at TV and seen them folks. On a talk show! As far as our growing up we didn't know nothing about those folks. [Her voice is higher and more assertive.] Not when I was growing up! . . . I have heard talk of them, but we ain't never had to deal with them. Oh no, no, no. All I know is they put a rag on their faces. . . . [*A rag on their face?*] Whatever that thing is they got! They put on their face and they peeping out of it! [Her voice is more agitated.] No, we ain't never had to deal with them. But I have heard a lot of talk about some people talk about them but we ain't never had to deal with them. . . . It's good in [our state]. It is not—we didn't have to deal with no Ku Klux. I ain't about or had to deal with no Ku Klux Klan. . . . [*So was it good for black folks here?*] Yeah. Yeah, they good. They was good. No hate. Never heard of that as far as I know, and I been around here a long time. I never heard of it. . . . They meet black people and don't even know you, and they meet you and they friendly with you. They just friendly with you. You don't know their name and they don't know your name. Probably never seen you before, but they are friendly. [Voice is softer, not excited.] Friendly people. Yep. Yep. (*Julia Rose, 70s*)

Rose reports excitedly that growing up in her southern town was a mostly positive experience for African Americans, despite much evidence from historical materials and others' contemporary recounting that it was otherwise. It is possible that Julia Rose's experiences with white extremist groups like the Klan were different from those of others in her community or that she is misremembering the bloody Klan actions of the past. Indeed, her account of whites treating African Americans with friendly pleasantries is more consistent with contemporary experiences in this area than during the Jim Crow time when she was younger. It is also possible that she is in significant denial about past experiences. Researchers Bryant-Davis and Ocampo suggest that trauma survivors often use denial as a means to protect themselves emotionally and psychologically and to prevent acknowledging their victimization.[12] Moreover, one also senses in her strong and insistent denial that she is perhaps at some level still fearful of the still existent (albeit small) Ku Klux Klan in her state and does not want to be seen as criticizing them, even in the present day.

ACTIVE RESISTANCE: SOCIALIZING CHILDREN

Childhood Ignorance and Avoidance

There is a difference between denial of Jim Crow atrocities and childhood ignorance of them. As we have seen previously, some interviewees discussed how their parents tried, to varying degrees, to keep racial disparities and violence hidden from them as children. One interviewee in the Southwest, Melvin Northup, recalls why he accepted a subordinate position in the legal segregation era:

> We never thought anything about not having a school bus. We didn't know anything about school buses and such. We saw the school buses go by going to the white schools, and it had "school bus" on it. Didn't mean anything to us. 'Cause we didn't have one so we didn't . . . at those times, you took what you had and you were satisfied with it, because that's all you knew. (*Melvin Northup, 60s*)

He describes his compliance as a child with the racial order because he didn't know any better. Black children could easily witness the racial divisions, yet were not always fully aware of the depths of whites' racist hatred or the origins and rationalizations supporting that hate.

Parenting was challenging to say the least. Parents wanted to protect their children's innocence, yet understood the importance and necessity to prepare them for a world of potential white violence—including physical, written, or spoken action inflicting or threatening to inflict injury on black individuals, especially on those who resist. Parents had various strategies for explaining and countering white supremacy. Some, like respondent Russell Butler in the Southwest, discuss a lack of lessons about barriers and norms in his case:

They stayed in they place and I stayed in mine. . . . Oh, "Negro, you stay in your place, you want something you go to the back door and get it. Don't come in here 'cause you ain't got no business in here." They had water fountains for the colored people, water fountains for the white folk. You go to town we had places we can go eat, where it was divided place. You come in, you go down this-a-way, and white folk go down this-a-way, sat there and eat. Mmm-hmm, you have to pay the man, and go on about your business. . . . Other than hard times that's about it, hard times. I'll tell you now, that's something my parents never did talk about too much around the children. What they talked about, they talked about it with grown folks, and we didn't sit there and listen to their conversation. They talk about it. You get up and go on out there somewhere and play. . . . They want you, they need you, they'll call you. . . . It was a hard time, but we made it. (*Russell Butler, 70s*)

As Butler poignantly describes, respect for elders and knowing their place in society were fundamental parts of the socialization of children by their parents. Black parents' frequent silence around their children served a dual purpose that included respecting the elders' private conversations, but also protecting the children from painful adult discussions of racial discrimination that could lead to secondary racial traumas.

An older woman, Joyce Bishop, describes well how her mother would make her leave the house when whites from a nearby store would come to her house to collect payment for certain products they sold:

When I was a little girl, and [white] people came to the house and talked to [my mother] real nasty, I remember that. Really nasty. I mean they called her nigger-this, nigger-that. . . . [My mother] made us leave the house. And I would cry. I would think, "Why are they picking on her?" When they left, we, me and my brother, would take off and run in the house. . . . If she was in tears, she wouldn't let us see. She protected us. And when she paid them she told me, "Whatever y'all do when you grow up, do not buy anything from [names store] because they are very, very prejudiced." . . . I don't think it's got no better [today] really. It's just hidden more. (*Joyce Bishop, 50s*)

The stress of helplessness is prevalent for the child and mother. As a child, she was unable to protect her mother from white abuse, and the mother attempted to protect her children from witnessing her mistreatment and trauma. In spite of her mother's efforts to protect her children, they were painfully aware of much that was taking place. In her interview Bishop notes that she teaches her own children about not patronizing hostile stores, and does not burden them with her hurt feelings.

Practical Advice: Community Representation and Two-Faced Whites

Many of the messages taught to children involved practical knowledge or explicit steps to succeed. In the Southwest Calvin Hunter explains how he was taught about the burden that he bore as a representative of his community:

> We were always told to conduct ourselves properly so we would be a good example and would not be a handicap for those coming behind us so we had to be formal in most situations and try to conduct ourselves in an exemplary manner so that we, because if one black did something wrong, then all the blacks were considered wrong. So we had that burden that we had to deal with and most of us handled it fairly well. [*Did you pass this advice on to your children?*] Yes. I think the way I worded it is the only way they can get to your dad is through you. Yeah, so you have to watch yourself because they know who you are and they know who your folks are. You are representing not only yourself but the community. And that was the same message that was given to me when I was growing up, the honor was more to it than just about me. I have three sons, which was scary, three sons. (*Calvin Hunter, 60s*)

This message of being a representative of your community and of your racial group is different from the dominant narrative accenting the importance of individualism. African Americans, then as now, knew the burden that their actions placed on black kin and strangers alike. Indeed, as discussed previously, many innocent African Americans were assaulted or murdered by whites either in a case of mistaken identity or in retaliation for what one African American had done. Given the frequency with which black men were assaulted or lynched, this father reasonably recounts that it was "scary" to parent black boys. Rather than use words like "joyous," "adventurous," or "exhausting," Hunter notes that this child-rearing was scary because of the high risk of white violence, incarceration, or early death. Again we observe the intergenerational character of the segregation stress syndrome. Black children in each generation likely come to feel their parents' fear in dealing with whites, from the transmission of both verbal and nonverbal parental messages.

Besides being taught about representing the African American community as a child, Frank Wilson notes that he was taught explicit messages about the two-faced nature of many whites:

> I was always told, "Don't trust the white man." To tell you the truth I don't trust him today, not too much. . . . My dad, and in [black] schools they [teachers] would tell you. . . . [*The teachers*?] . . . Yeah, they [the teachers] would tell you. They [the teachers] would just say, "Don't trust them because you might get hurt." (*Frank Wilson, 80s*)

According to most whites, black men and women were not to be considered as social equals or potential leaders, but mainly as a tool for working for whites, and on white terms. This interview reveals that African Americans were very aware of whites' variable performativity and trustworthiness and communicated that reality across the generations. Additionally, casual conversation between white and black acquaintances might be interpreted differently when whites were alone. The consequences of harmless banter between acquaintances could lead to white retaliation, including violence. Although the likelihood of that happening might have been rare, the threat was usually present: Offend whites and the welfare of one's person or family might be in danger.

Emphasizing this point, another respondent reports being taught in childhood similar strong lessons about whites. Florence Tyler, a childcare worker, emotionally recalls how going to work with her mother turned into a painfully frightening experience:

> My mother would wash clothes for Mr. Smith. . . . I would help my mother by using an iron to press the clothes. He always wanted his shirts cleaned and pressed. Back then you didn't have bleach. You had to use lye. We used a washing board to scrub the clothes. . . . I

remember one day, I don't know what happened, but there was one spot on the corner of his collar and he started cussing. . . . He just kept cussing and yelling at my mama. I was so scared for my mama. . . . She just kept saying, "I'm sorry sir, I'm sorry sir, it won't happen again. . . . Yes sir, yes sir, sir, I'm sorry. It won't happen again." She was begging and pleading with him. I remember that being my first memory. My mama told me to always keep my distance from white folks. . . . She said, "You can't trust them. . . . They will grin and smile in your face but they are not your friend." This is what I tell my children. (*Florence Tyler, 80s*)

She too explains parental lessons about whites being pleasant to your face, yet turning their backs when the relationship doesn't meet their needs. This experience occurred over 50 years in the past, yet she recalls it in significant detail. It has impacted her to the point where she still tells her children, to this day, not to trust whites.

Throughout her interview the negative effects of the segregation traumas became quite evident. Like other African Americans of her generation, she lives in a darkened house where the curtains are drawn so tight that it is difficult to see her face in the middle of a sunny day. She repeatedly asked for the audio recorder to be shut off, and she asked many questions about the use of the data, clearly needing confirmation of interview confidentiality. For many of our elderly respondents, the racially traumatic events that occurred in their youth have shaped their lives to the extent that they still fear the possibility of significant white retaliation.

More Family Socialization: Be Obedient

As we have already seen, numerous respondents exhibited trauma symptoms throughout their interviews. A retired domestic worker answered several questions with ease before she was asked the question, "Do you remember your first encounter with a white person?" At that moment she became tense, as sweat formed on her forehead. Elma Boyd could not recall her first encounter in the 1930s, but remembered the way in which she had framed her responses to whites:

During the time that I was coming up we were always taught to, always especially to a white person, they would tell us always be

obedient to them. "Yes sir, no sir, yes madam and no madam." . . .
That is the way I tried to bring my children up too. "Always be
obedient. Be obedient to them. Never be sassy." I tried to tell them,
"I have been obedient, and I have listened to a lot of instruction that
I got from my foreparents. I don't know how I would have brought
you all up if I had not been obedient." My dad and my stepmom
would always have us together, and he would talk to us about different things and how to be obedient . . . [to] white people during that
time, [or] they may find you dead somewhere. (*Elma Boyd, 70s*)

Boyd's composure shifted from comfortable to anxious as she shared
early lessons for surviving the brutality of Jim Crow patterns. Death was
indeed a potential consequence of not being compliant and deferential
to whites, so teaching obedience to children was critical. As we have
seen throughout this book, black southerners certainly knew "their
place." As have other scholars, we note in our interviews the unhealthy
paternalistic relationship in which whites often treated African
American adults as children by demanding that they be invisible, calling
them by their first names, and demanding submissiveness and obedience.

An interviewee in the Southeast, Edward Harris, shares with us how
his mother taught him lessons of being obedient and of submission to
whites:

It was important that you were respectful when you were out. . . . It
was important that you were not disrespectful to whites. . . . I heard
stories of the Ku Klux Klan . . . I didn't want to encounter those
things. [Blacks] did not want to encounter those things. . . . If you
meet someone [whites] down the street it was, "Yes sir," "No
ma'am." (*Edward Harris, 60s*)

During the legal segregation decades, whites in the Klan and other
white supremacist groups regularly engaged in violent or other discriminatory acts against blacks of all ages, often under the cover of darkness
or hidden behind hooded masks with identities concealed. As a result, it
was often difficult for African Americans to discern good whites from
whites who intended to cause harm. Thus, as this respondent makes
clear, obedience and deference were taught to children and were required in regard to all whites to ensure the safety of one's self, family,
and community.

Another elderly respondent, Maxine Shaw, echoes the previous respondent in discussing lessons on the importance of obedience from her grandmother and mother:

> I remember when I was little, the white kids for some reason used to come down the track going in [our] part of town. And we would fight them. We threw rocks at them, and they threw rocks back at us. We were small, and it was never anything . . . but my grandmama would always have a fit if she saw you doing something, you know. She'd tell you, "Oh, don't do that." She was just deathly afraid of [whites]. . . . And so was, so was my mother. She was afraid of whites. And I know why now. She was, she was an obedient [person] . . . I wouldn't say an Uncle Tom . . . because she had a lot of respect from whites in this city. (*Maxine Shaw, 70s*)

Childish pranks of throwing rocks took on a different meaning in Jim Crow situations where black children—after being warned by older family members—had to be concerned about violent repercussions from whites. Note too the reality of having to live being "deathly afraid" of what whites might do—again a vivid example of the visceral impact of white-imposed racial oppression. Quite a few respondents also noted a concern for coming across as an "Uncle Tom," a derogatory term for a black person who excessively attempts to please white oppressors. Maxine Shaw, like many others in our interviews, differentiates between obedience for the sake of survival versus obedience to gain favors from whites and at the expense of other black people.

Maxine Shaw also comments that whites in the city respected her mother. Another respondent, Loretta Price, who resides in the Southwest, explains that her grandfather worked hard to be in good favor with whites:

> We were taught to respect them, yeah. We [were] also taught that we were not their equals, they didn't consider us their equal, but we were always told that we were as good as anybody. We knew our place. Like I said, when we were in stores, we . . . had my father or my grandfather or whoever it was to get the item for us. We don't go through the store and pick up stuff. We did not, because we knew our place. [*What if you did?*] I would imagine that we would have gotten somewhat of a tanning because our parents were very strict on us. I mean, you just didn't disobey. . . . We were told the inferior

stories, I don't mean that he taught us that, we were told those stories [by whites]. . . . We were told [by my father] that we were as good as anybody else, but unfortunately that's the way it was. We lived in the country . . . and everything you got is coming from [whites]. The seeds that you're putting in the ground are coming from him. Your fertilizer is coming from him. The ties that you're getting is coming from him. The boots that you're getting . . . especially from these old black people, how are they going to get above that? There was just no outlet, like I told my father, my grandfather was a favored black man and that he had the help of judges, of lawyers, or people that just wanted to succeed. And that's why he was so successful. He was not an educated man. (*Loretta Price, 70s*)

Black children received contradictory messages about their racial identities and social placement. Their families told them that they were equally capable and as good as whites, but at the same time they were taught obedience to whites as a strategy of survival. Contrary to what they were taught by family members, whites constantly reminded them by their treatment that they were racially inferior. As Price explains, there was no outlet from white supremacy, as whites owned everything. Still, her grandfather became economically successful by hard work and with the help of some whites. These contradictory messages embody W. E. B. Du Bois's challenge of the black double consciousness: this "twoness" of being both a white-constructed "Negro" and a dignified human self, and viewing oneself constantly through both of these contradictory lenses.[13]

An interviewee in the Southeast, Joseph Brown, alludes to this double consciousness and the contradictory messages about being black in Jim Crow America:

You only interacted with your own, and it was like you internalized it. And you knew it was there but you tried to act human anyway. Because there was so much, you know to dehumanize you, so you would try to rise above it by dealing with your own dignity. And that was done through the church—that we were all God's children. I was [taught] I could be anything I wanted to be. All I had to do was work hard for it, and that there's going to come a time when all of this is going to melt away and that we'd be viewed as equal. . . . So it was a little thing that your parents were telling you and that the people in the community, they always encouraged kids in a positive way. Stay in school, go to church, listen to your parents, you can do anything you want to do. I know you are going to be a doctor or I know you are going to be a teacher. We had role models to emulate, you know, there was a trust for black people. (*Joseph Brown, 80s*)

Brown learned to hold his head high by ignoring the white messages of black inferiority and focusing on his humanity, prayer, education, and hard work. He claimed that the racial inferiority messages of Jim Crow would eventually "melt away," leaving one dominant perception rather than a contradictory double consciousness. He coped in the Jim Crow decades by obeying his parents, listening to teachers, turning to the church, and following successful black role models such as doctors, lawyers, and business owners.

Children Ignore Ramifications of Resistance

So far in this chapter we have the profiled coping strategies used to survive Jim Crow, and some of the messages that children received about enduring white supremacy. In this section we discuss certain active resistance strategies that African Americans used to chip away at white racial barriers and the racial hierarchy. Even as black parents sought to protect their children from the many messages of black inferiority, their children sometimes unknowingly resisted the imposed racist norms, such as Alvin Ford in the Southwest:

I was about 10 or 12 years old when I realized that I couldn't go in the front door of the café 'cause I was [black]. I went through there one day. Of course, they turned around and looked at me, but I kept on walking. And I knew, I knew I had to go to the back of the building. I don't know how I knew, but I knew I had to go to the back of the building to get served. But nobody there never said anything, and I got what I wanted. And I knew the lady there well. She made the best pie in the world. I knew her very well. But when I told mother about it she said, "Well, you really weren't supposed to do that." You know she told me not to do it again. And she said, "Ain't nobody said anything, but you can't ever tell when somebody gonna act crazy." So that's all she told me about it. And she didn't really put it, put it in [a] segregational context, you know. Just that the people might, might be thinking of something crazy. (*Alvin Ford, 70s*)

White social control over African Americans did not entail a guarantee of violence, but a guarantee of a potential for violence. This youngster pushed the boundaries of white supremacy unknowingly, yet he was vaguely aware that he was doing something wrong. While his mother did not explain the danger in terms of specific Jim Crow rules, she noted that it only took one or two volatile whites to cause him great harm.

Similarly, Benjamin Hayes, a retired teacher in the Southwest, remembers accidentally drinking from the wrong water fountains:

> It was at the [names store] when I accidentally drank out the wrong water fountain. . . . And we went to the store, and I got thirsty. And I just went to the first fountain I got to and they had signs that said "FOR WHITES," and I just ignored the sign. But my experience was not as bad as some may have encountered prior to me because a . . . white man warned me about drinking and sort of shouldered me as I ran off. [*Did you get in trouble by your parents?*] No, I was warned not to do it again. [*Did it ever happen again?*] Yeah, intentionally but I didn't get caught. [Laughs] (*Benjamin Hayes, 70s*)

Like the previous respondent, Benjamin Hayes's breach was an accident, yet he was vaguely aware that he was breaking the community rules. Ordinary whites, as here, policed the racial hierarchy to ensure that even children obeyed the signs. As an elderly man, he realizes that his childhood defiance of the white norms could have had much worse consequences. Developmentally, children and young adolescents may feel invincible and may be incapable of understanding the grave ramifications of some of their defiant actions, which only become apparent in retrospect.

This childlike sense of invincibility can be seen in our interview with Joan Mathis, a brave woman now in her 60s. She describes refusing to give up her seat on a segregated public bus in the Southwest:

> I was about 12 or 13 years old. We had to ride on the back of the bus. If a white person got on the bus, we had to move to the back of the bus and we had to stand up all the way. . . . Sometime a white person would get on there, every now and then, and when a white person would get on there, if it wasn't no seats for them to sit down, they'd ask you to move to the back, ask you to get up. I've been asked to get up and let them sit down there. Well, I just refused to get up. I say,

"I'm a woman just like she's a woman," and the bus driver stopped. He said, "If you don't let her sit down . . . when I move the bus, I'm going to call the police." I just still stayed there. They called the police, and they had me catch the next bus. Sure did. I had to get off the bus. (*Joan Mathis, 60s*)

Some psychological research points to adolescence as a time of invincibility orientation where young teens may be unable to differentiate between taking chances and being safe.[14] However, Mathis seems to have recognized at a fairly early age the fragility of the racial hierarchy that depends upon everyday individual acts to collectively uphold it. By chipping away at the racist norms in these small moments, blacks often created cracks in the foundation of racial oppression. Her actions, as well as hundreds of other small acts of resistance explained by the respondents, emphasize the cumulative *bravery* that it took to eventually tear down the segregation structures. Mainstream U.S. history books typically emphasize the courageous actions of a few black individuals like Rosa Parks and Dr. Martin Luther King, Jr., without paying the homage to the millions of everyday acts of resistance by ordinary African Americans, most never documented, that were essential to the eventual destruction of the nefarious realities of legal segregation.

MORE ACTIVE RESISTANCE: MAINTAINING INTEGRITY

Some of our respondents explained how they often resisted Jim Crow norms and institutions in more subtle and subversive ways. One interviewee, Clifford Gray in the Southwest, recalls how he resisted being reduced to subhuman:

My brother knows all about what went on. . . . Me and him were working for a guy baling hay. . . . So, we was working there, helping him tie the hay down and go put it in the shed. So all of a sudden we went home to eat. . . . So we did that and so the ole guy come out there, "Y'all ready to go back?" . . . We was going back to where he was baling the hay. He stopped and was talking to another white guy that was doing the same thing. And they was talking and he said, "Well, guess I better go see what my niggers are doing." Me and my brother looked at him. I said well, "I tell you what, this was it." So we just backed off right here and got out of the car, and walked back to the house. Then, when you were young men like we were . . . maybe 13 and 11, somewhere in there, you have to go through these things. And then they still like to made that statement, "Have to go see what my niggers are doing." So we left that alone. Instead of being treated like that, I'd rather not have a job. (*Clifford Gray, 60s*)

Although he was an adolescent who needed a job for extra money, he knew the job was not worth compromising his dignity and being reduced to a white man's N-word. Gray's actions of simply walking away from the situation spoke volumes about how he and his brother wouldn't stand for such blatant disrespect. However, numerous other respondents weren't able to walk away from jobs as adults, no matter how much they wanted to leave. They needed the jobs to support their families and were forced to endure much racist humiliation.

A respondent in the Southwest, Jeffrey Nelson, explained to us how African Americans looked out for each other in maintaining their dignity and integrity, and thereby subtly undercut white supremacy. He describes driving a truck with a white man when they decided to get something to eat:

He said, "Next stop is [names town], let's get something to eat." I said, "Okay." So we parked over there on the side . . . and go to the screen door. Well, he opened the door, and I walked in. Big fat old white lady sitting in there. She say . . . "You going to have to go around to the back for you to come in." I said, "It don't make me no difference where I eat just as long as I get me something to eat." . . . So I went back there, I told [the black waitress] I wanted some steak and french fries. That woman opened up that refrigerator, and she got a steak out of there, it went down her arm like this [demonstrates length of steak]. I thought she was going to put it on the damn thing and chop it, and just take half of it and cook it. No, she cooked that whole thing. I know why, the reason she done it. She done it because of [what] that white lady up front said to me when I come in. I couldn't eat all that steak. But now, when I get through eating, I can go through there and pay for it and go out the front door, mmm-hmm. But I can't come in the front door. (*Jeffrey Nelson, 70s*)

The white woman attempts to accent black inferiority by insisting that he walk through the back door, as was customary. However, the black restaurant worker, who was also likely mistreated at her work, subversively treats the black customer with an indulgence of more steak. This small act of resistance on the part of the waitress attempts to maintain the humanity of this black man. Nelson notes the inconsistency in the racist norms wherein he is not allowed to enter the restaurant from the front, but can go out the front door in order to pay. He notes later in his interview, "They don't care about you. All they want is your money." As in previous accounts, the power of money was sometimes a critical tool in coping with the realities of legal segregation. Money often trumped whites' disdain for black customers. Here it involved money for a meal. In other cases it involved walking away from a job and wages to maintain one's dignity, or not purchasing an item in a store from white clerks who behaved in a racist fashion.

Open Defiance by Individuals

A few respondents recalled open defiance of the racial hierarchy as a mechanism of resisting Jim Crow. A respondent in the Southwest, Martin Foster, recounts how he resorted to fighting to maintain his dignity:

> Fighting. Any white boy that . . . call you "nigger" or out of your name, they got a fight coming. And that way, you know on Saturday morning, they had these big shot football players playing at [names place], and all those, they come out on the park. And we'd go over there and we, you know scrimmage with them and play with them. We always end up fighting because somebody would say the N-word, and there's a fight. . . . Police come and took all the blacks and put them in jail and let the whites go. So, my answer to that is that I did fight it, whenever it happened. They found out, that in that community at that time when you disrespect a black guy, and call him out his name, you in a fight and that was just the way it is. [*What did you find was the least effective?*] By ignoring what you're going through. You didn't get anything solved going like that. [*Where did you learn the coping strategies . . . ?*] That come from me. My dad told us he didn't ever want to see us fighting and that he wasn't coming to get us out of jail. But that was my strategy, that came from me. He wasn't the kind that would start something, but me, I was the type that would start something. Me and my brothers. (*Martin Foster, 60s*)

Apparently, the white football players sometimes shrewdly antago-
nized the black players, knowing that the consequences would be a
fight—which would be followed by the black males being arrested.
Even so, Foster accents the importance of responding strongly when
one is called out by something other than their actual name, especially
by a demeaning racist epithet. We can see a possible generation shift
here, as his father's strategy was to maintain peace even at the expense
of his dignity.

Another respondent in the Southwest, Bessie Marshall, notes that
her parents wanted her to comply with the racist norms, yet she too
openly defied some influential whites:

> One time, I was grown then, we was at this schoolyard, and this
> police [officer] wanted to put me in jail. And he kept telling me to
> come on, come on. And I asked him, "Where do you want to come?
> To a room?" And he wanted to hit me, but he didn't hit me, there
> were too many blacks around. And he said, "Naw, I ain't that type of
> policeman." I said, "Well, you're talking like it." And that's the closest
> time I ever got to . . . somebody wanting to hit me. 'Cause when I
> was coming up . . . if someone said something to me I didn't like, I
> said it back. And my dad told me, you going to get your butt
> whooped one of these days. But I wasn't scared. I don't think none of
> my people was scared. . . . I always talked back to them [whites]
> when I felt like it. And my mama told me one day, we're going to be
> looking for you one day, and we ain't gonna find you because they
> done killed you. . . . Well, it still didn't scare me. . . . That's what
> made them [whites] so angry sometime, but they say, "You can talk
> to her as much as you want, that nigger ain't scared." I told one of
> them one day, "It takes a nigger to find a nigger." [laughing] . . . And
> then when I grew up to be a teenager, one of them cops that used to
> be mad and used to talk back to me, I found out he liked me. I told
> him I said, "I don't fool [with] no cops." Back when I was coming up
> I was mean. I didn't take nothing off of nobody. (*Bessie Marshall,
> 70s*)

Like the previous respondent, Marshall notes how she openly talked
back to powerful whites as her personal resistance strategy, thereby
defying the wishes of her more cautious parents. Neither she nor her
"people" were scared. Sometimes there is power in having nothing, for
you have nothing to lose in fighting back. Our respondents and others

who endured the horrific Jim Crow conditions should not be viewed though a simplistic lens as just meek victims, but rather as brave and active resistors who challenged white supremacy in overt, subtle, and covert ways when they could. Marshall wasn't scared at the prospect of making whites angry and seems to have realized that this strategy made many whites respect her and leave her alone. In addition, when she found out the white officer liked her, she resisted his advances, which was not surprising given the history of police assaults on African American women. For some, this interview account may come across as "angry," an interpretation that fits into the old white-racist framing of the "angry black woman." However, what many whites fail to realize is that they or their ancestors intentionally created the conditions to generate key aspects of this racist stereotype. Indeed, whites typically focused on this racist framing of black women and not on the extraordinarily oppressive environment within which their behavior was in fact quite normal and rational.

In the next interview, Dale Morgan, living in the Southwest, remembers planning a creative scheme to defy his boss's racist framing of African Americans:

> I remember I got a job, it was a luggage company. And they're selling suitcases and stuff like that. And I got a summer job working in there. So she say, "Boy . . . if you have to go to the bathroom, you can't go to that bathroom back there, what we use. You have to get out and go to the cafeteria down the street." Stuff like that. So I say, well, . . . I'll fix her. So you fight against this stuff in your own particular way. When I got ready to go, I [laughing] got my check that Friday evening, and I was working till about 2:00. And I got my check about my time, and . . . got ready to go. And I left, and I looked in there, and I saw she was sitting up there by the cash register. Wasn't nobody there but me and her. So what I did, I went back there, and I flush the bathroom. She thought I had . . . used the bathroom. [Laughing] And she jumped up! And she come running back that way! And she ran past me. I was hiding in the little hallway door, and she missed me! [Imitates woman] "Didn't I tell you!" And I was out the door, gone. [Laughing] So I don't know what happened after that but, she . . . just hated black folks. And I couldn't understand why they hated us so much. We don't do nothing to them, and they act like, what can I say, they act like we was dogs! (*Dale Morgan, 70s*)

He explains some ways that blacks resisted and fought back against oppressive conditions. Unlike a previous respondent, Clifford Gray, who had some freedom to walk away because his dad would take care of him, this young man, Dale Morgan, walked away from a needed employment situation where he was disrespected and devised an ingenious strategy to protest. Although flushing a toilet seems harmless, these small acts of defiance contributed to growing black empowerment and resistance that eventually resulted in the large-scale protests that toppled legal segregation.

Collective Resistance: The NAACP and the Church

There were many ways in which black communities rallied together to collectively resist Jim Crow oppression, such as through the NAACP, the church, and other social organizations. Respondent Phillip Bailey remembers NAACP meetings at the local church:

> The NAACP would send people through as representatives but . . . that was a hush-hush thing. And it was held at a church. And people were very quiet about where they were going to have these meetings because the church could be burned to the ground. (*Phillip Bailey, 60s*)

African Americans understood whites' investment in maintaining rigid segregation and often conducted their business in secret. Civil rights activists feared violent retaliation from whites enraged at the civil rights organizations attacking segregation. Just a few weeks after Dr. Martin Luther King, Jr., led the 1963 March on Washington, the Sixteenth Street Baptist Church in Birmingham, Alabama, was bombed before a Sunday service, killing four black girls. This terroristic bombing was likely done in retaliation for the growing civil rights movement there. Activists like King, Medgar Evers, Rosa Parks, and Juliette Morgan, the last a white activist, were often threatened with bodily harm if they continued to organize. Black southerners relied on sympathetic black and white northerners for organized resistance, including publishers of black newspapers and northern activists such as the Freedom Riders who rode newly integrated buses traveling across the South, often at great personal peril.[15]

An interviewee, Sadie Dixon, describes how the black church was a place to find much comfort and to organize resistance to racial segregation:

> The church was a very intricate part here, in this area. . . . In fact, during integration, that was where the NAACP meetings were held at the church. There wasn't a community center. . . . It was either done at the church or at the school. . . . If something happened, like if I say, Mrs. Patterson's son got beat up or killed, we would talk about that at church. The pastor and those people who were considered as the leaders, that was what they did. The first thing that was said was, "We need to pray." And then they would discuss among themselves how that could be corrected. There wasn't very much that could be done about it at first, because we didn't have a recourse. We talked about it in church, and how to deal with it, and that this is not the way that the Lord had intended for it to be, and those blacks who were willing to step up to the plate and speak out, then the ministers supported them, and urged their congregations to support them—that these people were about the business of trying to make a change for us, and it was for the better. . . . That was the young people who were trying to do that and it was formed inside our community in church. We were scared but we went out there and tried to make a change. Our families, they were afraid for us, but they felt that there needed to be a change, and as long as we weren't physically harmed they were supportive. We were a nonviolent group. (*Sadie Dixon, 50s*)

Black youth were critical agents of change during the civil rights era of the 1950s and 1960s. They had the most to gain from change, and they weren't burdened by providing a family wage. When faced with violent white retaliation, they earned greater sympathy from many whites than comparable black adults. As noted by Dixon, the black church was the heart of the community, and collective prayer, coupled with a strong belief in the benevolence of God, was a major coping mechanism used by many to survive the continuing white atrocities, including during the era of more frequent civil rights protests.

Numerous respondents emphasized how their religion came first in their lives, gave joy and solace, and helped them to resist internalizing the label of inferiority imposed on them by whites. Another respondent in the Southeast, Cynthia Jamison, explains this important response:

The only way you will get through anything, you've got to put God first. You have to. You have to. And you have to just ask for guidance, you have to pray, you have to read the Bible, and you—that's the only way you're going to make it. . . . That's what the Bible said: Seek ye first the kingdom of heaven, so the king is God and everything else will just fall into place. So, that's, nowadays, that's the only way they're going to make it. That's the only way, is stay in church. You know, pray, pray a lot. Because they not going to be able to make it out there on their own. . . . I was 13 years old when I came up here. I think, I remember going to the movie once we had to go to prayer meeting, choir rehearsal, Bible study, Sunday school, morning service, afternoon service, night service and our day was to sit in church all day on Sundays and that was it. (*Cynthia Jamison, 60s*)

From a young age many African Americans were raised in these busy church settings. Another respondent in the Southeast, Lila Wise, also recalls how people found communal strength in the church and in their devotion to God:

[My mother] lived for the Lord and she lived for him until she died. And I'm going to live for him until I die. . . . I know my sister will too. . . . We didn't have nothing else to look forward to but God. So she always told us about God. I think we just, we was strong because we believe in God. . . . That's what I think. . . . That's all we had to do was go to school and church. And we had to walk to church. We didn't have no car. 'Cause most of the time you stayed at church, well practically the whole day. And you walked there and you stayed. You had to walk 'cause we didn't have a car. . . . 'Cause there is no other place that you can go . . . mostly we go to church. And in the evening we get together and get more strength. . . . Like a fireplace when the fire in the fireplace, you put one log on there it burns bright. You put another log on there it burns a little bit brighter and when you all together like that it makes you strong. Without that I don't know, we didn't have nothing. Without God. Going to church was great. (*Lila Wise, 70s*)

Historically the black church has been a place of refuge, strength, and comfort. The church was the one segregated institution in which African Americans could thrive largely free of Jim Crow norms. As Martin Luther King, Jr., famously noted in a 1953 sermon, "eleven o'clock on Sunday morning is the most segregated hour in Christian

America."[16] Ironically, given the church segregation imposed by whites who claimed to be Christians, segregated black churches provided a major source of collective resistance for African Americans across the South.

Another respondent in the Southeast, Cynthia Payton, remembers the importance of religion in everyday responses to the harsh realities of Jim Crow:

> You just go along with life and pray you know. Ask the Lord to watch over you. A lot of whites want to know how you can come up with a smile all the time and you're happy. You know, black people, you always see them always laughing. They ain't got nothing but they're still laughing. [Whites] don't understand that part. That is our belief in God. He is our strength. (*Cynthia Payton, 80s*)

Payton's insightful comments again underscore the power of belief in a protective God, particularly in undergirding confidence and joy in life no matter how hard it was. This joy often surprised whites, who did not understand how someone who had little in the way of material things could feel they had everything that they needed. In particular, whites often marveled at or expressed resentment at black women's and men's strength in dealing with everyday realities. This resentment resulted in part from many whites' surveillance of African Americans to see if they had something that whites wanted—usually without any recognition of how much unjust enrichment whites already had. Great personal comfort resulted from this strong belief in a protective God and in Christian morality, as well as freedom from whites' moral dilemmas of the slavery and Jim Crow eras.

Cognitive dissonance is a psychological concept that describes the common disconnects between human beliefs and human actions, such as whites asserting that they are good and moral Christians, yet engaging in or failing to stop antiblack violence and other racial oppression. Many African Americans were aware of the contradictions between white assertions of Christianity and white oppression and prayed not only for their own survival, but also for the ability to forgive their oppressors. More than one respondent assessed Jim Crow situations with a comment like "whites didn't know what they were doing." The belief in a protective God and the ability to forgive and pray were very important coping mechanisms for the unimaginable horrors of this era.

Numerous respondents noted that their devotion to God and the church were instrumental in their surviving and resisting oppression in a variety of ways, small and large. A few spoke openly about participating in significant organized and confrontational resistance, even though such activities usually sparked further white attacks. One prominent religious leader, Theodore Roberts, now in his 80s, speaks in his interview to the importance of constant and confrontational black resistance, especially in the decades after World War II:

> You had to do that! You had to do that! In order to change the system you had to do that! You had to test it. You had to make them show their real color. . . . If you didn't keep protesting the system, [change] never would have happened and some of us just decided that we were going to test the system. It was dangerous to do it, but we did it. Yeah. We did it. . . . Schools were segregated. We wrote the school board and told them to consider integrating the schools. If they didn't integrate the schools, we were gonna file a suit. As time went on, we decided to file a suit. I went to several parents and told them we had to file a suit. I told them we had to have a particular child. All of them said "No!" My younger daughter was at [school] at that time. I said to her, "We've got to use a name on the lawsuit to file the suit. Don't tell your mother about it but would you agree to do this?" She said, "Yes." (*Theodore Roberts, 80s*)

From the 1940s through the 1960s, African Americans like Theodore Roberts and his child actively resisted segregation and pressed the larger black community to resist collectively. Like their predecessors, they showed that they were more than victims and demonstrated courage and creative agency in spite of the threat and reality of white violence. This leader was aware that he was putting his daughter at risk, yet also understood that it was in his daughter's best interest to push forward despite the almost insurmountable odds of success.

A respondent in the Southwest, Lewis Perry, similarly recounts significant activism on the part of African Americans, especially certain ministers:

> [One black minister] told the judge named Johnny Smith, was the judge then, he said, "If ya'll don't have those signs moved in 30 days I'm going to take you to court." He told them to have those signs down before 30 days, and they did too. He said, "Because when I go

to turn that water on to drink, this water fountain is clear." He said it was clear! It's not white. He said the same about these restrooms. "You got white and black. You don't see no tax white and black, on the tax it's the same." [He] went to all these schools [and saw] our books were outdated. And he went and checked on it. Some white folks got mad. . . . This bookstore right here on the corner . . . here, a white man had that store and so he said, "We've been treating you Darkies good all your life. Why ya'll going to push for integration?" One minister got up and said, "We're not pushing. We just want some of our schools to be somewhat good. We've been buying your groceries down through the years. [We] put you where you are now. You want to step on us! We're tired. We are tired." (*Lewis Perry, 70s*)

The stress of struggling with Jim Crow discrimination and inequality was clear in Perry's voice as he shared his recollections of the long fight for equality. He notes the power of organized resistance and of using resources like the courts against patterns of white supremacy, even though there was usually significant backlash. Additionally, many whites misunderstood the civil rights movement to be about a black desire to be integrated with and near whites. In contrast, Perry powerfully clarifies that the civil rights struggle was for equal access to important educational and other socioeconomic resources, particularly those that had helped to create white wealth. He concludes with the sharp point that much white prosperity had come from black customers and workers.

CONCLUSION

As we consider the everyday coping and resistance strategies that African Americans used during the long Jim Crow era, we should not be too quick to judge them with questions like "Why did they do that?" or "Why didn't they do this?" It is sometimes easy to critique their individual and collective choices from the safety of distant hindsight. In assessing the realities of and responses to extensive racial oppression, many contemporary analysts have fallen into a blaming-the-victim mode. However, instead of questioning the choices of these courageous African Americans who were stifled and subordinated under much Jim

Crow oppression, we need to keep in mind that their everyday choices were constrained by a truly totalitarian system that dominated almost every aspect of their lives—from sunup to sundown and from cradle to grave.

Surely, instead of asking "Why did African Americans respond by doing that?" the questions that need to be asked by many scholars and other analysts should actually be, "How could whites have perpetuated the extremely oppressive conditions imposed on African Americans?" and "How did whites cope with the cognitive dissonance of claiming to be moral and good Christians, yet inflict such violence-laced discrimination and unbearable pain on several generations of African Americans?"

7

FIFTY YEARS LATER

Jim Crow Unwilling to Die

It's better now than it was. Yeah, it's better now for everybody. But you know how, you know how the white folks is. The white folk, they've been having their foot right over your neck for years. They ain't going to get up nowhere soon, but they are raising they foot up a little bit now. You ain't choking as much as you was back then. They're going to let you get so far, and that's all you're going to get. (*Frank Wilson, 80s*)

Many white Americans, and some other Americans, now believe that the United States is a post-racial, colorblind society. They habitually cite the election of President Barack Obama, a political result they believe shows that civil rights efforts have cured the country's racial ills. With slavery's centuries, the "Black Codes" after the Civil War, and thousands of Jim Crow lynchings as the basis for comparison, yes, racial relations are undeniably better for Americans of color today. African Americans typically do not fear white home invasions—with the major exception of the police—or routinized sexual assaults by white men. However, as the 88-year-old respondent above notes, whites still maintain full dominance over African Americans, and they still regularly stifle their ability to enjoy full social, economic, and political citizenship.

In this final chapter we examine some of the many contemporary effects and impacts of our not-so-distant Jim Crow history. While numerous respondents remain hopeful for racial equality in the future, the

majority insist that we still have numerous Jim-Crow-type racial realities, albeit they are often dressed now in new clothes. In this final
chapter we trace out, somewhat briefly, how this contemporary racial
oppression (what a black pilot recently called "James Crow, Jr., Es-
quire")[1] looks through the eyes of our ever-astute respondents, who
have all survived overt, subtle, and covert racial injustices—from more
than 50 years ago to the present day. The respondents share with us
how they and other African Americans continue to experience contemporary manifestations of Jim Crow that African Americans fought to
eliminate before and during the 1950s–1960s civil rights era: hostile
white racial stereotyping and framing, an inferior and de facto segregated public educational system, lack of fair economic opportunity and
equity, significant political barriers, and constant surveillance and harassment from the police in most communities. These brave survivors of
Jim Crow oppression and their descendants regularly experience the
humiliation of being treated as second-class citizens and still struggle
with the long-term psychological and economic consequences of persisting racial discrimination. In addition, they connect the lack of necessary societal change with the deep-rooted belief that most whites are
unwilling to significantly change their attitudes, practices, and policies
of white superiority that condemn a great many African Americans to a
life of socioeconomic subordination and, literally, reduce their life
chances individually and collectively.

As we have shown throughout this book, the past and present symptoms of the segregation stress syndrome include a loss of trust for
whites and white-run institutions and feeling uncomfortable or afraid in
the presence of whites or in talking openly about racism. According to
our respondents, there is still a deep mistrust among many in African
American communities when it comes to establishing serious relationships with whites. Bear in mind, this is not the black "paranoia" of the
common white racial framing. There has been little acknowledgment or
apology by whites for the massive past injustices of the slavery and Jim
Crow eras. Additionally, there has been little acknowledgment by most
whites that major racial injustices in our economic, educational, criminal justice, medical, and housing institutions continue to exist today.

The many connections between contemporary racial patterns and
the Jim Crow century may come as a surprise to many, especially young,
readers of this book who have been raised with colorblind or multicul-

tural programming in schools and with many images of diverse celebrities and officials in the mainstream media. On the surface, much has
changed in this society over the past 50 or so years. However, just below
the surface much of the centuries-old racial hierarchy of power and
privilege persists. Structurally, the socioeconomic gap between white
and black Americans is in important ways now widening. In many areas
the racial segregation of public schools is greater today than during the
1960s. Recall that the white-black wealth gap for families has widened
since the legal segregation era, such that white families' median net
worth is now about eight times that of black families. In addition, there
is a higher rate of black male incarceration today than there was in the
Jim Crow era.[2] Today, it is not white lynchings and firebombings that
tear apart African American communities, but the intergenerational
transmission of unjust impoverishment and the chronic lack of black
access to important socioeconomic resources long available to whites.

Much systemic racism is currently in place but often remains somewhat concealed behind prison walls, in failing school systems, and on
downtown city streets. Whites continue to resist fully examining our
highly racist past and recognizing *how that past dramatically impacts
contemporary racial realities.* That denial of the past's legacies means
that most whites can rest comfortably feeling that we now live in a
(supposedly) racially egalitarian society based on meritocracy—one
where education and hard work will be rewarded with success—without any acknowledgment of whites' unearned benefits and unjust enrichment in the past and present. For most of our respondents, contemporary racist patterns and policies remain evident even without the
"whites only" signs. The subtle, hidden, and covert signs of white supremacy are hard for them to miss, even as they are sometimes harder to
fight against than in the Jim Crow era.

PROBLEMS IN THE PRESENT, HOPE FOR THE FUTURE

Given the scale and extent of the racial oppression that our respondents
have endured over many decades, it is striking how optimistic many of
them remain in the present day. Near the end of their interviews, our
interviewees were asked to comment on contemporary racial interac-

tions and patterns in comparison with the Jim Crow era. A few, such as Dora Maxwell in the Southwest, provide a clear message of hope:

> So you see everything here is better. And I appreciate that because, now that [whites] see that a black person is just as fast, just as beautiful as they are, they find out that they going to have to compete against [blacks] instead of dishing them off. They got to compete. So, it's really a change. . . . And it's going to get better, but it takes time. See, God don't give you stuff all at once. He kinda brings it down a little at a time, a little at a time. And if you just notice, you notice back then things were different, but every day it gets better. It gets better every day. But God ain't going to open your eyes up all at once, because we can't handle it. . . . He's opening our eyes, not only our eyes, but the white man's eye too. And the white man, *so* good at still segregating against us, until I bet you in the next 10 to 15 years they going to have to give that up, too. They have to open up everything to us. But you know they've got that white bash about them: "We are the white race, we, we are the best!" But they ain't no more than me [and] you. (*Dora Maxwell, 80s*)

Although Maxwell begins on a positive note of societal change, she nonetheless observes the prevalence of white discrimination and supremacy, the latter internalized by both whites and blacks—which she calculates will change in the future. Note too her faith in God as a means of coping with and resisting white racism.

Also recognizing the persistence of racial discrimination, Roberta Bass, a respondent in the Southwest, places her hope for the future on hard work and education:

> Always, always, show that you are an outstanding person. You are qualified to be equally as good or better as they are. . . . Things are better for us now, but it's still a lot of discrimination now. . . . We still are struggling, we still have a struggle. We've got a long way to go but if we keep studying and working hard, being fair with ourselves, helping each other, educating our people, we can be successful. (*Roberta Bass, 70s*)

This respondent echoes the most frequent response comparing the Jim Crow era with contemporary racism. Yes, things are better, but we still are not equal. Similar to Dora Maxwell, a previously cited respondent, Bass rejects the black inferiority stereotype created by whites in slavery and enforced throughout the Jim Crow era. African Americans are indeed qualified, capable, and smart. Blacks are under constant pressure to surpass whites' low expectations and must rely on hard work, education, and community reliance to succeed. Note too in her comments the continuing importance of collective action and support in trying to attain the proverbial "American Dream," one that for most remains a "dream deferred."

In his careful response, Steve McDonald, a respondent in the South-east, reflects even more optimistically on how things are better:

> I would say that things have gotten somewhere around 75 percent better. Not 100 percent, but 75 percent. We can do a lot of things today, and we don't have to worry about the white man too much these days. But, now when I was coming up you didn't have no rights. You didn't have no rights at all. Things are better. There a lot of them coming up today, a lot of young people coming up today that I see out in the streets. And the things that they doing today and the things that they saying to the white folks today, if they had of been coming up during the time I was coming up and they say them things to the white folk, they'd be dead. (*Steve McDonald, 70s*)

He explains that things are better because the basis of comparison is to a not-so-distant time when black southerners had no rights and faced frequent violence for minor infractions of racist norms. With a few exceptions, which have gotten media attention (such as Renisha McBride), African Americans are no longer likely to be killed by ordi-nary whites for racially related reasons.[3] However, as we discuss below, police brutality targeting black men remains a recurring problem in many towns and cities.

Other respondents also accented the societal changes, including the fact that African Americans are no longer required to be so deferential to whites. However, respondent Elizabeth Ware, a respondent in the Southwest, comments mostly on what has not changed:

> [Today] it's a little bit better, you know. . . . Like I said if you got some money you kind of buy your way around, you know. . . . But in these white folks' mind you're still a nigger. That's the way they think. That's the way they think. That's why I call them peckerwoods

and poor white trash. Crackers! That's what they are. (*Elizabeth Ware, 80s*)

Ware is excited to have the freedom to call whites some harsh pointed names. Some readers may take offense to such critical language, perhaps arguing it is equivalent to a white person using a racist epithet for black people. However, the key difference is the broader social context of racial oppression. In no historically white institutions—such as the economy, politics, or criminal justice system—do African Americans have widespread and oppressive control over the fate of whites, yet the opposite is often true. Ware asserts too that money is a resource to "buy your way around" some racism, yet regardless of social class African Americans are still often treated as racially inferior to and by whites.[4]

An elderly respondent, Lula Whitaker, living in a desegregated nursing home in the Southwest, reflects that, even though residents pay for the same services, whites receive preferential treatment. She begins by discussing racial relations today compared to the past:

> Oh yeah it's better, it's much better, much better. But it's still here, segregation is still here. I don't think it will ever die. I don't. I don't. I really don't. Of course you know just being, just being, you know, here [in a nursing home], and then you can see what's going on, you don't have to say a word. You can stop and just look, and just watch and you can tell it's different, different. [Whites] do their job. [But] they do you different. You're almost the last one to get something seen about you. But still they take you money for what we all in here for the same thing, 'Cause we can't take care of ourself. But it's different, it's different. (*Lula Whitaker, 90s*)

Things are better, but she regularly observes legacies of Jim Crow. A half-century ago, African Americans could see many overt signs of white supremacy and black subordination. Today, the signs are just as clear to them, yet are more hidden and subtle, at least for non-black observers, and are often operative behind a façade of colorblind organizational policies.

PERSISTING WHITE SUPREMACY

Our respondents have been witnesses to Jim Crow's widespread discrimination, lynchings, rapes, police violence, and home invasions. They or their relatives have suffered from the actions of groups like the white supremacist Ku Klux Klan. They also provide evidence that, despite the civil rights laws and important Supreme Court rulings on racial desegregation, many societal situations today regularly involve racial discrimination. Recall from an earlier chapter how one elderly respondent, Delores Fowler, begins to cry profusely in her response to our questions. She comments thus about the contemporary experiences of African Americans:

> I know that we have, the black-race people, and, you know, they had a hard time and, and it's still ain't what you'd call real good right now. 'Cause you still got, got that little segregation going on. They try to hide it, but it's still there. [*Her weeping grows, and there is pain in her eyes. I, too, begin to cry*] . . . [She states], "It's still there." [*I respond through tears, "I'm so sorry."*][5] (*Delores Fowler, 80s*)

The long-term psychological pain of the segregation stress syndrome is quite apparent as Fowler's crying several decades after the official end of Jim Crow segregation. She cries as she recalls memories about how whites have treated African Americans from Jim Crow to the present day. She is not alone in her assessment of the contemporary legacies of Jim Crow. The vast majority of respondents reiterated the sentiment that life today is better for African Americans, yet that it is nonetheless often white-dominated and racially oppressive.

As we have discussed throughout this book, the symptoms of the segregation stress syndrome include avoidance, hyper-arousal, anger, fear, and a loss of trust in whites who caused their racial trauma, as well as an intergenerational transmission of that trauma. Our elderly African American respondents who survived Jim Crow frequently exhibit some of these symptoms. Their often-expressed desire to warn their descendants about whites is rooted in the unchanged racial attitudes of most whites decades after Jim Crow. A respondent in the Southeast, Verna Steele, believes that today whites harbor feelings of racial superiority:

It [is] a lot better than what it used to be, but it ain't altogether perfect like it's supposed to be. . . . A lot of white people think that, they think that, they is over blacks and over the world. I guess, [in] the way they carry [themselves]. I don't know why they act like they do. I don't. I just can't get that. I just never could get it. Um-humm, why do they think they're so much of a God? . . . They the ones got to repent and die for themselves. You know, if you want to die that kind of way, that's you. I'm not. . . . I know it's surely not better 'cause there's a lot of things we think we got to do, [and] you can't do that. You can't do that. It don't look like nothing is changing yet. (*Verna Steele, 50s*)

Verna Steele begins by noting things are better, yet shortly remarks that "nothing is changing yet." This contradiction signals the complexity of the black experience today. This is not an either/or, but a both/and type of analysis. As noted by other respondents, the day-to-day interactions with whites are often much better and official Jim Crow norms are gone, yet major U.S. institutions remain firmly white-dominated and white-normed. This respondent contributes the lack of change to the white supremacist attitudes of most whites. This attitude has not changed much since the Jim Crow era, and many whites maintain much surveillance and control over the everyday lives of African Americans.[6]

PERSISTING SEGREGATION IN PUBLIC SETTINGS

During the Jim Crow era, black southerners were under the surveillance of ordinary white citizens and officials seeking to keep them in "their place." Overt signs that stated "whites only" clarified spaces where the African American presence was met with hostility. As Ernest Knight in the Southwest notes, there are places today where African Americans are not welcome:

I know at the time they didn't like blacks to go to like down by Ocean Drive here and all back over in there. You're going back into Ocean Drive and you were driving, I'm quite sure that in a lot of the hotels and places they didn't want you to come in there and eat. . . . I know it was a place down, right down, let me see, I think it's right down this street here, over there where they got that new courthouse built. They say that they didn't allow blacks to come in there and eat, eat

no food there. I don't know if they still go there because there's a
Confederate flag there. . . . And it's probably a lot of places right
here, right now, still don't like for us to come up in there. But, I
mean, I don't trust them. They got that biker's place down in town.
They say they don't too much care for blacks to come . . . in there.
So, I don't want them type of places. I still leave them alone right
today. It's still a lot of prejudice going on. You can tell that when you
walk in some of these hotels, right now, they don't care too much for
black folks. (*Ernest Knight, 70s*)

Although the "whites only" signs are removed, other symbols of
white dominance and racial framing remain, such as the commonplace
Confederate battle flag. Today, the display of this flag is an undeniable
legacy of earlier racial oppression, even though some whites claim it
only signals "southern pride." (They mean *white* southern pride.) This
Confederate flag was little seen until it was resurrected by whites in
their aggressive, often violent protests against racial integration during
the 1950s and 1960s, and especially by white supremacist organizations.[7] Even without such visual cues, African Americans are aware of
numerous places in their towns and cities that are unwelcoming, either
from warnings from other blacks or from picking up numerous nonverbal cues from whites. Additionally, displaying this flag can be viewed as
a type of assault on the many African American survivors of Jim Crow,
in whom it generates elements of the segregation stress syndrome.

A respondent in his 80s, Clifton Tate, raises questions about experiences in a white-run restaurant just a few weeks before his interview:

There is a restaurant . . . that I had been there a couple of times with
a lady. I went there about three or four weeks ago. The lady who was
seating us took us to a seat. She passed three booths where nobody
was sitting. She went to take us in the back booth. I said, "Where are
you going." She said, "I am taking you." [I said,] "No! You are not
taking [us] anywhere! You passed three booths up there. I am not
sitting back there." We went to [town] about four weeks ago. We
carried 20 children to a play. There were about 10 adults with us. We
had two vans. On our way back we stopped at a filling station to fill
up the vans. We filled the vans up with gas. The children went to go
to the restrooms. They said, "You can't go to the restroom. Not the
restrooms." I don't know why. [Long pause] I didn't do something

about it, but we went to another place to use the restroom after we had bought gas at that place. (*Clifton Tate, 80s*)

In these incidents we see some of the contemporary legacies of Jim Crow. Today, African Americans often report being seated in the back of certain restaurants and getting poor service in various types of public accommodations.[8] Like many people of color responding to discriminatory actions, this older man had mere seconds to decide how to respond to each troubling incident. As was evident in his long pause, that hurried decision weighed heavily on his mind some weeks afterwards. One might rationalize away the experiences in the restaurant and gas station as isolated or based on reasons other than whites' racial framing. Yet, these types of everyday discrimination, sometimes inaccurately called "subtle" slights and "microaggressions," remain commonplace and very painful for African Americans, even though too many whites are quick to dismiss them. Contemporary white aggressions have an added layer of complexity for respondents who lived during the legal segregation epoch. Contemporary racist incidents periodically reignite old memories and fears that come from surviving that extensive Jim Crow oppression.[9]

FAILING PUBLIC SCHOOL DISTRICTS

Given the fact that housing discrimination was legal in many areas before the 1968 Civil Rights Act banned most of it, and given the white flight to the suburbs in the decades before and after that act, today many neighborhoods continue to be racially segregated. Such segregated housing results, as researchers regularly find, in public schools on the whole being *more* racially segregated today than in the 1950s and 1960s.[10]

As much public school funding is derived from property taxes, more affluent (usually majority white) residential neighborhoods enjoy greater access to first-rate schooling resources. As a result, they are usually part of academically successful school districts as measured by test scores, graduation rates, more experienced teachers, college-oriented curricula, and college recruiters. In contrast, public school districts with high proportions of black and Latino students are likely to be impoverished and to have more inexperienced teachers, higher dropout rates, significant nutrition problems, greater exposure to area crime, and far fewer recruiters from employers and colleges.[11]

Some 85 percent of U.S. teachers are white.[12] Several respondents expressed concern about their grandchildren and other African American students being taught mainly by white teachers who often lack a serious commitment to the education of these students. One respondent in the Southeast, Theresa Glover, recalls certain *advantages* of her education during the Jim Crow era:

> Our teachers were black. We didn't have white teachers. . . . [Black teachers] paid more attention to us. You know, 'cause everybody knew each other. If we were late, professor used to line you up, and he'd get in the middle and went [She makes a swatting noise with her mouth, then laughs.]. [Black teachers] were interested because they knew this was the key for us, for blacks, you know. We had no other alternatives. We tried to get that education. . . . Teachers visited your home if you were having problems. (*Theresa Glover, 70s*)

The research is clear that a good education is a prime indicator for economic success, and African American teachers, then as now, understood its great importance for individuals and communities. Glover notes that the African American teachers were a part of the students' local community, to the point that they would go to a child's home.

In the Southeast a female interviewee in her 80s, Mamie Ramsey, eloquently expresses how children can feel when a teacher is not invested in their success:

> There are some things that are better and some things that are not. Okay, if a child is in an atmosphere where they feel loved, they are going to do anything the teacher asks them to do. Now, if you go to school, you have the feeling that this person is just putting up with me because I am here. Then . . . the one thing most of [the black teachers] did, they feel love for their students. And that's the one thing, all the children wanted to perform for their teachers. . . . Children did their homework, and they went to school with a desire to please their teacher. And if you have that, then there is going to be learning. No matter what, you're going to get something. (*Mamie Ramsey, 80s*)

This respondent is persuasive in her analysis of how children can feel if a teacher is not fully invested in their success. She experienced segregated schools, and school integration efforts in the 1950s and 1960s were often met with overt white resistance, including much violence. (Recall the infamous photos of white adults yelling at and spitting on black children.) These Jim Crow survivors recognize that their grandchildren and great-grandchildren are facing somewhat similar struggles in educational systems that are merely "putting up with" black youth and are frequently not invested in their educational success. According to numerous respondents, many white teachers today harbor a conscious or unconscious racial framing of black students. Typically, these teachers don't know their black students or their families, don't live in their neighborhoods, don't know their families, and don't care much about a black child's long-term success.

Government actions to change these educational conditions have been far from adequate. Thus, prominent education analysts such as Jonathan Kozol are critical of popular government programs like "Teach for America," which send recent, often privileged and white, college graduates with minimal teacher training to teach on a short-term basis in, mostly, inner-city school districts.[13] The major problem does not lie in these often idealistic young graduates, or more generally with teachers in thousands of underresourced public schools, but in the systemic racism that intentionally or indirectly creates huge disparities in school resources between most predominantly white communities and most predominantly black communities.

An elderly respondent in the Southwest, Sophie Goodwin, expresses concern for white teachers who do not want to teach black children:

> Things are better, but it's still discrimination. And I know things are better because we have the privilege of going in and out of the places that we used to couldn't go. We have access to the library, all of the nice places that we used to couldn't go. It's better for us. The only thing that bothers me is in the schools. I'm not pleased with the way that they handle a lot of the black children especially in the schools. There are slow children in the schools, and I feel like that they are not being treated fairly because most of the whites do not like to teach—that I have observed—the slow learner. All the children that they want, especially the black child, they want them to be on level. There are whites not on level; there are blacks not on level. And

when they find that they have blacks that are not on level, the first thing they want to do is have them tested and put them in special education. (*Sophie Goodwin, 70s*)

She continues a sharp assessment of what follows from this commonplace testing:

That's putting a label on them. And when they put them in special education you have to have a very, very good teacher, dedicated teacher to teach that child and bring that child up to level where he can come out of special education. If not, that child is labeled, and they end up not being able to go to college. Really some of them just haven't had a chance, but they are labeled and put in special education. . . . They are not giving the slow child a chance, and the sad thing about it is that I have observed it's always the black male. . . . I don't like that, and I think that more should be done to teach the slow learner regardless of the color of the skin, and especially blacks. I don't feel that they are treated fairly. Special education is not for all the slow learners. Some of the slow learners just need a better teacher, and a dedicated teacher. Because they haven't had a chance, but I feel if a lot of the slow learners had had a chance they would come out of special education. (*Sophie Goodwin, 70s*)

Goodwin expresses concern for black children who are slow learners and correctly notes the swift labels of "special education" or "learning disabled" that often are stuck on young black males. Black and Latino students compose most of those in special education classes. Boys are overrepresented in disciplinary actions; they are three times more likely to be suspended or expelled from school than their white peers. Additionally, black boys are significantly underrepresented in gifted and talented programs. They are much less likely to be enrolled in advanced high school courses compared with white peers earning identical achievement scores.[14]

Research studies suggest that similar school behaviors exhibited by white and black youth are often interpreted differentially and through a racial lens. For example, white apathy in class tends to be interpreted as a signal of boredom, too-easy material, academic exceptionalism, or the failure of a teacher. In contrast, similar apathetic behavior exhibited by African American students tends to be interpreted as a lack of intelligence, too-difficult material, or an attention disorder.[15] Overwhelmingly, contemporary educators, especially whites, view African American children through a deficit model as "problems to be managed," rather than children having significant educational potential that needs to be fully tapped. Across the country, in predominately black and Latino classes the emphasis is commonly on maintaining order in the classroom rather than on offering an interesting and rigorous curriculum for these children. Given this racial and educational climate, it is unsurprising that today fewer than half of black male students graduate from high school on time.[16]

DIFFERENTIAL TREATMENT AT WORK

Echoed throughout our interviews are stress, concern, and worry in regard to the future of young black Americans. The persisting inferior education of many young blacks usually translates into rather grim job prospects. Even for those with the educational credentials to succeed, African Americans of various ages today face institutionally racist barriers, as well as an array of white discrimination at the interpersonal level. One 70-year-old retired professor in the Southeast, Duane Hunt, recounts some of his discriminatory experiences more recently in the workplace:

> Well, there's no question about it. You see it. It's subtle, it's under the guises of policy, things of this nature. Hiring practices—there's always a way to circumvent state ways, meaning affirmative action and things like that. I'm a classic example. I was hired at a community college in the Southeast. You can have five tenure track lines, but you must hire minorities. They had no choice so I was one of the five and you could feel the tension when we got there. It reminded me of the integration demonstration that I used to participate in [during Jim Crow era]. The proof is in the pudding about the things that happen, you know. Like, am I being paranoid here? People are being *too* nice, kind of thing. (*Duane Hunt, 70s*)

With Jim Crow experiences in the back of his mind, he then talks about the critical step of promotion to tenure in his college position:

When I came up for tenure, I mean it was quite evident that they were trying not to keep me. I went in to the committee, I presented my application. This is my department now. These are my colleagues, okay. I've been working with these people for years, all right. And I go to meetings with them, professional meetings, interact with them on a daily basis. You got the "Pepsodent smile" you know, the laughing, the joking. But the mood turned . . . and you could feel it. So I have them, I presented my application to the chair of the department. I gave my presentation, question and answer time. I left. The vote was 50/50. Now, there is no way under normal circumstances that the vote should be 50/50. The vote should have been 100 [percent] in terms of tenure. And so, if it had not have been for my chair who was a decent and honorable person, who wrote a strong letter on my behalf to the faculty-wide promotion and tenure committee. One of the questions they asked me was why do you feel the vote was 50/50. I said, "I have no idea. You have to ask [my white colleagues]." . . . And the person who wrote not to approve was a friend of mine, office mate, who was quite obvious he didn't like me. And it was based on, you know, purely on race and his bigotry. . . . I had to fight for it, but I got tenure. (*Duane Hunt, 70s*)

He too connects his current experiences to those of the Jim Crow background. In the contemporary era he uses strategies he learned as a child to interact and deal with problematic whites at work. He references a Pepsodent toothpaste "smile," probably to indicate his accommodation to make whites comfortable. Yet, his attempts were not enough to convince half of his colleagues that he was their equal in achievements. Earning a Ph.D. and other credentials and doing well in his job didn't guarantee him freedom from the constant white judgments and the stress of knowing that in the minds of numerous white colleagues he was still racially "inferior."

Dr. Hunt continues his interview about the necessary deferential behavior in dealing with whites today, as it was in the legal segregation decades:

You had to give whites their proper respect and deference because they were the boss . . . . You were always treated so you always knew that you were colored and you had better act in a defined way. As soon as whites came into our midst, we just put that shield up 'cause we didn't know what was about to happen. You were always on your guard. . . . They were supervising you; you always was on your guard, always. Here again, what I was told as a kid, I still follow it today: You never told white folks what you were thinking. You always told them what you wanted them to know. It was kind of a reflex move against racism. . . . I worked at a cafeteria as a waiter, and just because you have on a white coat and a pair of tuxedo pants and black shoes, you were still viewed as a "nigger," and they let you know it. So you keep your thoughts and your feelings to yourself and you work for the few nickels you could get, but when you got off from work you talked to each other. You shared your stories but the moment you got into the midst of whites, you turn all that off and you went on about your business and you did your job. (*Duane Hunt, 70s*)

He essentially offers the listener a catalogue of the strategies African Americans have had to use in dealing with whites since the days of slavery, up to the present day. He was taught as a child to shift orientation when in the company of whites and to "put up a shield" to survive white racism. Unfortunately, this is still the case in our systemically racist society. The stress of being under constant white surveillance and "acting in a defined way" was one of the many realities of Jim Crow that African Americans had to learn deal with—and one that they still must deal with today. Numerous elderly respondents recalled that in the Jim Crow era they were under more or less constant surveillance in public spaces and in their neighborhoods by ordinary whites and white police officers and officials. The contemporary reality of "racial profiling" by whites of various statuses is not a new phenomenon for African Americans.

Assessing the contemporary era, our elderly respondents view whites' often more informal and subtle racist practices, as well as their still overtly racist policies, as having negative impacts on African Americans similar to those of the Jim Crow decades. Although legal segregation has been officially dismantled, the struggle for racial equality, including for equal economic security, is still ongoing for these survivors of Jim Crow and their many descendants. Thus, a retired teacher in the Southeast, Nora Dillard, expresses deep concern for the job opportunities for black men today:

I have a son, and he's a graduate of the [college], and I don't know. I don't. I think in some instances that things aren't too much better for black males. . . . There still seems to be a way of discriminating against them when it comes to jobs and opportunities. It just seems to still be very, very hard for black males. It makes me feel sad that that does exist. Well, I think that you have a different kind of discrimination, a more subtle kind of discrimination to deal with now. And the way you deal with that is to be aware of the facts. I mean, when I say facts, I mean things that are happening. Not something you think, but you look at what is really happening in job opportunities. Is there equal opportunity at that job or in the job market? Or that there's equal opportunity, but why is it I always wind up not getting that job? Why is that? So, I think it's more subtle now, and because our young people think that there is equal opportunity. Maybe I'm speaking for the young people. Maybe they already know there isn't equal opportunity out there. But, seemingly to me that our young people aren't aware of our history. If you're not aware of your history you can get lost out there. . . . If you don't have community and family—and when I say community I mean like the community that there used to be before integration came about there used to be a real community where black people get together and share and admit. And they acknowledge that these things do exist. (*Nora Dillard, 60s*)

Not surprisingly, Dillard expresses deep concern for black men and their lack of good employment opportunities today, which echoes other respondents' concerns for black boys and men in educational settings. Her feelings of sadness are rooted in recognizing the often more concealed and subtle aspects of contemporary discrimination. Black survivors of Jim Crow segregation are an aging group who are *the living experts* in regard to this country's history of systemic racism, and they typically recognize discrimination and other white racism despite its frequently more covert nature. This former teacher questions if young black people are adequately educated about the facts of U.S. racial history. Her intergenerational warning of "looking at the facts" is based on decades of relevant experience with systemic racism, including her experience in fighting to not internalize whites' racial framing of black inferiority.

Recent studies underscore the facts that this interviewee relates, including data on major racial disparities in hiring practices. Although some whites claim that there is much preferential treatment in job markets for African Americans and other people of color and assert falsely that there are currently racial quotas, the data indicate that preferential treatment is mostly given to whites, even among companies claiming to be "equal opportunity employers." For example, a study in Chicago and Boston found that, with other background characteristics being equal, people who had resumes with white sounding names (like Emily or Greg) enjoyed a 50 percent higher callback rate from employers than those with resumes with black sounding names (like Lakisha or Jamal). The study found that a white name alone was regarded by employers to be about the equivalent of an additional eight years of work experience.[17] Another study found that being black had a greater impact on employment chances than having a criminal record: White men with a criminal record were more likely to be called back for a job interview than black men without one.[18] This discrimination in hiring practices helps to explain employment disparities, such as black unemployment rates being double those of whites and employed blacks earning significantly less than comparable white workers.[19]

A respondent from the Southwest, Regina McDowell, believes that in some ways the prospects for equality are bleaker today than they were decades ago in the legal segregation era:

> It's disguised or hidden. Like they say everybody can go to school. You're looking at the rise of housing and the rising cost of fuel and stuff like that, and I don't think we take all of that into consideration when we have young people that are striving [for economic security]. In some ways it's more difficult for y'all now than when it was for us. . . . We knew it was going to be hard to get into a white institution and go to school. We knew that they would not accept us, but they got so many levels that are designed to distract or discourage you that it's really becoming more difficult now. It's going to be harder now to get black students through college I think than before. It is not a physical restraint; it's the economical things that [whites are] putting in place that's making it more difficult. Affirmative action is not being used—which means you don't get to get the breaks that we got. And I hate it when they start talking about affirmative action as unfair. I mean how are you going to level a playing field that has been lopsided ever since its inception? Whites will wait for over 200 years and then you think in 35 years that you are going to level the field because of affirmative action? I feel bad about some of my colleagues who benefited from affirmative action, and they're taking that away from [younger African Americans] so you can't utilize it as

a tool to get into areas that have been excluded. (*Regina McDowell, 60s*)

During the slavery and Jim Crow centuries, African Americans were subject to extensive physical and social restraints that prevented them and their families from attaining anything like economic security. Today, major racial barriers are still present, but sometimes are more covert and hidden behind ostensibly colorblind policies. A respondent in the Southwest, Faye Bishop, expresses some of these important concerns:

> There are some family members I know expressed that they were not treated fair because they are black. Several instances, where they heard of a job, they went there prepared, able to get the position, but when they got there, interviewed for the job, [whites] told them that the job had already been filled. Later on, they found out that it had not been, but they had hired a white person. So they felt like they had not been treated fairly about the job. (*Faye Bishop, 70s*)

Our survivors of Jim Crow testify that family members struggle with persisting racial discrimination in educational and employment settings and in accessing various government programs, such as those providing housing loans. As in the past, such discrimination limits their individual and family opportunities to become economically prosperous.

The façade of meritocracy asserts that working hard and getting an education is the pathway to success, still a mantra regularly touted by many whites. Numerous respondents argued that this pathway was often closed off for African Americans, no matter how hard they worked and played by the rules of the dominant group's employment game. One male respondent in the Southeast, Larry Kennedy, goes so far as to question if the fight for integration during the Jim Crow era was actually a mistake:

> It's important to have a college education, and yet blacks are out here picking up trash? Working back at the trash place. You lose your value, or your sense of the value of education. Don't give me no doggone B.S. or B.A. when I've got to work on the back of a truck picking up garbage. . . . It becomes degrading for America to say to me that education is the key to opportunity and upward mobility, but when I get it, because I'm black, there ain't no opportunity. Doors

closed. There is no opportunity. One of the brightest guys I ever met in [town], died several years back . . . [I'd] sit down and talk with him. He had a drinking problem, but he told me how he got that drinking problem. You see what I'm saying? You never know how many minds have been destroyed, I mean bright minds, have been destroyed behind that system. (*Larry Kennedy, 70s*)

He then accents the critical importance of black community organizations:

Black institutions that were out there, they were supreme institutions. They were doing some educating. Even with those inferior textbooks, they were doing some educating. Put in a whole lot of common sense and knowledge, not just theory. . . . How do you tell your child that I got a high school education, or I have two years of college, or I have three years of college and just couldn't make it, financial things were bad and everything, but you got an education. All those who had got a B.S. or B.A., and they had to ride around in the back of a trash truck. I'm not degrading that because they take care of their families. But that's not the idea of what education and degrees is all about. . . . Don't tell me to get educated when there is no opportunity for me to use my education. And particularly after we moved into "integration." [*Did the black community feel maybe integration wasn't the best thing for them?*] There's no question about it. Sometimes I wonder now why in the hell I was downtown [protesting Jim Crow] . . . all over downtown raising all that hell. What has it done to us? Materially, psychologically, and from within, we see now. Now, what it did to me in terms of raising my consciousness of acceptance of being "a first-class citizen." Nothing! (*Larry Kennedy, 70s*)

Kennedy shares with us the heavy psychological and material price that the black community has paid in attempts at racial integration now for decades. A component of the segregation stress syndrome is the shame and anger that comes along with decades of fighting for recognition as first-class citizens and realizing that has not actually happened. In this man's account we observe evidence of racial trauma based on past lived experiences during the Jim Crow decades, on present experiences with the lack of racial equality, and on a realization that the future is still bleak for many young African Americans.

The wealth gap between African Americans and whites today in the seemingly "democratic" United States is greater than the racial inequality in South Africa at the peak of legal apartheid.[20] Recall that in the 2010 survey of Consumer Finances the median wealth of white families was about eight times that of black families. This wealth gap has grown considerably since the Jim Crow era. In addition, illustrating the intergenerational component of the wealth gap, even white high school dropouts have on average more wealth than blacks with a college degree.[21]

The significant, sometimes growing inequalities between white and black Americans since the official end of legal segregation are easier to understand when we consider the larger societal picture. As we explained earlier, given the Jim Crow legacy of neighborhood segregation and the fact that housing taxes fund public schools, a majority of African American children suffer from inferior or absent educational resources. In addition, whites receive much preferential treatment in securing good jobs in the economy. Recent research by Nancy DiTomaso has demonstrated well the white networking patterns that reproduce much racial inequality in employment. Hundreds of white respondents admitted that they had used their exclusive white networks to get most jobs they had over their lifetimes. They had not gotten most of these jobs only because of their personal "skills, qualifications, and merit."[22] She also found that white opposition to aggressive racial integration of U.S. employment settings was substantially based on white fear that *their exclusionary white networks* would be significantly eliminated.

Not surprisingly, thus, whites have much more in the way of socioeconomic resources passed across the generations of white families who have been unjustly enriched by an array of white "affirmative action" programs—including many government programs over more than a century, such as homestead land, home loan, and veterans' programs. Moreover, although whites today engage in more criminal (blue-collar and white-collar) activities than blacks, black Americans are under greater surveillance from agents of the criminal justice system. As a result, they are more likely to be caught up in the extensive U.S. prison-industrial complex, which some call the "new Jim Crow"—thereby removing them from much political engagement, many economic opportunities, and important family connections.[23]

CONTINUING BLACK SURVEILLANCE: RACIAL PROFILING

As in the Jim Crow decades, black parents today often teach their children how to react and interact with often dangerous white police officers. Indeed, there are several guidebooks and pocket reminders available to assist black parents in efforts to keep children safe in interactions with police. Numerous respondents commented on the assumption still made by many police officers today about African American criminality. A respondent in the Southeast, Forrest Watts, believes things are better today, but not yet equal:

> I don't think that it ever will be equal—in the courts and different things that we're supposed to have, that we don't have. I tell you like this: If a cop stops you, it's a different approach than if a cop stops a white man. I'm not saying all cops are bad, I'm not saying that, but I have seen the way young cops ridicule black people. I think it's better but . . . I don't think it's equal. And I don't think it will ever be really equal. . . . Well, it's not ever going to be equal cause [whites are] trying to keep you down. But we, we better get out from under that, you understand. (*Forrest Watts, 80s*)

Other respondents shared their personal experiences of differential treatment with white police officers today, such as Allan Myers in the Southeast:

> About six weeks ago, I'm on my way to work. I drive every day. . . . I pull up to the stop sign, make a right turn, I looked up, there was a trooper behind me. His lights came on. They said I was doing 80 [mph]. I said, "No, I wasn't. I come this way every day, I wouldn't do 80." So that was one of those "driving while black" things. He said, "Let me see your license. Where you coming from?" I said, "I live [here]. I come this way every day. Here's my [college] identification card." There's that apartheid thing again. I've got to validate myself. I said, "Here's my ID card. I teach at the community college. Come this way every day. I know where you guys sit. Why would I speed?" He said, "All right, Mr. [name], I'm gonna let you go this time." Let me go? I haven't done anything! Then I was stopped a few days later. (*Allan Myers, 60s*)

This educator calls our attention to important remnants of white Jim Crow thinking in this law enforcement incident. He cites the need for more than the usual identification, which reminds him of the old apartheid system of South Africa. (Tragically, that South African apartheid system was actually modeled in part on the U.S. Jim Crow system.)[24] Although the respondent was released—apparently there was little evidence to proceed—unwarranted stops nonetheless create undue emotional stress and loss of time and energy, as well as perpetuate the old white framing of black criminality.

Black women and couples often face similar police profiling and harassment. An interviewee in the Southwest, Bettie Tyson, shares with us a similar experience she had with law enforcement:

> There are a number of black people that I know would report . . . they have been discriminated by the police. And one incident that I really recall, and that was about two years ago. My husband and I . . . came through a little town, and we saw the policeman sitting under the tree in his car in this little town. Of course we never break the rules, because we don't want to pay no fine. We always stayed with the rules and the regulations of the law, we never break the law. So we passes him; we're looking at him on the highway. When we got down about three blocks here, this patrolman coming behind us with his lights on. My husband said, "Wonder what in the world is he stopping us for? I don't understand this." So we pull over. My husband asks, "What are you stopping me for?" He stated, "You were going one or two miles over the speed limit." (*Bettie Tyson, 70s*)

Then she recounts her elderly husband's courageously assertive response:

> [My husband] said, "Just wait a minute, I'm almost three blocks [away], and you are just now stopping me? Why didn't you stop me when I just passed you? Do you think that I would be speeding looking at you? No! What are you doing? Racial profiling me? What are you doing?" He said, "No, you were speeding." My husband said, "No, I was not speeding, and if you are going to write a ticket, you write the ticket, and I will meet you in court." (*Bettie Tyson, 70s*)

Then she responds firmly and with some contextual information for the white officer:

So I said to him, "What is your name?" He said, "Here's my name; here this is my badge." I said, "You know what? I'm a taxpayer in this county where you're working. I know your grandparents. I'm an old citizen here, I know your grandparents." I said, "So you know what? I know my husband was not speeding. You know it too, but you are racially profiling because we are old blacks." He said, "Oh no, no." I said, "Oh yes, you are too, because I'm hearing about this, but I tell you what, you write the ticket, and we will meet you in court." He said, "Well, I'm not going to write you a ticket this time. I'm going to let you by, but be careful up the road because my brother is a patrolman in the next town, and he might pick you up in the next town." (*Bettie Tyson, 70s*)

These rather daring older African Americans, emphatic that they were undeserving of police accusations of wrongdoing, reminded the officer of their social connections within the local community. The officer says that he is not racial profiling, but warns them that his brother in the next town might pull them over. As discussed previously, the equal-justice-under-law ideal is for people to be held accountable only when they actually engage in criminal activity, and to be unburdened when innocent. However, much contemporary social science research suggests that African Americans are regularly and disproportionately stopped and/or searched when they are innocent.[25] Ironically, this commonplace policing discrimination ensures that some whites' criminal activities are ignored, thereby putting all citizens' safety at risk.

A respondent in the Southwest, Elbert Houston, recalls his experiences with the police and how racial profiling will likely always exist:

It's getting better, and we still have long ways to go. There is racial profiling. I don't care what they say, it's going to always exist. They [police] gonna always respond to a situation where there's black crime in a white neighborhood quicker than they would if it was black-on-black crime. But I have seen strides under the present administration where they are making a concerted effort to do better . . . where they are starting to hire more blacks in the [police] force. But then . . . it's like being a part of a fraternity, and you know you don't rat on a fraternity brother. I mean I think they're making strides with some things that they're doing within the department itself that they are gonna crack down on those people who would use their authority unwisely. . . . If it's very overt, then it's something that you address but you have to make sure that you go through the proper channels. For instance, if you have a patrolman stop you for what you consider is not a necessary stop, and they do not have justifiable cause—for any reason they can just stop you and inquire. But if you think it's unjust, you learn to cope, and you actually write a complaint in. And you get the officer's name and number, and you go through the formal channels of doing that. That was one of the things you learned to do rather than subject yourself to unfair treatment by overreacting at the stop. The same thing in a restaurant, if you feel like you are being treated unfairly, rather than being boisterous and drawing a lot of attention, just simply ask for the manager. The manager comes over, and you talk to him. We learned how to do things through channels, and I think we are being more effective. (*Elbert Houston, 60s*)

Houston emphasizes some contemporary strategies available to African Americans to resist white discrimination and dominance. Assertiveness is now more possible without the severe penalties of resistance that usually accrued to courageous resistors under legal segregation conditions. With their Jim Crow experiences often in the back of their minds, our respondents understand that they have been under surveillance all of their lives by white police officers and many other whites.

This police surveillance, profiling, and harassment has translated into an African American community that is nationally crippled by the great expansion of the prison-industrial complex, one in which African Americans are incarcerated at nearly six times the rate of whites. Criminologists have regularly underscored the lack of relationship between the racial character of prison populations and actual crime rates by racial group. In recent decades crime rates have stabilized or declined, yet prison populations have increased, often dramatically.[26] For example, although whites use illegal drugs about as often as blacks, the latter are incarcerated for illegal drug offenses at a much higher rate than whites. Indeed, African Americans make up about 12 percent of the general population, and about 13 percent of illegal drug users, yet they make up 38 percent of those arrested for drug offenses. Even more strikingly, African Americans make up 55 percent of those convicted for these offenses, and an incredible 74 percent of those sentenced to prison for them.[27] This extreme and highly discriminatory overrepresentation in incarceration for drug use comes at an enormous cost to the individual, family, and community. It has a very substantial cost for the larger society, including the taxpayer burden of the great cost of expanded incarceration, as well as the many costs in the form of lost human talents. Researchers like Michelle Alexander have shown that these inegalitarian prison realities result from the racially discriminatory policies of the contemporary "justice" system, policies often hidden behind a colorblind framing of society.

Actually, contemporary racial discrimination has often replicated the old Jim Crow norms and practices, if often in somewhat newer forms. Today African Americans face highly discriminatory policing and imprisonment, confront bleak employment opportunities, are frequently blocked from important housing and student loan opportunities, and encounter increasing political and voter disenfranchisement. We may live in a "new Jim Crow" era, *but* it has all too many similarities to the old Jim Crow era.

EMPOWERING BLACK CHILDREN: LESSONS FROM JIM CROW

The teaching of strategies of resistance to discrimination also connect the Jim Crow era to the present day. As we saw in chapter 6, our respondents accent the need to teach younger generations important lessons of survival and resistance. As some respondents noted, in the Jim Crow era black children were usually taught by black teachers who cared greatly for them and passed along lifesaving strategies for surviving overt racial oppression and for being proud of themselves. Today, black children frequently do not have this traditional support. They are more likely to be taught by white teachers who are ignorant of or, worse, indifferent to the systemic racial barriers that blacks currently face in society. Given this reality, many respondents explained how critical it was for children to receive an authentic education about this country's Jim Crow history of oppression and resistance.

A retired nurse in her 70s, Della Kirkland, explains well the value of such a critical education:

> I think the children need to know that the strides that were made by black folk during a period of Jim Crow was so great . . . hard fought,

hard battles, [and] suffering. All of the things that we fought for . . . they are enjoying now. But the battle isn't over! They don't know we had the stamina and the strength and the fortitude to fight through those 100 years. Young blacks think they've arrived, and they don't still have a battle! See, I am blown away when I hear people say, "Oh, I don't need affirmative action." Ha, ha, ha, you don't need affirmative action [is] the way they explained it. They explain affirmative action as taking somebody without skills. I don't know any affirmative action that took anybody who didn't know. Affirmative action is that you get your foot in the door, then you prove you know what you're going to do. . . . But we get these little kids. . . . I am appalled when they don't know the history. And they need to know it because they didn't arrive all by themselves. They came on my back. I came on my mama's back. She suffered more than I suffered. But I suffered more than my children suffer. But my children tell the history. My son was in class, and his teacher wasn't telling it right. And he says, "Wait a minute, my mama says . . ." [laughs] He said, "No, you're telling it the wrong way. My mama said so . . ." But that's why I think it's important. You can't keep life going if you don't have the "get-skill" demon. (*Della Kirkland, 70s*)

Her emphatic response that the "battle isn't over!" is an acknowledgment that even with some civil rights victories, the war for racial equality must continue. She is aware too of the intergenerational transmission of suffering, as well as of the strategies needed to navigate discrimination and cope with its trauma. She emphasizes the importance of understanding the Jim Crow times in which older African Americans lived, survived, and fought—and in educating contemporary "educators" about this often covered-up or misunderstood historical heritage.

In her long interview Della Kirkland is especially astute; she draws on her Jim Crow experiences and continues with more intergenerational advice to young African Americans today:

We have to look at a black man trying to be a black man when there's nobody gonna respect him. And his out may not have been the out that he wanted, but he's looking for it. That's why I tell black women, "Hold him up." Hold black men up. Talk about how good they are. I know black daddies that comb hair, wash dishes, wash clothes . . . took care of sick wives. . . . My daddy drove two generations to school. I know black daddies who did a lot. But when you see TV and every black man is lying on the ground with their handcuffs on, the whole white world thinks all black men do that. And if black women and their children don't hold them up, who's going to do it? (*Della Kirkland, 70s*)

She adds, with yet more sage insight, advice on the support of black men:

If they're not doing right, when you get them home you can take care of that. You can talk about what the issues are. But you don't need to go out in front of the whole world and say, "Oh, he's a black, he ain't no good." That is not helping anybody. And when I grew up, my parents taught me that you don't tell white folks all your business no how. That was the order of the day. . . . I was doing my nursing, and these white nurses were doing all this research on black folks. And they wrote all this stuff, and I knew it was all wrong. . . . I told my teacher, I say, "This is not evidence. . . . Because that white person went in there, and so all these black people told her what they wanted her to know." 'Cause it wasn't her business to get into their business. . . . So I think that we have to tell the story. I tell grandmas now, "Sit down and talk to the children. Tell them how you washed clothes. Tell them how far you walked to get to work. Tell them what you got paid. Tell them how it felt to only be able to dress up on Sunday and be called Miss Smith, because all the week they called you Doris or Aunt Sukie or Auntie or worse, you know. Tell them about the respect." That's why the respect is important to the old folk. They had already paid the price by being called by their first name by little white five- and six-year-olds. (*Della Kirkland, 70s*)

Again we observe the importance of the intergenerational transmission of warnings, lessons, and strategies that have been passed down for many decades since the Jim Crow era. Kirkland is painfully aware of the historical and contemporary lack of respect that has been given to black men and women. Given the spatial segregation of U.S. society, where most whites do not have regular egalitarian and sustained relationships with African Americans, false or exaggerated media images of black people become an "educational" source for whites and often perpetuate a damaging and racist framing of African American men and women.[28] Kirkland accents the urgency in challenging many educators' white-centered perspectives. She has a deep understanding of the necessity of recounting well the historical realities of white racism, and she emphasizes the need to pass along the coping strategies from the Jim Crow era that are still applicable and necessary today.

A respondent in the Southeast, Jennie Harrell, describes the destructive consequences of people not interrupting the racially framed and culturally ingrained messages of African American inferiority. She describes her experiences today as compared to those of the legal segregation era:

> As far as something that's better, you basically have that feeling of little bit more freedom. You're not as low as [whites] been telling you've been, because you're learning that you're not what they've been telling you that you are. And people are learning that more, that you are somebody. Even with your black skin you're still somebody. But I guess down the years the black people been brow-beaten so much and told that you're nothing. Some older people don't tell the kids that you are somebody so they still pass it down to their kids that you're nothing. And I think that's the harm that's being done to the black kids today. That they're not told enough that they can be anything they want to be, and they are somebody. It's like from generation to generation, like an abused husband passes down to his son, then he passes it down to his son, and it's just like abuse [from] people from another race. It just passes down from generation to generation. (*Jennie Harrell, 60s*)

Similar to the intergenerational transmission of wealth and poverty, we see an intergenerational transmission of white supremacy and black inferiority. The recurring trauma associated with this constant "browbeating" of black Americans gets passed along to subsequent generations unless it is actively countered and disrupted. Just as the symptoms of racial trauma are passed along, so too can be the important strategies of black resistance and opposition to white abuse and discrimination.

A respondent from the Southeast, Blanche Jackson, elucidates the survival strategies she learned in the legal segregation decades, strategies she now passes along to her daughter, who has experienced contemporary workplace discrimination:

> I think there is still a lot of prejudice out there. I see it here, all the time. You've got to. You can see it. It ain't gone. I don't think it's got no better really. It's just hidden more. It's kinda like under some-

thing, instead of just being right up front. . . . They do it undercover-like. Behind your back they'll say one thing. To your face, they'll say something different. To me that's still in the prejudice line. [*How do you deal with discrimination today?*] It's kinda hard. It's hard. It's really hard. Sometimes you have to give up the right for the wrong. And I'm finding myself doing that a lot . . . certain things I do, or don't do. . . . When I know I'm right, I have to back down, I'm running into that all the time. . . . And people can almost walk over you and almost not say anything, and I'm not used to that. I'm used to being cordial and nice to everybody. I told [my children] that they can't fight back, and say word for word on someone [who] is not treating them properly, fairly. You have to just hold some of the comments you want to make. You have to hold them. My daughter called me this morning. She was saying that she was having a meeting with one of her bosses. And she said, "I'm gonna tell that . . ." And I said, "Don't you say it! Don't you dare say it! You don't go in there doing that—not with that attitude! Because it's going to backfire on you. They've got the upper hand, and you've got to be humble." She said, "Momma, you're right. . . . You took all that a long time ago. But I'm not going to take it now." But still, you cannot do that. . . . It's a daily thing. You just have to smile and keep going. Sometimes I don't retaliate. But every now and then, I have to . . . I don't want them to think I'm a total . . . you know. It's hard. It's hard. (*Blanche Jackson, 60s*)

Jackson discusses the intergenerational transmission of racial trauma and of the Jim Crow strategies learned as a child—to smile, be cordial, silent, or invisible to whites. Her daughter validates the respondent's experiences and coping strategies, in spite of her desire to use a more assertive approach with her bosses. Survivors of Jim Crow often utilize earlier coping strategies in interactions with whites and pass them along to their descendants. Those born after the 1950s–1960s civil rights movement often incorporate these resistance strategies of the past, along with newer resistance tactics, in dealing with whites today.

In passing along strategies of survival and success over the generations, a few respondents accented the importance of this smiling, cordiality, and being humble even today. One respondent from the Southeast, Rosa Lee Johnson, explains her views thus:

I would say what I say to a lot of children: If you give away a smile, most of the time you get it back. If you think a smile then you think different than if you think a frown. I guess that would be my simple way of putting it. Give a smile away with all that goes with a smile. And, you know, now when we say give a little love, this means you clap and jump up and down. I think people can feel this. (*Rosa Lee Johnson, 80s*)

Similarly, a respondent in the Southwest, Myrtle Jones, describes how she responds to discrimination today: "The way I would respond is I would be cordial, hoping that they [whites] would do the same, and most of the time if you are cordial they know that you mean right, and mean to be nice and cordial. They will fall in line most of the time" (*Myrtle Jones, 70s*). We observe the prominence in these intergenerational transmissions of being cordial, smiling, and laughing, the old strategies that African Americans learned for their survival. In earlier decades many of these elderly black women raised white children, some of whom are now the employers of African Americans. They understand the polite strategies often needed to keep the racial peace. A superficial reading of these narratives might suggest that this is simply a matter of common courtesy. There is certainly a gendered component to much smiling, for women are expected to appear pleasant lest they be labeled a "bitch." Yet, as several excerpts from our interviews in previous chapters suggest, black men were, and are, also expected to smile so as to make whites more comfortable. In the Jim Crow era whites didn't understand that strategy, but African Americans knew that ensuring white comfort was fundamental to long-term survival.

THE CASE FOR REPARATIONS FOR JIM CROW OPPRESSION

Thus far, we have provided some history of Jim Crow; offered much evidence from many of Jim Crow's survivors on the centrality of white discrimination, exploitation, theft, and violence; and demonstrated from their testimony the individual and collective psychological consequences we term the segregation stress syndrome. We have also demonstrated the harsh legacies of Jim Crow segregation in the many contemporary patterns of white racial discrimination that are faced by our respondents, their descendants, and other African Americans.

As we have seen repeatedly, a majority of our experienced respondents feel that their families and communities are in some significant ways not much better off than they were some 50 years ago. At some point in their interviews, the majority discuss witnessing their children or grandchildren struggle with contemporary racial barriers similar to those that they experienced in the Jim Crow era. They often see their children and grandchildren, and others like them, struggling with discriminatory policing, failing schools and inadequate teachers, lack of good-paying jobs and other economic resources, second-class political citizenship, and an overall disregard by many whites of the impacts of discrimination on black individuals, families, and communities.

We do want to accurately represent views of these brave folks who were willing to share with us their extraordinarily difficult Jim Crow experiences in spite of their fears and reservations. We combed through the interviews to find answers from the respondents on how to achieve serious remedies for the social injustices that they experienced under Jim Crow and for the racial injustices that they and their younger family members are still experiencing now. Significantly and surprisingly, we didn't find anything in the interviews that referenced large-scale reparations and monetary compensation for what happened to these older African Americans under Jim Crow totalitarianism. It is quite telling that they are not thinking in terms of reparations. For us, this is an implicit but powerful message, especially given the pervasive white notion that African Americans are always looking for some sort of government handout, for "something for nothing." What, then, do they indicate that they want to see in terms of remedies for this white-controlled society's systemic injustices? In point of fact, all these courageous Jim Crow survivors ever say that they want to see now is equal access for themselves and their descendants to educational opportunities, good jobs, and first-class citizenship in all important areas of society. Most especially, they want the life chances—especially the societal opportunities and access to resources—to be much better for their children and grandchildren.

The overwhelming majority made very clear throughout their interviews that they didn't hate white folks, but instead prayed for them, forgave them, and looked to a higher power to help survive the white oppression they have faced and currently face. Their revealing and difficult life narratives offer up a powerful message of humanity, forgiveness, and the human ability to look past the great pain caused by white oppressors to the creation of a truly liberty-and-justice U.S. system, one to which they are greatly committed.

We understand and agree with their reasonable desires and expectations for dramatic societal change in the direction of *real* liberty and justice for all. However, as scholars of U.S. racism with decades of research experience examining this society, we also understand how the racial oppression of the slavery, Jim Crow, and contemporary eras has a foundational and systemic reality in U.S. society. Four centuries of racial oppression have created such deep-lying racial inequalities, such extensive and rooted unjust enrichment for whites as a group and unjust impoverishment for blacks as a group, that a very large-scale commitment by those in power in this society to substantial government and corporate reparations for centuries of racial oppression are not only warranted but also necessary to begin the movement of this racist society toward our respondents' goals of a truly just, free, and egalitarian society.

By way of conclusion, thus, let us consider briefly some arguments offered against major government reparations for African Americans. These arguments almost always focus on reparations for what was done to African Americans in the slavery era and largely ignore the long era of antiblack oppression under Jim Crow, as well as contemporary patterns of white racism. Consider these mainly erroneous, usually whitewashed, arguments about reparations for African Americans who had enslaved ancestors: (1) too much time has passed for reparations redress; (2) all victims of slavery are dead and living African Americans do not deserve reparations; (3) whites today are not responsible for injuries inflicted on African Americans during slavery; (4) locating the victims and calculating reparations are impossible; and (5) African Americans need to be more independent of government anyway.[29] Sadly, even otherwise astute white scholars do not perceive the moral and societal need for current reparations, as in this recent comment by influential political scientist Ira Katznelson: "The brutal harms inflicted by slavery and Jim Crow are far too substantial ever to be properly remedied. . . . There is no adequate rejoinder to losses on this scale. In such situations, the request for large cash transfers places bravado ahead of substance, flirts with demagoguery, and risks political irrelevance."[30]

Like almost all white analysts of reparations issues, Katznelson ignores the reasonable arguments about reparations *for the Jim Crow era,* which he actually brought up, arguments that do not face these major objections. Having just probed deeply into the extremely destructive realities of Jim Crow, the reader will understand why we see much of the white objection to reparations as so highly self-interested that whites do not see, or do not want to see, what is remarkably obvious to us. Clearly, the arguments about too much time having passed for racism redress is *not so relevant* in considerations of reparations for Jim Crow segregation. Patterns of legal segregation ended officially with the significant implementation of 1960s civil rights laws, the final one being the 1968 civil rights act on housing. Yet, even these important laws did not bring an immediate end to some overt Jim-Crow-like discrimination, which lasted openly into the 1970s in numerous towns and cities.[31] Thus, extreme U.S. racial apartheid ended less than five decades ago.

A related argument against reparations for black Americans is that the victims of oppression are supposedly "long dead" and, thus, that living black Americans do not deserve such reparations.[32] This argument allows white (and other) contemporary analysts to focus on slavery, thereby ignoring the more recent Jim Crow era. However, the material and psychological impact of Jim Crow totalitarianism remains very evident. As we have demonstrated, the segregation stress syndrome continues to disrupt and harm many African American lives, those of the Jim Crow generation and those of their descendants. Consequently, linking the current mental and physical health problems of many African Americans to this destructive Jim Crow past is a reasonable and relevant way of making a strong case for contemporary reparations.[33]

Arguments against reparations for black Americans also often overlook the salient fact that the U.S. government has already supported some reparations in a number of precedent-setting cases—for racialized oppression that overlapped in time with Jim Crow totalitarianism faced by African Americans. For instance, the U.S. government has paid (modest) reparations to the Japanese Americans who were imprisoned for essentially racist reasons in U.S. concentration camps during World War II. The U.S. government has also provided some monetary compensation to certain Native American groups for stolen lands and returned some lands, as a modest type of reparations for U.S. government land theft and treaty violations. In addition, under great U.S. government pressure, the contemporary German and Austrian governments have compensated some Jewish and other Nazi Holocaust survivors (and the State of Israel) in the form of significant monetary reparations.[34]

Moreover, a recent U.S. Supreme Court case, *Republic of Austria v. Altmann* (2004), set a precedent that can be applied to African Americans who are seeking reparations for the unjust enrichment of whites at their expense through centuries of past wrongdoing.[35] The high court held that certain government actions in the distant past could be *retroactively remedied* under later legislation (the 1976 Foreign Immunities Act), a U.S. decision permitting a lawsuit by Maria Altmann against the contemporary Austrian government that seeks to recover valuable paintings stolen by German Nazis and put into an Austrian museum. In this and similar cases involving the highly racialized actions of 1930s–1940s Nazi government officials, the statute of limitations has been considered as not applying because of the character of Nazi "crimes against humanity"—which included extensive imprisonment, torture, murder, and property theft. In our view such legal reasoning can be applied to the case of African American suffering and material loss from the also totalitarian oppression of the U.S. Jim Crow era—with its pervasive discrimination, widespread imprisonment, torture, murder, and theft of land and labor. These too were large-scale "crimes against humanity" that involved very extensive violations of human rights. For many decades the African American residents of Jim Crow areas could not even be plaintiffs seeking any reparative justice for the immediate, frequent, and openly discriminatory white actions they long had to endure. In our view it is well past time for them to have this basic human right in the United States.[36]

We might note, too, that recent lawsuits filed against specific U.S. corporations—Aetna Insurance Company, JP Morgan, and the Brown and Williamson Tobacco Corporation—show evidence of the various strategies being utilized to fight for African American reparations, but almost always in reference to the connections of these companies to major benefits from slavery.[37] On occasion, nonetheless, some compensation or apologies have flowed from these cases, and some white executives and government officials now recognize, to varying degrees, the salience of black reparative demands. Moreover, considering the slavery centuries, some African American leaders have called for a major government apology for slavery that is coupled with substantial reparations, while others just seek the reparations. Assessing slavery, for example, Randall Robinson has argued that white individuals should be held personally responsible for the slavery actions and enrichments of their white ancestors. Robinson also insists that these crimes against humanity, which were often carried out or collaborated in by white government officials, constitute "crimes that should not be touched by statute of limitations, because when governments commit such crimes, they have a certain immortality."[38] In 2009, belatedly and under pressure from black organizations and lawmakers, the U.S. Senate did issue a brief apology to African Americans: "The Congress (A) acknowledges the fundamental injustice, cruelty, brutality, and inhumanity of slavery and Jim Crow laws; (B) apologizes to African-Americans on behalf of the people of the United States, for the wrongs committed against them and their ancestors who suffered under slavery and Jim Crow laws."[39] This brief Senate resolution, unfortunately, was not supported with a similar House resolution, and it only apologized for slavery and Jim Crow, and no more than that. Indeed, these mostly white senators added a specific provision to the apology resolution that barred African Americans from seeking reparations for the admitted U.S. government role in the centuries of African American oppression.

This negative government reaction to Jim Crow and slavery reparations needs to be changed to a positive consideration of such remedial actions. Recall again that millions of *living* African Americans suffered through Jim Crow totalitarianism, and millions of *living* whites participated in its everyday discrimination, including frequent acts of white violence. Our respondents offer much evidence on the costs of this extensive white discrimination over several decades. Moreover, research by Elliot Jaspin, James Loewen, and others cited in previous chapters has demonstrated that significant groups of whites often drove large numbers of blacks, sometimes *whole* black communities, out of numerous southern and border state towns, thereby securing black lands and other property at little or no cost.[40] Strikingly, whites in these communities today have mostly hidden, suppressed, or destroyed records of these substantial "racial cleansings" in the Jim Crow era.

The oppressive events of the Jim Crow era are often recent enough to allow for some contemporary tracking of the black victims and their white oppressors. African Americans who lived through that era can typically share in detail what happened to them, where it was done, and who did it. In addition to testimony from African American individuals, there are also newspaper and other archival sources that can provide evidence on how, when, and to whom African American families lost their lands, other property, and sometimes family members' lives. The Holocaust-like oppression many faced was not some vague reality now lost in the mists of history, but was carried out by specific white individuals and groups—many of them, and their descendants, profiting greatly in the present off of unjust enrichment gained during long years of Jim Crow and earlier racial oppression.

Moreover, in its everyday operation that extreme white oppression was not marginal to otherwise "just" and "democratic" U.S. institutions. The actions of, and laws made by, many white local, state, and federal government officials regularly created, maintained, and/or allowed the totalitarian oppression that millions of African Americans faced in the legal segregation era. We should note too, that in the long century from the 1870s to the 1970s, in areas where there were no official Jim Crow laws, there was much informal Jim-Crow-type discrimination against African Americans. For example, many powerful whites in the North, including those at the helm of government agencies, were implicated in the destruction of black opportunities to build up wealth. Richard Rothstein has summarized how the creation of racially segregated communities by white government action, in the North and South, has often been covered up. History books rarely include discussions of how our highly segregated housing patterns were *intentionally* created by white government, real estate, and banking decision makers over the Jim Crow decades. "The federal government purposefully placed public housing in high-poverty, racially isolated neighborhoods to concentrate the black population, and with explicit racial intent, created a whites-only mortgage guarantee program to shift the white population from urban neighborhoods to exclusively white suburbs."[41] The Internal Revenue Service buttressed this discriminatory action by giving tax exemptions to community-segregation organizations, and state-licensed real estate agents and mortgage agencies channeled blacks into black communities and whites into white communities, while police organizations often ignored violent actions by whites designed to drive black families out of white neighborhoods. Not until the late 1960s did the federal government ban overt housing discrimination. By then, the underlying structure of U.S. housing segregation was firmly in place, a racially segregated pattern persisting in the present.[42] In the North and the South, we observe the heavy involvement of white officials in the racialized segregation of African Americans, involvement that has played a very important role in reducing their chances of securing first-rate schools and other community services—and thus in building up family capital and wealth.

Unsurprisingly, this relatively recent historical reality is typically ignored or suppressed, often aggressively, by our contemporary white-run governments, in our public discussions about the morality of racism, in most mainstream history books, and indeed by the mainstream movie studios and other mainstream media. Quite clearly, new and extensive reparations laws need to be passed by the U.S. Congress, which itself needs to become much more desegregated in terms of representatives of all racial and ethnic backgrounds. Among others, Elliot Jaspin has suggested the need too for a U.S. counterpart to South Africa's recent Truth and Reconciliation Commission, which heard testimony from black and white South Africans on the extreme oppression that blacks faced there in the brutal apartheid era.[43] Considering the U.S. Jim Crow era, in place of those black Americans who are now deceased, qualified researchers could publicly document and assess the many black expulsions from white-run towns. We suggest, too, that the same could be done for the many other ways in which whites stole black land, other property, labor, and lives over the long Jim Crow century. Remedies for the costly impacts of the totalitarian Jim Crow oppression can be specific and designed to compensate for specific wrongs to living black individuals, by living whites or white-controlled companies—however difficult and expensive such legal procedures might be.

CONCLUSION

Whites often make many arguments for inaction in regard to substantial reparative actions on behalf of contemporary African Americans, but most of these derive from the highly privileged white position in the centuries-old system of racial oppression. Such arguments buttress the persisting unjust structures of white power and privilege against real structural change. The common white argument that African Americans must be more independent of government and more enterprising is neglectful of this country's history. For centuries white Americans were the exclusive beneficiaries of government "affirmative action" that raised many into the middle class. In contrast, for three and a half centuries black Americans have had to be independent of the oppressive white-run governments and to be independently enterprising even to survive this country's extensive racial subordination. In spite of that oppression, and its consequent high costs and incredible pains, African Americans have developed strategies of resistance and survival for themselves, their families, and their communities. They have frequently organized to protest the state generated and privately generated oppression that whites have targeted at them. Thus, calls by whites for black Americans to become less dependent on government programs are not only hypocritical but also do nothing to bring solutions for the country's large-scale, persisting, and unjust racial inequalities. Such black "independence" would not address the overwhelming magnitude of white-imposed discrimination and of the extensive racial inequalities that have been cumulatively created by white discrimination and passed along over many generations and about four centuries.

It's too easy for whites to minimize the long-lasting effects of past and present discrimination by referencing the apparent success of a few prominent African Americans, such as Oprah Winfrey or Barack Obama. Whites typically ignore, or do not know, the truncated and harmed lives of the millions of African Americans who have struggled for many decades with substantial racial discrimination and much consequent unemployment and impoverishment. Whites routinely turn a blind eye not only to the centuries-old reality of systemic racism, but also to its severe socioeconomic and psychological impacts on African Americans past and present.[44] Full individual and family freedom, justice, and equality for African Americans has *never* been allowed by the U.S. system of racism. During and after the Jim Crow era, most African Americans found themselves dealing daily with extreme social, political, and economic constraints of large-scale racial discrimination, as well as the serious psychological impacts of the fear, anxiety, anguish, and shame that are persisting manifestations of the segregation stress syndrome.

There are some people who argue, "We can't put a price on pain and all that has been lost to African Americans." However, as noted previously, white government officials have agreed on reparations for some of the losses of the Japanese American survivors of World War II internment camps and on some reparations for Native Americans who lost much land to white violence and chicanery. In addition, many whites have fought for reparations to the Jewish survivors of the Holocaust and to punish severely the Nazi war criminals. Thus, the argument for not calculating the costs of past racial oppression is fallacious and yet another deflective defense for the current racial injustices of this society. Clearly, a few historically oppressed groups have been successful in capturing, to varying degrees, the moral sense of powerful people outside their own group.

In conclusion, we suggest that African Americans likewise need to gain such moral support for major reparations from their white oppressors, including reparations for those who have survived Jim Crow and their descendants. Undeniably, large-scale government reparations are one way for unjustly enriched white government and private sector leaders, together with other affluent whites, to present unjustly impoverished black neighborhoods with an abundance of much-deserved and much-needed socioeconomic resources that can help them to overcome some systemic impacts of centuries-old white racism.[45] A central issue here is why the mostly white leaders at the helm of most federal, state, and local governments do not see such socioeconomic reparations to be just, necessary, and urgent. They are urgent, for time is of the essence, as the African American survivors are growing older. Some of our respondents have died without any public recognition of or official apology for their extensive suffering. Time-wasting plays into the hands of oppressors and buttresses their hypocritical excuses for government inaction. Certainly, too, social scientists should document and disseminate yet more African American accounts of Jim Crow totalitarianism, for they often make a very powerful case for such long-overdue government reparative action. They provide both voice and validation of the extraordinary lived experiences of millions with systemic white racism.

The inability of the mostly white-run U.S. government to create new laws and policies that will facilitate a just and reparative resolution for the Jim Crow survivors and their descendants strongly supports the belief among these and other African Americans that the deep-lying antiblack attitudes of whites have changed too little in recent decades. Because of whites' still-common belief in white superiority and civilizational exceptionalism, most will not turn the racial mirror around and look carefully at themselves and the centuries of racial atrocities created and facilitated by an oppressive white-racist system. According to our respondents, most whites' perception of white superiority and others' inferiority has not changed nearly enough and is in truth hindering the meaningful implementation of the "liberty and justice for all" that white America has promised all Americans, including African Americans, for two and a half centuries. Importantly too, a truly just, free, and democratic society must attempt to heal the deep wounds of its highly racialized past. When such deep wounds and their expanding impacts are left untreated, they don't go away, they don't heal, and the festering grows until something is done or the society self-destructs. The time for reparative change is now. The time is right for tending to deep wounds of our racialized past.

NOTES

I. INTRODUCTION

1. All names are pseudonyms, derived from Internet resources combining the most common names in the 1920s and the most common African American last names. Any connection to persons living or deceased is entirely coincidental. Traditionally social science research relies on first names only; to give due respect to the participants, we use first and last names. The written quotations are all taken from oral interviews, and thus have numerous indications of spoken dialogue. To maintain these voices of the participants, we intentionally don't use "[*sic*]" in their narratives, even when there are grammatical errors. Also, we lightly edited the responses to improve readability (for example, utterances such as "uhhh" and repeated words not used for emphasis, such as "She was a, was a teacher") were deleted. For each narrative we include the respondents' ages in decades (50s, 60s, 70s, 80s, or 90s).

2. In this book we use "black Americans" and "African Americans" interchangeably.

3. See Bruce Hoffman, "Inside Terrorism," accessed January 24, 2014, http://www.nytimes.com/books/first/h/hoffman-terrorism.html.

4. See John Hope Franklin, *Runaway Slaves: Rebels on the Plantation* (New York: Oxford University Press, 2000).

5. See Joe R. Feagin, *Systemic Racism: A Theory of Oppression* (New York: Routledge, 2006); Melvin Oliver and Thomas Shapiro, *Black Wealth/White Wealth: A Perspective on Racial Inequality* (New York: Routledge, 2001).

6. Leon F. Litwack, *Been in the Storm So Long: The Aftermath of Slavery* (New York: Vintage Books, 1980); Franklin, *Runaway Slaves.*

7. Stanley A. Elkins, *Slavery: A Problem in American Institutional and Intellectual Life* (New York: University of Chicago Press, 1959); David J. Knottnerus, D. L. Monk, and E. Jones, "The Slave Plantation System from a Total Institution Perspective," in *Plantation Society and Race Relations: The Origins of Inequality*, ed. T. J. Durant and J. D. Knottnerus, 17–29 (Westport, CT: Praeger, 1999).

8. Erving Goffman, *Asylums: Essays on the Social Situation of Mental Patients and Other Inmates* (Garden City, NY: Anchor, 1961), 12.

9. See Joe R. Feagin, *Racist America: Roots, Current Realities, and Future Reparations*, 3rd ed. (New York: Routledge, 2014).

10. Douglas A. Blackmon, *Slavery by Another Name: The Re-Enslavement of Black American from the Civil War to World War II* (Norwell, MA: Anchor, 2009).

11. Leon F. Litwack, *Trouble in Mind* (New York: Random House, 1998).

12. See Feagin, *Systemic Racism*.

13. Goffman, *Asylums*, xiii.

14. Ibid.

15. See Herbert Spencer, *Principles of Sociology* (Hamden, CT: Archon, 1969); Bertram W. Doyle, *The Etiquette of Race Relations in the South* (Chicago: University of Chicago, 1937); Robert E. Parks, *Race and Culture: Essays in the Sociology of Contemporary Man* (New York: Free Press, 1950); Erving Goffman, *The Presentation of Self in Everyday Life* (New York: Anchor, 1959).

16. For example, J. William Harris, "Etiquette, Lynching, and Racial Boundaries in Southern History: A Mississippi Example," *American Historical Review* 100, no. 2 (April 1995): 387–410; Adrienne Johnson Gosselin, "Racial Etiquette and the (White) Plot of Passing: (Re)Inscribing 'Place' in John Stahl's *Imitation of Life*," *Canadian Review of American Studies* 28, no. 3 (1998): 47–67.

17. James R. McGovern, *Anatomy of a Lynching: The Killing of Claude Neal* (Baton Rouge: Louisiana State University Press, 1982); Howard Smead, *Blood Justice: The Lynching of Charles Mack Parker* (New York: Oxford University Press, 1986); Laura Wexler, *Fire in a Canebrake: The Last Mass Lynching in America* (New York: Scribner, 2003); Timothy B. Tyson, *Blood Done Sign My Name* (New York: Three Rivers Press, 2004); Patricia Bernstein, *The First Waco Horror: The Lynching of Jesse Washington and the Rise of the NAACP* (College Station, TX: TAMU Press, 2005).

18. For example, Audrey Olsen Faulkner, Marsel A. Helser, Wendell Holbrook, and Shirley Geismar, *When I Was Comin' Up: An Oral History of Aged Blacks* (Hamden, CT: Archon, 1982); John Langston Gwaltney, *Drylongso: A Self-Portrait of Black America* (New York: New Press, 1993); Litwack, *Trouble in Mind*; William H. Chafe, *Remembering Jim Crow* (New York: New Press,

2001). There are also recent books, which we cite later, on rape, resistance, and African American women. See Charlotte Pierce-Baker, *Surviving the Silence: Black Women's Stories of Rape* (New York: Norton, 2000) and Danielle L. McGuire, *At the Dark End of the Street: Black Women, Rape, and Resistance—A New History of the Civil Rights Movement from Rosa Parks to the Rise of Black Power* (New York: Knopf, 2011).

19. The requirements for a diploma then often differed from present-day high school diploma requirements.

20. The gender disparity in our sample reflects the fact that among older African Americans women outnumber men. This project started as the dissertation project of Ruth Thompson-Miller and expanded from there. Prior to her successful interviewing, Joe Feagin had encouraged numerous students, of various backgrounds, over the years to undertake this type of project. Thompson-Miller was the first to be able to undertake such a project successfully. She found that being black and female was often critical to establishing rapport with the respondents and seemed to help to minimize their stress in talking about white racism.

2. THE REALITY AND IMPACT OF JIM CROW

1. Thomas R. Dye, "Rosewood, Florida: The Destruction of an African American Community," *Historian* 58 (Spring 1996): 605–22.

2. Maxine D. Jones, "The Rosewood Massacre and the Women Who Survived It," *Florida Historical Quarterly* 76 (Fall 1997): 193–208.

3. See, for example, Thema Bryant-Davis and Carlota Ocampo, "Racist Incident-Based Trauma," *Counseling Psychologist* 33 (2005): 489–90.

4. Findings from the National Vietnam Veterans' Readjustment Study, National Study for PTSD, accessed November 10, 2013, http://www.ptsd.va.gov/professional/pages/vietnam-vets-study.asp.

5. See James W. Loewen, *Sundown Towns: A Hidden Dimension of American Racism* (New York: New Press, 2005).

6. Joe R. Feagin, *Racist America: Roots, Current Realities, and Future Reparations*, 3rd ed. (New York: Routledge, 2014).

7. Elliot Jaspin, *Buried in the Bitter Waters: The Hidden History of Racial Cleansing in America* (New York: Basic Books, 2007), 222.

8. See Loewen, *Sundown Towns*; *Banished*, directed by Marco Williams (2007; New York: Two Tone Productions), DVD. Transcripts were taken from closed-captioning viewing.

9. In the quotes, the interviewer's comments appear in brackets and italicized text.

10. Danielle L. McGuire, *At the Dark End of the Street: Black Women, Rape, and Resistance—A New History of the Civil Rights Movement from Rosa Parks to the Rise of Black Power* (New York: Knopf, 2011), 51.

11. Shaun L. Gabbidon and Helen Taylor Greene, *Race and Crime*, 2nd ed. (Thousand Oaks, CA: Sage, 2009).

12. "Abraham's Shadow Hangs Low over Tallahassee: His Mother Can't Forget Him," *Baltimore Afro American (1893–1988)*, June 20, 1959, 3.

13. Sean Alfano, "Race an Issue in Katrina Response," *Associated Press*, September 3, 2005, http://www.cbsnews.com/news/race-an-issue-in-katrina-response.

14. Maurice Halbwachs and Lewis Coser, *On Collective Memory* (Chicago: University of Chicago Press, 1992), xxi.

15. Sharon Wasco, "Conceptualizing the Harm Done by Rape: Applications of Trauma Theory to Experiences of Sexual Assault," *Trauma, Violence, & Abuse* 4 (2003): 309–22.

16. See also Jennifer Ritterhouse, *Growing Up Jim Crow: How Black and White Southern Children Learned Race* (Chapel Hill: University of North Carolina Press, 2006).

17. See Joe R. Feagin and Melvin P. Sikes, *Living with Racism* (Boston: Beacon, 1994); Carole Marks, *Farewell—We're Good and Gone: The Great Black Migration* (Bloomington: Indiana University Press, 1989); Stewart E. Tolnay and E. M. Beck, "Racial Violence and Black Migration in the American South 1910–1930," *American Sociological Review* 57: 103–16.

18. Teresa Evans-Campbell, Karen D. Lincoln, and David T. Takeuchi, "Race and Mental Health: Past Debates, New Opportunities," in *Mental Health, Social Mirror*, ed. William R. Avison, Jane D. McLeod, and Bernice A. Pescosolido, 169–90 (New York: Springer, 2007), 173.

19. Gerald Darring, *Jewish Experience of the Holocaust: In Their Own Words* (Mobile, AL: Wilhelm, 2013), 258.

20. "Saving Private Ryan Brings Painful Memories to Combat Veterans," WRAL.com, July 27, 1998, accessed December 1, 2013, http://www.wral.com/news/local/story/127913.

21. Peggy A. Thoits, "Dimensions of Life Events That Influence Psychological Distress: An Evaluation and Synthesis of the Literature," in *Psychosocial Stress: Trends in Theory and Research*, ed. H. B. Kaplan, 33–103 (New York: Academic, 1983).

22. Joe Feagin, *The White Racial Frame: Centuries of Racial Framing and Counter-Framing* (New York: Routledge, 2010); Phillip Dray, *At the Hands of Persons Unknown: The Lynching of Black America* (New York: Modern Day Library, 2003).

23. C. Y. Johnson, J. Bowker, G. Green, and H. Cordell, "Provide It but Will They Come? A Look at African American and Hispanic Visits to Federal Recreation Areas," *Journal of Forestry* 105 (2007): 257–65; C. Y. Johnson and J. M. Bowker, "African-American Wildland Memories," *Environmental Ethics* 26 (2004): 57–76; P. A. Taylor, B. D. Grandjean, and J. H. Gramann, *National Park Service Comprehensive Survey of the American Public, 2008–2009: Racial and Ethnic Diversity of National Park System Visitors and Non-Visitors* (Fort Collins, CO: U.S. Department of the Interior National Park Service Science, 2011).

24. *Diagnostic and Statistical Manual of Mental Disorders*, 5th ed. (New York: American Psychiatric Publishing, 2013).

3. EVERYDAY SURVEILLANCE AND RACIAL FRAMING

1. Joe Feagin and Clairece B. Feagin, *Racial and Ethnic Relations*, 9th ed. (Upper Saddle River, NJ: Prentice-Hall, 2011), passim.

2. Vincent P. Mikkelsen, "Coming from Battle to Face a War: The Lynching of Black Soldiers in the World War I Era" (Ph.D. dissertation, Florida State University, 2007), 7.

3. Mikkelsen, "Coming from Battle to Face a War," viii.

4. Joe R. Feagin, *The White Racial Frame: Centuries of Racial Framing and Counter-Framing* (New York: Routledge, 2010).

5. "Say My Name: An African-American Family History," 2006, accessed January 16, 2014, http://www.freewebs.com/jencessa/thefirststep.htm.

6. Kent L. Sandstrom, Daniel D. Martin, and Gary Alan Fine, *Symbols, Selves and Social Reality: A Symbolic Interactionist Approach to Social Psychology and Sociology* (New York: Oxford University Press, 2010).

7. Erving Goffman, *Asylums: Essays on the Social Situation of Mental Patients and Other Inmates* (Garden City, NY: Anchor, 1961), 18.

8. Debra Van Ausdale and Joe R. Feagin, *The First R: How Children Learn Race and Racism* (Lanham, MD: Rowman & Littlefield, 2001).

9. See William H. Chafe, Raymond Gavins, and Robert Korstad, *Remembering Jim Crow: African Americans Tell about Life in the Segregated South* (New York: New Press, 2011).

10. Richard Wright, *Black Boy: A Record of Childhood and Youth* (New York: Harper and Brothers, 1945), 16.

11. See Joe R. Feagin, *Racist America: Roots, Current Realities, and Future Reparations*, 3rd ed. (New York: Routledge, 2014), ch. 2–4.

12. One of many critiques include Claire Potter, "For Colored Only? Understanding 'The Help' through the Lens of White Womanhood," *Tenured Radical*, August 21, 2011, accessed January 21, 2014, http://chronicle.com/blognetwork/tenuredradical/2011/08/for-colored-only-the-role-of-white-women-in-the-help/.

13. See Joe R. Feagin and Zinobia Bennefield, "Systemic Racism and U.S. Health Care," *Social Science & Medicine* 103 (2014): 7–14.

14. Joe R. Feagin and Karyn D. McKinney, *The Many Costs of Racism* (Lanham, MD: Rowman & Littlefield, 2005).

15. See Feagin, *Racist America*.

16. Vernellia R. Randall, *Dying while Black* (Dayton, OH: Seven Principles Press, 2006).

17. See Nessa Carey, *The Epigenetics Revolution: How Modern Biology Is Rewriting Our Understanding of Genetics, Disease, and Inheritance* (New York: Columbia University Press, 2013).

18. Janet Price and Margrit Shildrick, eds, *Feminist Theory and the Body: A Reader* (New York: Routledge, 1999).

19. "Infant Mortality and Low Birth Weight among Black and White Infants—United States, 1980–2000," Centers for Disease Control and Prevention, *Morbidity and Mortality Weekly Report* 51, no. 27 (July 12, 2002); "Births: Final Data for 2003," Centers for Disease Control and Prevention, *National Vital Statistics Reports* 54, no. 2 (September 8, 2005), http://unnaturalcauses.org/assets/uploads/file/UC_annotd2.pdf.

20. Nancy Adler et al., *Reaching for a Healthier Life: Facts of Socioeconomic Status and Health in the U.S.* (San Francisco: John D. and Catherine T. MacArthur Foundation Research Network on Socioeconomic Status and Health, 2007), accessed January 21, 2012, http://www.macses.ucsf.edu/downloads/reaching_for_a_healthier_life.pdf.

21. William Marsiglio and Sally Hutchinson, *Sex, Men, and Babies: Stories of Awareness and Responsibility* (New York: New York University Press, 2002); see also Ausdale and Feagin, *The First R*.

22. Michael Cunningham, Craig Marberry, and Maya Angelou, *Crowns: Portraits of Black Women in Church Hats* (New York: Doubleday, 2000).

23. See, for example, Jane M. Richards and James J. Gross, "Emotion Regulation and Memory: The Cognitive Costs of Keeping One's Cool," *Journal of Personality and Social Psychology* 79, no. 3 (2000): 410–24.

24. *4 Little Girls*, directed by Spike Lee (1997; Brooklyn, NY: 40 Acres & A Mule Filmworks and Home Box Office), DVD. Transcripts were taken from closed-captioning viewing where the quote was copied verbatim.

25. Feagin, *Racist America*.

26. Joe Feagin and Eileen O'Brien, *White Men on Race: Power, Privilege, and the Shaping of Cultural Consciousness* (Boston: Beacon, 2003), 35.

4. MORE SURVEILLANCE OF BLACK BODIES

1. Jennifer Ritterhouse, *Growing Up Jim Crow: How Black and White Southern Children Learned Race* (Chapel Hill: University of North Carolina Press, 2006), 169–70.

2. Eduardo Bonilla-Silva and Tyrone Forman, "'I Am Not a Racist But . . .' Mapping White College Students' Racial Ideology in the USA," *Discourse and Society* 11, no. 1 (2000): 50–85.

3. Leslie Houts Picca and Joe R. Feagin, *Two-Faced Racism: Whites in the Backstage and Frontstage* (New York: Routledge, 2007), ch. 3 and passim.

4. Irving M. Allen, "PTSD among African Americans," in *Ethnocultural Aspects of Posttraumatic Stress Disorder: Issues, Research, and Clinical Applications*, ed. A. Marsella, M. Friedman, E. Gerrity, and R. Scurfield (Washington, DC: American Psychiatric Association, 1996), 209–38; and Robert T. Carter, "Racism and Psychological and Emotional Injury: Recognizing and Assessing Race-Based Traumatic Stress," *Counseling Psychologist* 35, no.1 (2007): 13–105.

5. Debra Van Ausdale and Joe R. Feagin, *The First R: How Children Learn Race and Racism* (Lanham, MD: Rowman & Littlefield, 2001); and Ritterhouse, *Growing Up Jim Crow*.

6. Robert M. Entman and Andrew Rojecki, *The Black Image in the White Mind: Media and Race in America* (Chicago: University of Chicago Press, 2001).

7. Patrick Chiroro and Tim Valentine, "An Investigation of the Contact Hypothesis of the Own-Race Bias in Face Recognition," *Quarterly Journal of Experimental Psychology* 48, no. 4 (1995): 879–94; and Diane P. Ferguson, Gillian Rhodes, Kieran Lee, and N. Sriram, "'They All Look Alike to Me': Prejudice and Cross-Race Face Recognition." *British Journal of Psychology* 92, no. 4 (2001): 567–77.

8. Rory McVeigh, *The Rise of the Ku Klux Klan: Right-Wing Movements and National Politics* (Minneapolis: University of Minnesota Press, 2009).

9. Bill Maxwell, "More Young Blacks Are Suicidal," *Role Models Today*, 2003, accessed January 6, 2014, http://rolemodels.jou.ufl.edu/rolemodels/publisher/suicidal.shtm.

10. Allan G. Johnson, *Privilege, Power, and Difference*, 2nd ed. (New York: McGraw Hill, 2005); and J. G. Bernburg, M. D. Krohn, and Craig J. Rivera, "Official Labeling, Criminal Embeddedness, and Subsequent Delinquency: A

Longitudinal Test of Labeling Theory," *Journal of Research in Crime and Delinquency* 43 (2006): 67–90.

11. Danielle L. McGuire, *At the Dark End of the Street: Black Women, Rape, and Resistance—A New History of the Civil Rights Movement from Rosa Parks to the Rise of Black Power* (New York: Knopf, 2011).

12. Shannon Meyer and Randall H. Carroll, "When Officers Die: Understanding Deadly Domestic Violence Calls for Service," *Police Chief* 78 (May 2011): 24–27.

13. Callie Marie Rennison and Sarah Welchans, "Intimate Partner Violence," *Bureau of Justice Statistics Special Report*, NCJ 178247, May 2000, accessed January 4, 2014, http://www.bjs.gov/content/pub/pdf/ipv.pdf and "Fact Sheet: Intimate Partner Violence (IPV) in the African American Community," IDVAAC, accessed January 4, 2014, http://www.idvaac.org/press/factsheet.html. See also Shondrah Tarrezz Nash, "Through Black Eyes: African American Women's Construction of Their Experiences with Intimate Male Partner Violence," *Violence against Women* 11 (2005): 1427, and "Women of Color Network: Domestic Violence," accessed January 25, 2014, http://www.nhcadsv.org/uploads/WOC_domestic-violence.pdf. On the stereotypes of black women, see Joe R. Feagin, *Racist America: Roots, Current Realities, and Future Reparations*, 3rd ed. (New York: Routledge, 2014), 109–14 and passim.

14. William J. Harris, "Etiquette, Lynching, and Racial Boundaries in Southern History: A Mississippi Example," *American Historical Review* 100, no. 2 (April 1995): 387–410.

15. Stewart E. Tolnay and E. M. Beck, "Racial Violence and Black Migration in the American South, 1910–1930." *American Sociological Review* 57 (1992): 103–16; Fitzhugh Brundage, *Under Sentence of Death: Lynching in the South* (Chapel Hill: University of North Carolina Press, 1997); and James Allen, J. Lewis, L. F. Litwack, and H. Als, *Without Sanctuary: Lynching Photography in America* (Santa Fe, NM: Twin Palms, 2005).

16. Edward L. Ayers, *The Promise of the New South: Life after Reconstruction* (New York: Oxford University Press, 1992), 158.

17. Claudia Adrien, "The Newberry Six," *Gainesville Sun*, September 4, 2005, accessed February 1, 2014, http://www.gainesville.com/article/20050904/DAYBREAK/50904013?p=1&tc=pg#gsc.tab=0 (page 4 notes the reference to "Lynch Hammock").

18. Lisa Lindquist Dorr, *White Women, Rape, and the Power of Race in Virginia, 1900–1960* (Chapel Hill: University of North Carolina Press, 2004), 5.

19. Robert A. Gibson, "The Negro Holocaust: Lynching and Race Riots in the United States, 1880–1950," *Yale-New Haven Teachers Institute*, Curricu-

lum Unit 79.02.04, accessed January 24, 2014, http://www.yale.edu/ynhti/
curriculum/units/1979/2/79.02.04.x.html.

20. Dorr, *White Women*; and McGuire, *At the Dark End of the Street*.

21. Dorr, *White Women*, 181.

22. Feagin, *Racist America*.

23. Christopher Myers, "Killing Them by the Wholesale: A Lynching Rampage in South Georgia," *Georgia Historical Quarterly* 90, no. 2 (Summer 2006): 214–35; and "Remembering Mary Turner," accessed January 5, 2014, www.maryturner.org.

24. Henrietta Vinton Davis, "Black Women Who Were Lynched in America," weblog posted August 1, 2008, accessed January 6, 2014, http://henriettavintondavis.wordpress.com/2008/08/01/black-women-who-were-lynched-in-america/.

25. See Feagin, *Racist America*; Tolnay and Beck, "Racial Violence," ix; George C. Wright, *Racial Violence in Kentucky, 1865–1940: Lynchings, Mob Rule, and "Legal Lynchings"* (Baton Rouge: Louisiana State University Press, 1990).

26. Feagin, *Racist America*.

27. Signe-Mary McKernan, Caroline Ratcliffe, Eugene Steuerle, and Sisi Zhang, *Less Than Equal: Racial Disparities in Wealth Accumulation* (Washington, DC: Urban Institute, 2013), 5.

28. See, for example, B. E. Carlson, "Children Exposed to Intimate Partner Violence: Research Findings and Implications for Intervention," *Trauma, Violence and Abuse* 1, no. 4 (2000): 321–40; and Izaskun Orue, Brad J. Bushman, Esther Calvete, Sander Thomaes, Bram Orobio de Castro, and Roos Hutteman, "Monkey See, Monkey Do, Monkey Hurt: Longitudinal Effects of Exposure to Violence on Children's Aggressive Behavior," *Social Psychological and Personality Science* 2, no. 4 (2011): 432–37.

29. Thomas R. Dye, "Rosewood, Florida: The Destruction of an African American Community," *Historian* 58 (Spring 1996): 605–22.

30. Raymond A. Winbush, *Should America Pay? Slavery and the Raging Debate on Reparations* (New York: HarperCollins, 2003), 48.

31. Ibid.

32. William A. Darity, Jr., and Dania Frank, "The Economics of Reparations," in *African Americans in the U.S. Economy*, ed. C. A. Conrad, J. Whitehead, P. Mason, and J. Stewart (Lanham, MD: Rowman & Littlefield, 2005), 335.

33. Stephen Smith, Kate Ellis, and Sasha Aslanian, "Remembering Jim Crow," *American RadioWorks*, November 2001. See the section "Blacks Remember Jim Crow: The Land," accessed January 10, 2014, http://americanradioworks.publicradio.org/features/remembering/blacks.html.

34. Mary Mitchell, "Reclaiming Land May Be Bigger Than Reparations," posted June 5, 2005, accessed January 10, 2014, http://www.africanamerica. org/topic/reclaiming-land-may-be-bigger-than-reparations.

35. James W. Loewen, *Sundown Towns: A Hidden Dimension of American Racism* (New York: New Press, 2005).

36. Thema Bryant-Davis and Carlota Ocampo, "Racist Incident-Based Trauma," *Counseling Psychologist* 33 (2005): 479–500; see Joe R. Feagin, *Systemic Racism: A Theory of Oppression* (New York: Routledge, 2006); James R. Grossman, *A Chance to Make Good: African Americans, 1900–1929* (New York: Oxford University Press, 1997), 48.

37. Bryant-Davis and Ocampo, "Racist Incident-Based Trauma," 489–90.

5. RAPE AND RAPE THREATS

1. R. Pain, "Space, Sexual Violence and Social Control: Integrating Geographical and Feminist Analyses of Women's Fear of Crime," *Progress in Human Geography* 15, no. 4 (1991): 415–31.

2. Jennifer B. Wiggins, "Rape, Racism, and the Law," *Harvard Women's Law Journal* 6 (1983): 103–41.

3. Rachel F. Moran, *Interracial Intimacy: The Regulation of Race and Romance* (Chicago: University of Chicago Press, 2003); Phyl Newbeck, *Virginia Hasn't Always Been for Lovers: Interracial Marriage Bans and the Case of Richard and Mildred Loving* (Carbondale, IL: Southern University Press, 2008); and Peter Wallenstein, *Tell The Courts I Love My Wife: Race, Marriage, and Law—An American History* (New York: Palgrave MacMillan, 2002).

4. Paul Finkelman, "Treason against the Hopes of the World," in Peter S. Onuf, ed., *Jeffersonian Legacies*, 181–224 (Charlottesville: University Press of Virginia, 1993).

5. Randall Robinson, quoted in Raymond A. Winbush, *Should America Pay? Slavery and the Raging Debate on Reparations* (New York: HarperCollins, 2003), 3; Patricia Hill Collins, *Black Feminist Thought: Knowledge, Consciousness, and the Politics of Empowerment*, 2nd ed. (New York: Routledge, 2000); Angela Y. Davis, *Women, Race, and Class* (New York: Vintage, 1983).

6. S. E. Anderson, *The Black Holocaust: For Beginners* (New York: Writers and Readers, 1995).

7. Paul R. Spickard, *Mixed Blood: Intermarriage and Ethnic Identity in Twentieth Century America* (Madison: University of Wisconsin Press, 1989), 239.

8. John Langston Gwaltney, *Drylongso: A Self-Portrait of Black America* (New York: New Press, 1993); Joel Williamson, *New People: Miscegenation*

and Mulattoes in the United States (Baton Rouge: Louisiana State University Press, 1995); Stephan Talty, *Mulatto America: At the Crossroads of Black and White Culture: A Social History* (New York: HarperCollins, 2003).

9. John Brown, *Slave Life in Georgia: A Narrative of the Life, Sufferings, and Escape of John Brown, A Fugitive Slave, Now in England,* ed. L. A. Chamerovzow (London: 1854), 132–33, accessed February 2, 2014, http://docsouth.unc.edu/neh/jbrown/jbrown.html.

10. See Catherine Clinton, *Harriet Tubman: The Road to Freedom* (New York: Little, Brown, 2004); Harriet Jacobs, *Incidents in the Life of a Slave Girl* (New York: Dover, 2000); Patricia McKissack and Fredrick McKissack, *Sojourner Truth: Ain't I a Woman?* (New York: Scholastic, 1992); and Davis, *Women, Race, and Class,* 55.

11. See Henry Wiencek, *An Imperfect God: George Washington, His Slaves, and the Creation of America* (New York: Farrar, Straus and Giroux, 2003), 72–79, 84–85, 284–85, 301–5.

12. Catherine Clinton, *The Plantation Mistress: Woman's World in the Old South* (New York: Pantheon, 1984), 110–11 and 121–22.

13. Mary Frances Berry, "Judging Morality: Sexual Behavior and Legal Consequences in the Late Nineteenth-Century South," *Journal of American History* 78, no. 3 (1991): 835–56; Peter W. Bardaglio, "'Shameful Matches': The Regulation of Interracial Sex and Marriage in the South before 1900," in *Sex, Love, Race: Crossing Boundaries in North American History,* edited by Martha Hodes, 112–40 (New York: New York University Press, 1999); Newbeck, *Virginia Hasn't Always Been for Lovers*; Robinson, quoted in Winbush, *Should America Pay?*

14. Newbeck, *Virginia Hasn't Always Been for Lovers,* 38.

15. Patricia Hill Collins, *Black Sexual Politics: African Americans, Gender and the New Racism.* (New York: Routledge, 2005), 65.

16. Danielle L. McGuire, *At the Dark End of the Street: Black Women, Rape, and Resistance—A New History of the Civil Rights Movement from Rosa Parks to the Rise of Black Power* (New York: Knopf, 2011).

17. Charlotte Pierce-Baker, *Surviving the Silence: Black Women's Stories of Rape* (New York: Norton, 2000). See also McGuire, *At the Dark End of the Street.*

18. Martin S. Weinberg, Rochelle Ganz Swensson, and Sue Kiefer Hammersmith, "Sexual Autonomy and the Status of Women: Models of Female Sexuality in U.S. Sex Manuals from 1950 to 1980," *Social Problems* 30, no. 3 (February 1983): 312–24.

19. See, for example, Office of Policy Planning and Research, "The Negro Family: The Case for National Action" (Washington, DC: U.S. Department of

Labor, March 1965); this report is more commonly known as "The Moynihan Report" after its lead author Daniel Patrick Moynihan.

20. Shirley Ann Hill, *Black Intimacies: A Gender Perspective on Families and Relationships* (Lanham, MD: Rowman & Littlefield, 2005).

21. See "White Man Charged with Rape of Eight-Year-Old Girl," *Chicago Defender*, October 23, 1915, 1.

22. Sharon Wasco, "Conceptualizing the Harm Done by Rape: Applications of Trauma Theory to Experiences of Sexual Assault," *Trauma, Violence, & Abuse* 4 (2003): 309–22; Holly E. Barnes, "Preventing the 'Second Rape': Rape Survivors' Experiences with Community Service Providers," *Journal of Interpersonal Violence* 16, no. 12 (December 2001): 1239–59.

23. Bessel van der Kolk, Alexander McFarlane, and Lars Weisaeth, *Traumatic Stress: The Effects of Overwhelming Experience on Mind, Body, and Society* (New York: Guilford, 2006), 31.

24. McGuire, *At the Dark End of the Street*, 33.

25. Associated Press, "Lawmaker Wants Alabama to Apologize to Rape Victim," *Black Entertainment Television*, March 17, 2011, accessed January 11, 2014, http://www.bet.com/news/national/lawmaker-wants-alabama-to-apologize-to-rape-victim-.html; see also National Public Radio, "Hidden Pattern of Rape Helped Stir Civil Rights Movement," February 28, 2011, accessed January 3, 2014, http://www.npr.org/templates/story/story.php?storyId=134131369.

26. McGuire, *At the Dark End of the Street*, 2.

27. See Tamara Beauboeuf-Lafontant, *Behind the Mask of the Strong Black Woman: Voice and the Embodiment of a Costly Performance* (Philadelphia: Temple University Press, 2009).

28. "White Man Rapes Girl: Thirteen Year Old Girl Criminally Assaulted by Farmer," *Chicago Defender*, April 29, 1916, 1, col. 3.

29. Rebecca L. Skloot, *The Immortal Life of Henrietta Lacks* (New York: Crown, 2010); Stewart E. Tolnay and E. M. Beck, "Racial Violence and Black Migration in the American South, 1910–1930," *American Sociological Review* 57 (1992): 103–16; Phillip Dray, *At the Hands of Persons Unknown: The Lynching of Black America* (New York: Modern Day Library, 2003).

30. McGuire, *At the Dark End of the Street*.

31. "White Man Rapes Six-Year-Old Girl: Culprit Entered Home in Absence of School Girl's Parents," *Chicago Defender*, May 31, 1919, 1.

32. McGuire, *At the Dark End of the Street*.

33. Angela Browne and David Finkelhor, "Impact of Child Sexual Abuse: A Review of the Research," *Psychological Bulletin* 99, no. 1 (January 1986): 66–77; Joseph H. Beitchman, Kenneth J. Zucker, Jane E. Hood, Granville A. DaCosta, Donna Akman, and Erika Cassavia, "A Review of the Long-Term

Effects of Child Sexual Abuse," *Child Abuse & Neglect* 16, no. 1 (1992): 101–18.

34. "White Man Rapes Colored Orphan Employed by Him," *Philadelphia Tribune*, July 24, 1920, 7.

35. Charles Johnson, *Backgrounds to Patterns of Negro Segregation* (New York: Harper and Row, 1943), 71; Michelle Alexander, *The New Jim Crow: Mass Incarceration in the Age of Colorblindness* (New York: New Press, 2010).

36. McGuire, *At the Dark End of the Street*; George C. Wright, *Racial Violence in Kentucky, 1865–1940: Lynchings, Mob Rule, and "Legal Lynchings"* (Baton Rouge: Louisiana State University Press, 1990).

37. "Order Mississippi Jury to Spare White Rapist of Girl," *Philadelphia Tribune*, August 6, 1960, 2.

38. Alexander, *The New Jim Crow*.

39. Mason I. Lowance, *A House Divided: The Antebellum Slavery Debate* (Princeton, NJ: Princeton University Press, 2003), 459. See also Joe R. Feagin, *Racist America: Roots, Current Realities, and Future Reparations*, 3rd ed. (New York: Routledge, 2014).

40. Plessy v. Ferguson, 163 U.S. 537 (1896).

41. "White Rapist Is Called Insane," *Atlanta Daily World*, March 27, 1932, 1; see also Wright, *Racial Violence in Kentucky*, 301.

42. "Girls Reveal Story of Brutal Crime," *Chicago Defender*, March 6, 1926, 1.

43. Wright, *Racial Violence in Kentucky*, 301.

44. "Would Be 'First' in Nation: Death for White Rapist—Really?" *New Journal and Guide*, July 4, 1959, 1–2.

45. "S.C. Judge Gives White Marine, Negro Rapist Electric Chair," *Philadelphia Tribune*, July 4, 1959, 12.

46. "Core Leader Demands End of Executions," *Los Angeles Sentinel*, July 30, 1959, C4.

47. Anonymous author in *Black Women in White America*, ed. Gerda Lerner (New York: Vintage, 1972), 172.

48. Ralph Ginzburg, *100 Years of Lynchings* (Baltimore, MD: Black Classic Press, 1996), 91.

49. Wright, *Racial Violence in Kentucky*.

50. Kristen M. Lavelle, *Whitewashing the South: White Memories of Segregation and Civil Rights* (Lanham, MD: Rowman & Littlefield, forthcoming).

51. Benjamin Bowser, *The Black Middle Class* (Boulder, CO: Lynne Rienner, 2006), 48.

52. See also Gwaltney, *Drylongso*; Williamson, *New People*; and Talty, *Mulatto America*.

53. Clinton, *Plantation Mistress*.

54. Gerda Lerner, ed., *Black Women in White America* (New York: Vintage, 1972), 156.

55. See Hill Collins, *Black Feminist Thought*.

56. Newbeck, *Virginia Hasn't Always Been for Lovers*.

57. McGuire, *At the Dark End of the Street*.

58. Ibid.

59. Ibid., 132.

60. Ibid., 106.

61. See Chana Kai Lee, *For Freedom's Sake: The Life of Fannie Lou Hamer*, Women in American History (Urbana: University of Illinois Press, 1999), 88–98.

62. McGuire, *At the Dark End of the Street*.

63. Ibid., 29 and 114.

64. Brittany C. Slatton, *Mythologizing Black Women: Unveiling White Men's Racist and Sexist Deep Frame* (Boulder, CO: Paradigm, 2012).

65. Hill Collins, *Black Feminist Thought*.

6. COPING AND RESISTANCE STRATEGIES

1. Marilyn Frye, "Oppression," in *The Politics of Reality: Essays in Feminist Theory* (Trumansburg, NY: Crossing Press, 1983), 1–16.

2. Associated Press, "Racial Attitudes Survey," October 29, 2012, 19, http://surveys.ap.org/data/GfK/AP_Racial_Attitudes_Topline_09182012.pdf; Associated Press, "Majority of Americans Harbor Prejudice against Blacks: Poll," *New York Daily News* (October 27, 2012), accessed January 30, 2014, http://www.nydailynews.com/news/national/u-s-anti-black-attitudes-article-1.1193641.

3. Marcia Alesan Dawkins, *Clearly Invisible: Racial Passing and the Color of Cultural Identity* (Waco, TX: Baylor University Press, 2012).

4. In the quotes, the interviewer's comments appear in brackets and italicized text.

5. See Dawkins, *Clearly Invisible*; and George Yancey, *Who Is White? Latinos, Asians, and the New Black/Nonblack* (Boulder, CO: Lynne Rienner, 2003).

6. See Leslie Houts Picca and Joe R. Feagin, *Two-Faced Racism: Whites in the Backstage and Frontstage* (New York: Routledge, 2007).

7. Douglas A. Blackmon, *Slavery by Another Name: The Re-Enslavement of Black American from the Civil War to World War II* (Norwell, MA: Anchor, 2009).

8. Ibid.

9. Ibid.

10. Joe Feagin and Eileen O'Brien, *White Men on Race: Power, Privilege, and the Shaping of Cultural Consciousness* (Boston: Beacon, 2003).

11. Patricia Hill Collins, *Black Feminist Thought: Knowledge, Consciousness, and the Politics of Empowerment* (New York: Routledge, 2008).

12. Thema Bryant-Davis and Carlota Ocampo, "Racist Incident-Based Trauma," *Counseling Psychologist* 33 (2005): 488.

13. W. E. B. Du Bois, *The Souls of Black Folk* (1903; repr., Oakland, CA: Eucalyptus Press, 2014).

14. M. E. Wickman, N. L. Anderson, and C. S. Greenberg, "The Adolescent Perception of Invincibility and Its Influence on Teen Acceptance of Health Promotion Strategies," *Journal of Pediatric Nursing* 23, no. 6 (2008): 460–68.

15. Philip A Klinkner and Rogers Smith, *The Unsteady March: The Rise and Decline of Racial Equality in America* (Chicago: University of Chicago Press, 1999).

16. Susan Englander, ed., *Advocate of the Social Gospel, September 1948–March 1963 of the Papers of Martin Luther King, Jr.* This reference refers to the 1953 service at Ebenezer Baptist Church in Atlanta, GA.

7. FIFTY YEARS LATER

1. See Louwanda Evans, *Cabin Pressure: African American Pilots, Flight Attendants, and Emotional Labor* (Lanham, MD: Rowman & Littlefield, 2013).

2. Signe-Mary McKernan, Caroline Ratcliffe, Eugene Steuerle, and Sisi Zhang, *Less Than Equal: Racial Disparities in Wealth Accumulation* (Washington, DC: Urban Institute, 2013), 5; Michelle Alexander, *The New Jim Crow: Mass Incarceration in the Age of Colorblindness* (New York: New Press, 2010), 6–7.

3. See, for example, Kate Abbey-Lambertz, "Theodore Wafer Will Stand Trial for Death of Renisha McBride," *Huffington Post*, December 19, 2013, accessed January 28, 2014, http://www.huffingtonpost.com/2013/12/19/theodore-wafer-trial_n_4472885.html.

4. See Joe R. Feagin, *Racist America: Roots, Contemporary Realities, and Future Reparations*, 3rd ed. (New York: Routledge, 2014), passim.

5. The "I" in italics is the first author, the interviewer.

6. For evidence, see Feagin, *Racist America.*

7. James W. Loewen and Edward H. Sebesta, *The Confederate and Neo Confederate Reader: The Great Truth about the "Lost Cause"* (Jackson: University Press of Mississippi, 2010), 13.

8. See Joe R. Feagin and Melvin Sikes, *Living with Racism: The Black Middle Class Experience* (Boston: Beacon, 1994).

9. Derald Wing Sue, *Microaggressions in Everyday Life: Race, Gender, and Sexual Orientation* (Hoboken, NJ: Wiley, 2010).

10. Doug Massey, *Categorically Unequal: The American Stratification System* (New York: Russell Sage, 2008).

11. See Gary Orfield, John Kucsera, and Genevieve Siegel-Hawley, *E Pluribus . . . Separation: Deepening Double Segregation for More Students* (Los Angeles: UCLA Civil Rights Project, 2012), 7–9.

12. Gary Orfield, "U.S. Schools Are More Segregated Today Than in the 1950s," *Project Uncensored*, accessed January 12, 2014, cited in http://www.projectcensored.org/2-us-schools-are-more-segregated-today-than-in-the-1950s-source/.

13. See Jonathan Kozol, *Savage Inequalities: Children in America's Schools* (New York: Broadway, 2012).

14. Statistics from Tim Wise, *Affirmative Action: Racial Preference in Black and White Positions*, Education, Politics, and Culture (New York: Routledge, 2005), 51; and "Race against Time: Educating Black Boys," *Focus On Blacks*, accessed January 12, 2014, cited in http://www.nea.org/assets/docs/educatingblackboys11rev.pdf.

15. Wise, *Affirmative Action*, 57.

16. "Race against Time."

17. Marianne Bertrand and Sendhil Mullainathan, "Are Emily and Greg More Employable Than Lakisha and Jamal? A Field Experiment on Labor Market Discrimination," *American Economic Review* 94, no. 4 (2004): 991–1013.

18. Devah Pager, *Marked: Race, Crime, and Finding Work in an Era of Mass Incarceration* (Chicago: University of Chicago Press, 2009).

19. Bertrand and Mullainathan, "Are Emily And Greg More Employable?, 991–1013.

20. Jon Jeter, "Worse Than Apartheid: Black in Obama's America," *Black Agenda Report*, October 29, 2013, accessed January 27, 2014,http://blackagendareport.com/content/worse-apartheid-black-obama%E2%80%99s-america.

21. Thomas Shapiro, *The Hidden Cost of Being African American* (New York: Oxford University Press, 2004).

22. Nancy DiTomaso, *The American Non-Dilemma: Racial Inequality without Racism* (New York: Russell Sage, 2013), 64–66.

23. Alexander, *The New Jim Crow*, passim.

24. See P. Eric Louw, *The Rise, Fall and Legacy of Apartheid* (Westport, CT: Praeger, 2004). Also see Nikki M. Brown and Barry M. Stentiford, *The Jim*

Crow Encyclopedia: Greenwood Milestones in African American History (Westport, CT: Greenwood, 2008).

25. Tim Wise, "Racial Profiling and Its Apologists," *Z Magazine*, March 2002, 40–44.

26. Alexander, *New Jim Crow*.

27. NAACP, "Criminal Justice Fact Sheet," accessed January 27, 2014, http://www.naacp.org/pages/criminal-justice-fact-sheet.

28. Charles A. Gallagher, "Color-Blind Privilege: The Social and Political Function of Erasing the Color Line in Post Race America," *Race, Gender & Class* 10, no. 4 (2003): 1–17.

29. Vincene Verdun, "If The Shoe Fits, Wear It: An Analysis of Reparations to African Americans," *Tulane Law Review* 67 (1993): 597.

30. Quoted in Wise, *Affirmative Action*, 157–58.

31. See Feagin, *Racist America*.

32. See Verdun, "If The Shoe Fits, Wear It."

33. See also Joe R. Feagin and Karyn McKinney, *The Many Costs of Racism* (Lanham, MD: Rowman & Littlefield, 2003).

34. Raymond A. Winbush, *Should America Pay? Slavery and the Raging Debate on Reparations* (New York: HarperCollins, 2003); Rhoda E. Howard-Hassmann, "Getting to Reparations: Japanese Americans and African Americans," *Social Forces* (2004): 823–40; Feagin, *Racist America*.

35. Republic of Austria v. Altmann, 541 U.S. 677 (2004).

36. Winbush, *Should America Pay?*

37. Alfred L. Brophy, *Reparations: Pro and Con* (New York: Oxford University Press, 2006).

38. Randall Robinson, quoted in Winbush, *Should America Pay?*, 73; Randall Robinson, *The Debt: What America Owes to Blacks* (New York: Penguin, 2001).

39. The Senate resolution, accessed June 24, 2009, is at http://www.opencongress.org/bill/111-sc26/text.

40. Rick Shenkman, "Interview with Elliot Jaspin: Racial Cleansing in America," accessed December 18, 2013, http://hnn.us/article/35900#sthash.riHhwapj.dpuf; Elliot Jaspin, *Buried in the Bitter Waters* (New York: Basic Books, 2008); see also James W. Loewen, *Sundown Towns: A Hidden Dimension of American Racism* (New York: New Press, 2005); *Banished*, directed by Marco Williams (2007; New York: Two Tone Productions), DVD. Transcripts were taken from closed-captioning viewing.

41. Richard Rothstein, "Truth as Well as Reconciliation," *Economic Policy Institute Newsletter*, December 12, 2013, accessed December 18, 2013, http://www.epi.org/blog/truth-reconciliation.

42. Ibid.

43. Shenkman, "Interview with Elliot Jaspin"; see also Loewen, *Sundown Towns*.

44. Robert Westley, "Many Billions Gone: Is It Time to Reconsider the Case for Black Reparations?" *Boston College Law Review* 40 (1998): 429.

45. See David R. Williams and Chiquita Collins, "Reparations: A Viable Strategy to Address the Enigma of African American Health," *American Behavioral Scientist* 47, no. 7 (2004): 977–1000.

INDEX

ABOUT THE AUTHORS

Ruth Thompson-Miller, assistant professor at University of Dayton, has conducted research on the era of Jim Crow in the south and South African apartheid. She has written several articles and book chapters on the topic. She has presented the research at more than 30 conferences, both nationally and internationally. She has participated in two documentaries about Jim Crow. She is a McNair Scholar and a three-year recipient of the National Institute of Mental Health Minority Fellowship through the American Sociological Association. In 2013, she was the chair of the Society for the Study of Social Problems Lee Scholar Travel Fund and Mentoring Program.

Joe R. Feagin, Ella C. McFadden Professor at Texas A & M University, has done much research on U.S. racism issues. He has written 65 scholarly books and 200-plus scholarly articles and reports in his areas of sociology of racism, sexism, and urban issues. His books include *Systemic Racism*; *Liberation Sociology*; *White Party, White Government*; *The White Racial Frame*; *Latinos Facing Racism*; and *Racist America*. He is the recipient of a 2012 Soka Gakkai International-USA Social Justice Award, the 2013 American Association for Affirmative Action's Arthur Fletcher Lifetime Achievement Award, and the American Sociological Association's 2013 W. E. B. Du Bois Career of Distinguished Scholarship Award. He was the 1999–2000 president of the American Sociological Association.

Leslie H. Picca, associate professor of sociology, is chairperson for the Department of Sociology, Anthropology and Social Work at the University of Dayton. She has publications in the areas of racial relations and adolescent sexuality, including the book *Two-Faced Racism: Whites in the Backstage and Frontstage*. Her research on racial relations has been nationally recognized, and she has been interviewed by CNN, the Associated Press, *Congressional Quarterly*, *Inside Higher Ed*, and *Journal of Blacks in Higher Education*, among others. She is a HERS-Bryn Mawr Summer Institute alumna, and a founding board member for the nonprofit Warm Welcomes Foster Care Outreach.